American Indian Nations
from Termination to
Restoration, 1953–2006

American Indian Nations from Termination to Restoration, 1953–2006

ROBERTA ULRICH

UNIVERSITY OF NEBRASKA PRESS | LINCOLN AND LONDON

Library of Congress Cataloging-
in-Publication Data
Ulrich, Roberta.
American Indian nations from
termination to restoration,
1953–2006 / Roberta Ulrich.
    p. cm.
Includes bibliographical
references and index.
ISBN 978-0-8032-3364-5
    (cloth: alk. paper)
1. Indians of North America—
Government relations—1934–
2. Indian termination policy.
3. Indians of North America—
Cultural assimilation. I. Title.
E93.U45 2010
323.1197'07309045—dc22
2010011367

Set in Quadraat.

This book is dedicated to the late Alvin M. Josephy Jr. His work was an inspiration and his help invaluable.

Contents

Illustrations

following page 146

Klamath men's traditional dancers
Grand Ronde cemetery shed
Grand Ronde governance center
Ponca Agency building

Acknowledgments

I am deeply indebted first of all to those tribal people who shared their life stories with me, illustrating how termination—and later restoration—had affected their lives. Their experiences are the core of this book, and I value the time they gave me and the honesty of their accounts. Even more, I am in awe of their resilience and courage. So my thanks to Don Arnold, Thomas Ball, George Barton, Leaford Bearskin, Gordon Bettles, Bensell Breon, Bill Brainard, Ron Brainard, Doris and Bud Chase, Gail Chehak, Edison Chiloquin, Howard Crombie, Theodore Crume, Michael Darcy, Taylor R. David, Verna Fowler, Roy Gilkey, Jesse Gonzalez, Don Ivey, Morris Jimenez, Robert Kentta, Charles E. Kimbol Sr., Russ Leno, Fred LeRoy, Billie Lewis, Dorene Martineaux, Sue Masten, Linda Mecum, Edward Metcalf, James Metcalf, David Miller, Elwood Miller, Jeff Mitchell, Charlie Moses, June Olson, Viola Pack, Sharon Parrish, Keith Pike, Bill Ray, Michael Rondeau, Cheryl Seidner, Sue M. Shaffer, Gerald Skelton, Carolyn Slyter, Joe Thomas, Leon Tom, Phil (Bill) Tupper, Laurie Voshall, Bob Watson, Donald Whereat, Jackie Whisler, Leona Wilkinson, Nancy Williams, Bob Younker, and Violet Zimbrick. I also thank former commissioner of Indian Affairs Kenneth Smith and tribal officials Llewellyn Boyd, Carlos Bullock, Helen Christie, Rod Clarke, David Lewis, Kim Mueller, and Gary Robinette for information and assistance. I have tried to do them justice.

Special recognition is due Barbara Alatorre, historian for the Klamath Tribes, who painstakingly kept tribal records through the wilderness of termination and did a prodigious amount of research on her tribe's travails. She generously shared information with me. Her diligence has kept her people's story alive. Her consultation was invaluable.

My particular thanks go to Kathryn Harrison of the Grand Rondes, Allen Foreman of the Klamaths, and Ada Deer of the Menominees, who provided entrees to their communities as well as their own stories. They are leaders of uncommon ability who also are able to convey their tribal experiences, values, and aspirations to a wider world.

It was nearly a decade ago that my friend and former newspaper colleague Jeanie Senior proposed that I write this book. Her suggestions, encouragement, and assistance over the years were key to bringing it to publication.

Those nontribal people who had been involved as government officials, tribal attorneys, or other advisers brought insights and information that I could have acquired in no other way. I owe LeaAnn Easton, Elizabeth Furse, Edwin Goodman, Roberta Hall, Alvin M. Josephy Jr., Michael Mason, Doyce Waldrip, Dennis Werth, Donald Wharton, and Hiroto Zakoji great thanks.

Librarians and archivists have long been high on my list of favorite people, and I had the assistance of many, some of whose names I never learned. John Ferrell of the National Archives and Records Administration—Pacific Northwest Repository in Seattle deserves special gratitude for his untiring work in organizing and cataloguing the Bureau of Indian Affairs files there. Joseph Schwarz of the National Archives in College Park, Maryland, also was especially helpful. James Fox and Linda Long of the University of Oregon Libraries Special Collections guided me through the massive files donated by Alvin M. Josephy Jr. and collections from key figures in the termination saga. The staffs at the Multnomah County Library, Portland State University Library, Boley Law Library at Lewis and Clark College, Oregon State Library in Salem, Beaverton, Oregon, City Library, and Oregon Historical Society Library all provided excellent help, as did those in charge of records for the Grand Ronde, Coos, and Coquille tribes.

I am grateful to Jane Curran for her meticulous, perceptive, and comprehensive editing of the manuscript.

And finally, thanks to my companion, John R. Lynch, whose patience, encouragement, and ability to unsnarl computer problems made this all possible.

Prologue: The Experiment

"What I remember growing up was going to a lot of funerals."[1]

With that one sentence Klamath Indian Gerald Skelton summed up the effects of the federal government's massive mid-twentieth-century social experiment known as termination. Skelton was not yet born when Congress voted in 1954 to terminate the Klamath Tribes of southern Oregon. However, his family story is a searing example of the traumatic and long-lasting effects of the policy under which the government ended its relationship with dozens of Indian tribes and bands. In the name of "freeing" the Indians from government restrictions Congress removed the tribal status of more than nine dozen tribes with nearly 13,000 members from Oregon to South Carolina and from Wisconsin to Texas. The result was thousands of Indians from rich tribes plunged into poverty and despair and thousands more from poor tribes sinking even deeper into hopelessness.

Skelton later became the cultural resources director for the restored Klamath Tribes, but his road there, as for his tribe, was long and convoluted. He remembered growing up in Klamath Falls twenty-five miles from what had been the million-acre Klamath Indian Reservation. "The main problem growing up was just being treated as a lesser person by the white folks," he said. "I learned to work with it and use it to my advantage. Someone, I think it was my mom, told us, 'don't do what they expect.' White people expected the worst of us."

In some cases the worst is what they saw. The Indians were poor people who suddenly had wealth from the sale of reservation land. But most had no experience managing money. Some, like Skelton's mother and her sisters, were teenagers. The money did not last. "Alcoholism skyrocketed right after termination," Skelton said. "People had debts," and the money paid those off.

Skelton's childhood memories were of his parents taking turns, one working while the other stayed with him and his brother and sister, and of his aunts sometimes helping out. "What I really remember," he said, "about 1966 or 1967 I started losing my aunts. I had five aunts, and between 1967 and 1985 they all died. They were young." He added, "They got all that money when they were just young girls."

Termination destroyed the tribal members' sense of identity. "In just my family, my grandfather and grandmother died early," Skelton said. "The family started to disintegrate. That left you with a question of who you are. That is heavy handed. It led to a sense of instability." Today, he added, "a lot of folks of my mother's generation aren't around. They were lucky if they lived to be thirty. My generation grew up with that instability."

Skelton's parents divorced when he was thirteen, and he went to live with non-Klamath grandparents. His brother went to prison, and he believed his sister had not lived up to her potential. "It's part of termination mentality," he said. "Part of it is you're told you're not this, not that." Other tribes labeled the Klamaths "sellouts." They were considered to be no longer Indians and were not eligible to be part of larger Indian organizations. But they were not accepted in the white world either. There seemed to be no place where they belonged.

While the Klamath people were probably the most tragically affected by termination, other tribes across the nation also suffered, economically and socially. Their stories are told in the following chapters.

American Indian Nations
from Termination to
Restoration, 1953–2006

1. BREAKING THE TIES

1 Policy

Kill the Indians

Joe Thomas described the history of the U.S. government's Indian policy as a series of "tions"—that is, "annihilation, assimilation, integration, termination, restoration."[1]

A member of the once-terminated Coquille Tribe on Oregon's southern coast, Thomas was the chief of security for CEDCO, the Coquille Economic Development Corporation. He also had been a teacher and a deputy sheriff. Just out of high school, he was part of another "tion"—relocation that went hand-in-hand with termination.

Termination was the post–World War II version of what had been the goal of European immigrants to the New World from the time the first of them settled on the Atlantic Coast: get rid of the Indians. The policies varied from the vicious—"the only good Indian is a dead Indian"—to assimilation—"kill the Indian, save the man."

When the newcomers to America were settled mostly on the eastern seaboard, their policy was to move the Indians westward, first beyond the Appalachians, then beyond the Mississippi. When whites wanted the western lands, too, national policy confined Indians to pieces of land called reservations. From there, Indian children were sent to boarding schools with the avowed purpose of removing every bit of Indian tradition, culture, language, clothing, and religion. Although it did not reach every reservation, the allotment policy begun in the late 1800s "devastated the Indian land base" by breaking up tribal land holdings to give each Indian a parcel of land that at best was subsistence level in both size and quality. Any "left-over" land the government offered to their white neighbors. This General Allotment Act resulted in a decrease of Indian-owned land from 138 million acres in 1887 to 52 million acres in 1934.[2]

Interspersed with these programs were scattered attempts to annihilate the tribal people through warfare, disease, or eliminating their food supply, such as the buffalo. Whether through massacre (Wounded Knee, Sand Creek) or breaking up tribal lands, the goal was getting rid of Indians. If they could not be destroyed, they must be turned into docile Christian tillers of soil. "And when an Indian learns to comply with one set of rules and regulations, they are changed so that he is compelled to begin again," said Thomas L. Sloan, a founder and president of the Society of American Indians.[3]

At the end of all these efforts, Indians were still here, mostly poor and afflicted with all the problems of poverty—ill health, alcoholism, and lack of education—but still defiantly Indian, many clinging to scattered bits of their homelands. In varying degrees they had adopted or adapted European-American culture and religion into their lives while retaining many of their age-old tribal traditions and customs. By 1950 there were an estimated 343,000 Indians in about two to three hundred tribes.[4]

The ties between the federal government and Indian tribes had been largely established through treaties and other agreements written into law in which the Indians relinquished vast amounts of land in exchange for retaining specified areas and guarantees of their right to continue hunting and fishing on traditional lands, plus education, health care, and economic assistance. No formal treaties were made after 1871, but as the U.S. government continued to confine additional tribes to reservations it made promises similar to those contained in treaties. In fulfilling its obligations to tribes the federal government created a vast bureaucracy, most recently lodged in the Department of the Interior and titled Bureau of Indian Affairs (BIA).[5]

Efforts to divest the government of its responsibilities to Indians began to sprout long before World War II. For example, proposals to extinguish the Wyandotte Tribe apparently began with the signing of the tribe's treaty in 1850. More generally and much later, in 1917, Indian Commissioner Cato Sells decided it was time for "competent" Indians to be freed from guardianship and for "incompetent" Indians to get more attention from the federal government. So the federal government established boards to decide whether each individual was "competent." In 1924 Congress conferred blanket citizenship on all Indians, but it did not lift some restrictions, such as the prohibition against buying alcohol.[6] Two years after the citizenship act the Institute for Government Research began a study of the needs of the Indian population. Its findings, known as the Meriam Survey, called for policies that would allow Indians to merge with "the prevailing [white] civilization" or to live beside it "with a minimum standard of health and decency." If adopted, such a policy would give Indians a choice—assimilate into white society or retain their culture and a decent standard of living. That report led to the Indian Reorganization Act of 1934, which gave tribes the option of establishing governments and assuming some control over their affairs.[7]

On most reservations, however, tribal enterprises were nominally operated by tribal governments but almost entirely run by BIA employees, few of whom were Indians. Nearly twenty years after tribes were promised more control over their business, the situation in the Northwest was typical. In June 1953 the Bureau of Indian Affairs Portland Area's budget officer noted that Pacific Northwest tribes had responsibility for allocating just 17.6 percent of the tribal and government funds spent on tribal programs in the region.[8] Despite this continuing low level of tribal authority, the new policy and the attention that New Deal Indian Commissioner John Collier gave to Indian problems had begun to improve conditions for tribes by the late 1930s.

World War II intervened to submerge most domestic issues, such as Indian policy, but in the late 1940s the stage should have been set for a resurgence of tribal development. During the war many Indians served in the armed forces, and many others moved from their reservations to work in war industries. Despite these experiences and having won citizenship, most Indians remained "wards of the government."

As such, they were subject to BIA decisions on their spending, their education, their health, their land, their housing. In this period an Indian still could not legally buy liquor and, in some states, could not marry a non-Indian. In a few states Indians could not vote. They chafed under these strictures, and many tribes agitated for a greater voice in managing their own assets. Some tribes sued the government for mismanaging their resources.[9]

Tribes were not the only ones dissatisfied with BIA management. The agency had long been a favorite whipping boy of Congress. Even during World War II the Senate Indian Committee staged a sweeping investigation of the BIA, concluding in 1943 that all property owned by individual Indians should be removed from federal trust protection and a number of Indian programs ended. In the first year after the war, a few members of the Klamath Tribes, encouraged by an attorney representing local government interests, made an abortive attempt to sell the Klamath Reservation and divide the proceeds among tribal members.[10]

At the end of the war Congress and the executive branch both engaged in a new approach to solving "the Indian problem" once and for all. This attitude converged with other factors and, driven by the relentless ideology of a U.S. senator, resulted in a social experiment on a scale that was as startling in its magnitude as it was devastating to the experimental subjects. The financial, emotional, and physical toll was tremendous.

It is easy, but an oversimplification, to place the blame for termination entirely on Arthur V. Watkins, a Republican senator from Utah, and Douglas McKay, President Dwight D. Eisenhower's secretary of the interior. However, efforts to cut the federal ties to tribes long preceded the entry of either Watkins or McKay on the national political scene. Watkins arrived in the Senate in 1947 amid a flurry of legislative proposals designed to get the government "out of the Indian business." McKay did not get to Washington until 1953. Even so, both men were instrumental in turning the idea of relinquishing federal control of Indians into reality.[11]

In the post–World War II period Americans went optimistically about creating a better world, rebuilding Europe and Japan while encouraging governments around the world to embrace democracy. Seeking to improve government at home, too, President Harry Truman established the Commission on Organization of the Executive Branch of Government to recommend ways to streamline all federal programs, including those dealing with Indians. The commission, popularly known by the name of its chairman, former president Herbert Hoover, issued its report in 1948, recommending that Indian tribes eventually be freed from government supervision. The document recognized that few, if any, tribes had enough members with sufficient education or business experience to take over full management of their own affairs any time soon. The Hoover report advocated "progressive measures to integrate Indians into the rest of the population as the best solution to 'the Indian Problem.'"

The proposal was framed as a long-term project, and the goal appeared to be cutting government expenses by eliminating payments for Indian programs and putting Indian property on tax rolls as much as it was making life better for Indians. For instance, the report recommended that during the transition to complete integration of the Indians, the administration of social programs for Indians should gradually be transferred to the states, with the federal government continuing to pay the costs "until Indian taxes can help carry the load." The recommendations envisioned adequate education and standards of living for Indians along with reductions in their mortality rates—then, as now, higher than those of the general population. Tribal property was to be transferred to Indian-owned corporations, and tax exemptions for Indian land were to be ended.

In addition, the commission report stated: "Young employable Indians and the better cultured families should be encouraged and assisted to leave the reservations and set themselves up on the land or in business."[12] At least in the case of the Klamath Tribes of Oregon, a number of tribal members who had "set themselves up on the land" lost it all with termination.

Congress also delved into Indian policy. Indian problems had always occupied a good deal of Congress's attention. Commerce with the Indians, after all, was one of the specific areas carved out for the federal government in the Constitution. As Congress resumed dealing with domestic problems after World War II, one of its first acts established the Indian Claims Commission, allowing tribes to sue for compensation for lands taken from them illegally or purchased for an unfairly low price. Dealing with 370 petitions, the commission eventually awarded $800 million to tribes. Despite its stated aim of redressing long-standing injustices, the commission was in the end a part of the effort to end government involvement with tribes.[13]

In 1947 alone the *Congressional Record* shows 135 items related to Indians—bills, resolutions, and special entries. Of 25 bills regarding Indians that were introduced in the Senate that year, 15 would have ended federal supervision and granted full citizenship rights or transferred jurisdiction to states. Three more would have transferred supervisory functions of certain programs to the Public Health Service, Agriculture Department, or Bureau of Reclamation. One would have repealed the Wheeler-Howard Act that provided for tribal governments, and one would have reduced spending by the Indian Bureau. Three additional House bills would have granted citizenship or transferred jurisdiction to states. Senators William D. Langer of North Dakota and Hugh A. Butler of Nebraska introduced separate bills to remove federal supervision over Indians, as did Watkins.[14]

Also in 1947, under orders from Congress, the assistant commissioner of Indian Affairs, William Zimmerman, drew up a list of tribes that he believed could be removed from federal supervision immediately, tribes he thought could function with little or no federal supervision within ten years, and tribes that would require ten years or more under federal supervision. Ten tribes were on Zimmerman's list of those ready for "immediate freedom," and two dozen on his list were tribes that could be ready in ten years.[15]

There is no evidence that Zimmerman consulted with the Indians in making his lists. There is ample evidence that he was monumentally wrong. Congress, when it got around to terminating tribes, made its own list.

In 1952 both major national political parties addressed the Indians' future in their platforms. Although neither party called specifically for ending the federal-tribe relationship, both spoke of allowing Indians to enjoy the full rights of citizenship. The Republicans stated, "We shall eliminate the shameful waste of the Bureau of Indian Affairs. . . . We pledge to undertake programs to provide the Indians with equal opportunities for education, health protection and economic development." The Democrats promised to "continue to use the powers of the federal government to advance the health, education and economic well-being of our American Indian citizens." The Democrats also said, "The American Indians should be completely integrated into the social, economic and political life of the nation" and promised final settlement of Indian claims.[16]

Administration and congressional policies converged in 1953 with the inauguration of Republican Dwight Eisenhower as president and new Republican majorities in both houses of Congress. Although Watkins was far from the only congressional proponent of termination, he was the member who pushed through the bills that ended tribal relations with the federal government. McKay, a former Oregon governor, enthusiastically put the laws into effect.

Both men appear to have been sincere in their belief that the Indians would be better off if they gave up tribal communities and either became farmers or went off to the cities and found jobs. Watkins also seemed convinced that Indians' only reason for wanting to retain their treaty status was to avoid paying state taxes on their land and property. McKay, who as governor had set up a council of Indians to meet with state officials on a somewhat regular basis, seemed to have a better understanding and more sympathy for the Indians. Historian Kenneth R. Philp notes that termination "reflected the conservative and nationalist mood of the Cold War era that resonated with the ideologies of individualism and capitalism." Indian law expert Charles Wilkinson cites also the shocking poverty on reservations and the ineptitude of the Indian Bureau.[17]

Looking back at the era leading to termination, the American Indian Policy Review Commission in its 1977 report said it was "impossible to assign one reason" for termination but listed "several explanations that were offered at the time." Among them were the following:

- "the notion that relatively well off tribes did not need a special relationship" with the government;

- "the notion that the way to relieve poverty among the Indians was to integrate them into American Society";
- Indian and congressional disapproval of the BIA;
- concern over "undefined law and order" jurisdiction around reservations;
- non-Indians' desire to obtain tribal lands;
- an overall desire to "reduce 'big government'"[18]

The commission barely mentioned two things that government records indicate also were major reasons behind the push for termination. One was concern, mostly by the BIA and a few organizations interested in Indian problems, that reservations could not support the growing Indian population. The number of Indians had dropped to a historic low of 237,196 in 1900 and then began to rise.[19] Although seldom mentioned in later discussions of termination, the issue appears in numerous documents in the 1940s and 1950s. The files of the Indian Office contain a 1942 report from the Administration Committee of the Association on American Indian Affairs on the Indian economic program. "Land is not the answer," the report said. There was not enough of it, and its ownership had been fractionated by inheritances.[20] Only slightly later, in the midst of World War II, the Department of the Interior was studying its postwar resources. Among those studies was a paper, completed in 1945, by James M. Stewart of the Office of Indian Affairs titled "How Can We Improve the Government Policy to Make the American Indians Economically Independent Faster, at the Lowest Cost?" Stewart said the underlying philosophy that Indians' future lies on the land needed reconsideration. Citing predictions that the Indian population, then 387,970, would grow by 120,000 in twenty-five years, he said, "Land acquisition cannot possibly meet this need." In fact, he said, the agency's land acquisition program could not even meet current needs, which had been listed in 1934 as 9.7 million acres.

Stewart outlined a program that would lead to ending government services for most Indians. "The overcrowded reservations, with no economic outlet available, if allowed to continue will quickly result in human misery, malnutrition on a tremendous scale, loss of self reliance and the will" to improve their lot.[21] In 1947, Representative Georgia Lusk of New Mexico entered into the *Congressional Record* a paper prepared by Mrs. John J. Kirk, president of the New Mexico State Welfare Board, for delivery to the National Conference on Indian Welfare. Titled "Withdrawal of Federal Supervision over Indian Affairs," her paper argued for moving Indians into mainstream society. Kirk said there was too little Indian land for the tribes to have a land-based economy.[22]

By 1956, with the termination program well under way, the government was using the lack of land argument to persuade Indians to agree to termination. In a meeting with western Washington tribes in Seattle that year, Indian Commissioner Glenn L. Emmons told the delegates the Indian population was growing too much for their reservations to support. He said he wanted to develop Indian lands to support the maximum number of people "on a decent plane of living" and encourage industry to locate near reservations to provide jobs. He also made a pitch for the relocation program, another effort to break up tribes by inducing Indians to leave their reservations for city jobs.[23]

The other reason behind termination not mentioned by the policy review commission was the desire of state and county governments to get Indian land onto their tax rolls. Counties from at least half a dozen western states banded together in 1947 to demand that Indian lands be subject to taxation. Testifying at a 1947 Senate hearing on an unsuccessful attempt to liquidate the Klamath Reservation in Oregon, Judge (commissioner) J. R. Heckman of Lake County, one of the two counties containing the Klamath Reservation, said, "The time has come for county government in the West to get into the problem and protect the public interest" by getting Indian land onto tax rolls. "The Association of Oregon Counties is going to work on this until it is finished."[24] Another witness, rancher Will Vernon, noted that Klamath County, the other county containing the Klamath Indian Reservation, had joined with counties in Arizona, Montana, Utah, California, "and other Western states" to try to end tax exemptions on Indian land.[25]

In 1950 sixteen states formed the Governors Interstate Council on Indian Affairs with one of its aims to "bring an early end to federal wardship." The National Governors' Conference approved creation of the council and its aims within a few months.[26] That same year Indian Commissioner Dillon S. Myer conceded, "Taxation of Indian lands is an issue that must be addressed." Watkins brought up the tax issue at every hearing he conducted. In fact, a Spokane Indian delegation told Commissioner Emmons in 1955 that Senator Watkins had explained to them a few months earlier that "the real idea [behind termination] was to put Indian land on the tax rolls."[27]

Those few members of Congress who took an interest in Indian issues had varied motivations for ending Indian programs. Some wanted to get Indian land onto state tax rolls. Some looked at tribally owned property and saw shades of communism. These people considered such community ownership positively un-American. Communism, in the form of ideology and a country—the Soviet Union—had replaced fascism, in the form of the Axis nations, as America's perceived enemy in the late 1940s and 1950s. And finally, to some, there was the cost of the Bureau of Indian Affairs and Indian programs. All those ideas meshed neatly into Watkins's crusade. As the movement for termination gained support, former Indian commissioner John Collier wrote a paper titled "Why Federal Services to Indians Should Be Continued." Prepared as suggestions for topics to be covered by Interior Secretary Oscar Chapman in a 1947 town hall meeting, the paper noted previous government efforts to "liquidate its responsibilities for large groups of Indians." Each led to poverty and demoralization for the Indians, he said. "This history would repeat itself if the United States should again repudiate its obligation," Collier wrote. It was an accurate forecast of the results of the 1950s termination policy.[28]

During those postwar years pressure increased on the BIA to work its way out of existence. The agency drew up a plan in 1948, not carried out, to end its programs for California Indians.[29] Indian Commissioners John R. Nichols and Dillon Myer both began to work toward the Hoover Commission goals. Nichols in 1949 told BIA employees to direct reservation programs toward termination of federal activities "at the appropriate time."[30] The next year Myer, Nichols's successor, began planning for a "step by step transfer" of BIA functions to other entities.

In 1950, with the Bosone Resolution (named for Utah Democrat Reva Beck Bosone) the House told the BIA not only to provide a list of tribes that could be terminated, but to recommend "some method of procedure whereby the termination of Federal supervision and control over Indians may be effected." The Senate failed to act on the resolution, however. Secretary of the Interior Oscar Chapman endorsed the resolution but cautioned against "precipitate withdrawal of guarantees protecting property rights or by termination of Federal services" before other services were available.[31] The next year Congress considered a measure to remove from the Constitution the congressional power to regulate commerce with the Indians and another measure to abolish the BIA. Despite strong opposition from tribes and intertribal organizations, both houses of Congress approved the Bosone Resolution in 1952 and provided the BIA with $50,000 to begin planning termination of tribes.

That set the stage for the 1953 passage by unanimous consent of House Concurrent Resolution 108, calling for an end to 164 years of relations between the federal government and Indian tribes. The resolution stated that federal supervision of tribes should be terminated "as rapidly as circumstances will permit." The hearing on the resolution had consisted almost entirely of testimony from tribes seeking to be omitted from the termination list. Among those cited in the resolution as presumed ready for immediate termination were the timber rich Menominees of Wisconsin and Klamaths of Oregon.[32]

With passage of HCR 108 Watkins became the dominant figure in the termination drive. A Mormon attorney, sometime ranch manager, newspaper editor, and organizer of water districts, Watkins was considered a moderate Republican when he entered the Senate. Historian R. Warren Metcalf describes Watkins in *Termination's Legacy: The Discarded Indians of Utah* as a man whose beliefs were firmly grounded in the Mormon Church and the Republican Party. Although he had lived near a reservation, he had little contact with Indians and no understanding of their views. "He did not betray the slightest concern for the economic needs of the Paiutes," Metcalf wrote.[33] Most accounts of Watkins's life list the major role of his Senate career as chairmanship of the committee that recommended censure for Senator Joseph McCarthy, the Wisconsin Republican who gave his name to an era with wide-ranging accusations that the nation was riddled with communists.

Watkins won respect from all sides in his handling of the committee investigation and report. He exhibited no such even handedness in dealing with the Indian issue. Almost immediately after he was sworn into office in January 1947, he became chairman of the Senate's Indian subcommittee and within months was holding extensive hearings on a proposal to withdraw federal supervision of the Klamath Tribes. Like many western members of Congress in both parties, he supported reclamation projects and voted to spend federal money on many. But he saw money spent on Indian programs as promoting socialism while the government was fighting communism.

Watkins viewed himself as a champion of Indian "freedom" and had little tolerance for those who disagreed. Witnesses before his subcommittee who agreed with him were treated with courtesy and given extended time to testify. He bullied Indian witnesses who disagreed until he got an answer he wanted. Other witnesses who disagreed also faced harsh questioning and an abrupt end to their testimony.

Where the Hoover Commission had recommended a period of years to prepare tribes to administer their own programs, Watkins wanted the government to shed its responsibilities as quickly as possible. He had support both from colleagues in Congress and from the executive branch, moderately from the Truman administration and enthusiastically from the Eisenhower administration. Nothing much came of Watkins's efforts during his first term. However, after he was reelected in the Eisenhower landslide of 1952, he found an administration sympathetic to his ideas on Indians and eager to support his push for termination.[34]

President Eisenhower named as the secretary of the interior Douglas McKay, a Salem auto dealer who had been elected Oregon governor after serving as president of the State Senate. McKay took on the task of dismantling Indian tribes. As governor, McKay had expressed the view that Indians "should assume the responsibility and duties of full citizenship"[35]—a phrase generally used to mean "their land should be taxed." In an interview in Washington DC a few months after he took office, McKay pledged he would "free the nation's 400,000 Indians from federal trusteeship" as soon as possible. He was quoted as saying, "The sooner we stop making government wards of them the sooner we can start making first class citizens of them."[36] To give the administration its due, both Eisenhower and McKay said that no tribe should be terminated without its consent.

Watkins had a different view. He thought if a tribe was "ready" in his estimation, it should be terminated whether the tribe favored such action or not. "Congress is of a mind to see that the Indians get more responsibility even if they don't want it," Watkins was quoted as saying in 1947.[37] At some of Watkins's hearings there was no testimony from any Indian. He considered treaties no obstacle. He was, in short, a man who knew how the world should be managed, and he set out to organize it along his lines, using as his victims probably the politically weakest group in the nation.[38] It was Watkins who kept the issue alive, often holding hearings alone or with a single colleague. As chairman of the Senate Subcommittee on Indian Affairs, he pushed ten bills through Congress cutting the federal ties to tribes and sending them out into the white world, ready or not. Most were not.

Congress showed no particular logic as it decided which tribes to remove from federal rolls. Although HCR 108 listed specific tribes that should be targeted for termination, only three large tribes and a number of small California bands from that list were actually cut from federal supervision. The remainder of the tribes ousted from federal protection were neither listed in the bill nor among those on Zimmerman's list of tribes ready for independence.[39] There were tribes considered the wealthiest. There were destitute tribes in which few people spoke English. There were tribes the BIA had ignored for years and tribes where the BIA agency headquarters was staffed by dozens of federal employees.

Zimmerman had recommended four criteria, including a tribe's degree of acculturation and its economic status. The House Committee on Interior and Insular Affairs, however, rejected those on the grounds that the standards were based on tribes, not individuals. "In essence, the Committee scrapped the use of any specific criteria," the Policy Review Commission stated. Instead, it "relied upon the subjective reports of BIA field agents."[40] In none of the extensive congressional hearings did Watkins or any other member of the House and Senate Indian subcommittees explain why the choices were made. Survivors in each tribe have opinions about why they were targeted, but there is little or no documentation of any reasons. Some believe industry wanted the tribal resources, mostly timber; others believe whites wanted Indian land.

By the time the program of termination had become thoroughly discredited, nearly 13,000 people in nine dozen Indian tribes and small bands had been pushed into a society in which many of them were ill prepared to cope. The largest and richest of the terminated tribes were the Menominees in Wisconsin, among the first to feel Watkins's zeal in 1953, and the Klamaths of Oregon. Also pushed out of the federal nest were four poverty-stricken small Utah tribes whose members had little education, little arable land, and little chance of success. The "mixed blood" Utes of Utah worked out a split of tribal assets with the full-blood tribal members and, according to congressional records, accepted termination. That is the only group that was denied a return to tribal status.

One catch-all bill ended federal supervision of more than thirty small California tribes and bands; no one seemed sure then or later exactly how many were affected. Another such catch-all bill listed sixty small Oregon tribes, including the Cow Creek band of Umpqua Indians who had never been fully acknowledged by the federal government. Years later, the Cow Creeks used the fact of their termination to prove their existence as a tribe and win a place in the family of federally recognized tribes. Also cut loose were the Catawba Tribe of South Carolina, the Alabama-Coushattas of Texas, and the Peoria, Ottawa, and Wydanotte tribes of Oklahoma. The last caught in the termination trap was the Northern Ponca Tribe of Nebraska, cut out in 1963 long after Watkins's 1958 defeat in his bid for a third term.[41]

Each of the terminated tribes was different in history and economic and social status, but some things were common to all, or almost all. Most of the affected tribal members had no idea what termination was or what it would mean in their lives. Few of the tribes were prepared to manage their tribal business on their own. Few tribal members in many tribes were prepared to deal with ordinary economic matters such as taxes, credit, banks, and determined salesmen. Some Indians saw a bright side to termination, hoping that an end to Indian programs and tax exemptions would end prejudice against them. It did not. They found that jobs and credit were still out of their reach. Some tribes fought against being terminated and won. Others resisted but were blackmailed into acceptance with threats to withhold payment of court-ordered claims settlements. Some felt termination was inevitable and accepted it. And some scarcely realized what was happening to them until it was too late.

Along with termination, other measures also were being taken to push the Indians into the mainstream of American society. Congress passed Public Law 280 in 1953, allowing several states to assume law enforcement and civil legal authority on reservations, replacing BIA and tribal administration. Agreement between each state and the federal government was required, but the affected tribes did not have to be consulted. Congress also began steps to remove Indian health care from the BIA to a new Indian Health Service within the Public Health Service. The BIA stepped up its contracts with states to educate Indian children in public schools rather than in reservation and BIA boarding schools established in the late 1800s.

BIA intensified another program, a "tion" from Joe Thomas's list. Relocating Indians to urban areas, usually far from reservations, for jobs and education had its beginning in the 1930s, was renewed after World War II, and was intensified in the early 1950s during the drive for termination. Most of the more than 200,000 people relocated between 1950 and 1968 had spent their lives in rural areas or small towns. They were sent mostly to large cities—Denver, San Francisco, Chicago, Dallas, Boston, Philadelphia.[42]

For individuals used to living among extended families the experience of being alone in unfamiliar surroundings was often overwhelming. Many dropped out and went back to the reservation. For those who stayed, the feeling of isolation remained. The pull toward home was evidenced decades later when tribes began building casinos that provided hundreds of jobs. Many of the relocated tribal members went back to their reservations.

Too often both relocation and termination of tribal status meant separation of Indian families and neighbors and a loss of shared culture, the destruction of a way of life with neither knowledge nor means to fully adapt to the larger society.

Members of Congress generally couched termination in terms of "freedom" for the Indians, of "liberating" tribal members from supervision by government and from the traditions of tribe and culture. The government did not label the program "termination" until late in the process. Instead, officials called it at various times readjustment, withdrawal, relinquishment of supervision, emancipation, release from restrictions, liquidation. There was little indication in any of these labels or the laws or hearings that the politicians understood anything of Indians' deep ties to their land and the importance of extended families and tribal relationships. Nor was there any consideration in evidence for Indian culture, tradition, and the importance of their hunting and fishing rights.

It was the loss of these intangibles that made many tribal members feel they had lost their identity and were adrift in a world they did not understand. It is that loss that is the subject of this book.

2 Menominees

Ambush

The Menominees were ambushed.

The three-thousand-member Menominee Indian Tribe asked Congress to approve a $1,500 payment to each member from its own tribal —not government—funds. Instead, the Wisconsin tribe got legislation severing its relationship with the federal government. That action brought the "Menominee people to the brink of economic, social and cultural disaster."[1] The effects were still felt half a century later.

There had been warnings. In 1947 the tribe was among ten that Assistant Commissioner of Indian Affairs William Zimmerman placed on a list of tribes ready for immediate "emancipation." However, nothing had been done about that list by either Congress or the Truman administration. Two decades earlier the Meriam Report had proposed creating a corporation to operate the tribe's profitable forest and lumber mill "as a great national asset." Tribal members would own shares in the corporation, but government officers would control the board of directors.[2] The Menominees had long wanted more control of their own activities including the timber and sawmill operations that paid most of the cost of operating the reservation. Before declaring their independence, however, the Indians wanted to invest in improving the business and their reservation's infrastructure. They were thinking long term. Suddenly Congress and the Bureau of Indian Affairs were demanding "now."

In 1951 the Menominees won a multimillion-dollar settlement from the federal government for mismanagement of the tribe's rich pine forest during the early years of the twentieth century. Under federal law, the tribe could not automatically collect the money resulting from the lawsuit; Congress had to appropriate funds for payment. In January 1952 a tribal delegation presented the BIA with a proposal to spend $9.5 million in tribal funds for a three-point program of reservation development. Included in the program were per capita payments of $1,000 to tribal members. The BIA responded that it would not recommend congressional approval because the proposal did not specifically include steps toward termination. After that rebuff, the Menominees asked Congress to approve part of the judgment money as a $1,500 per capita payment to tribal members. Again, the BIA opposed the Menominees' request "until there was a comprehensive termination plan." Congress took no action. However, it did put the Menominees on the list of tribes it considered ready for immediate release from federal supervision when it passed House Resolution 108 making termination the official policy in August 1953.[3]

One of the tribal delegates to Washington, Monroe Weso, explained later during a congressional hearing what happened next: "So far as I know this problem of withdrawal of Federal supervision started out in December 1952 when the Menominee Tribe selected a delegation to proceed to Washington to obtain legislation under which the Menominee tribal members were to receive $1,500 each of the tribal funds on deposit in the United States Treasury. A simple per capita bill, designed to achieve the desires of the tribe was drafted and introduced by Congressman [Melvin] Laird. This was in February 1953."[4]

The House passed the bill described by Weso. The Senate, at the behest of Senator Arthur Watkins, amended the House-passed bill by substituting termination of federal supervision for

the requested payment. The amended bill, approved by committee without a hearing and passed by the Senate, set a deadline of
December 31, 1958, for ending the Menominees' status as a federally recognized Indian tribe. "The Menominee Tribe objected stren-
uously to such an early termination date," Weso testified at the 1954
joint hearing by the House and Senate Indian Affairs subcommittees. Watkins told the tribal delegates "he would not arrange for action on the bill until he obtained a commitment from the tribe that it
would agree to withdrawal of federal supervision," Weso said. "We
had no authority to commit the tribe." Wisconsin Republicans Laird
and John Byrnes prevented the House from approving the Senate
version, and "our tribal delegation went back to the reservation to
draft a bill in lieu of" the Senate measure, Weso said. Laird said he
opposed the amended bill because a hundred years earlier the U.S.
government agreed the tribe could possess its reservation without
taxes. "Careful consideration is needed to modify that agreement,"
he said. He added, "Congress is under moral obligation to consider
the views of the tribe and state before altering treaties. I believe the
tribe's views should be honored if they are reasonable. I believe the
Menominee views are reasonable."[5]

The tribe, Laird, and the state of Wisconsin proved no match for
Watkins, who was chairman of the Indian Affairs Subcommittee of
the Senate Public Lands Committee. The Menominees won some
delays, but in 1961 the tribe that had successfully resisted removal
from its ancestral lands in the mid-1800s and the fracturing of its
reservation through allotments in the late 1800s and early 1900s fell
victim to the newest Indian policy—termination.[6] Ten years later the
Indians were poorer in money, health, and education. Even worse,
their social fabric was in tatters.

Tribal member Ada Deer, then a college student and later the
commissioner of Indian Affairs, recalled the tribal members' pain,
"a litany of terrible consequences." "Termination affected the whole

tribe," she said in a 2001 interview in her office at the University of Wisconsin in Madison, where she headed the American Indian Studies Program. "The tribal hospital closed because it didn't meet state standards. Mother [who was not Indian] was fired as a nurse for her activity. Personally, our family suffered because she got fired from her job. All the tribe suffered because they didn't have access to medical care. Funds for education were gone. Land became subject to taxation. If I hadn't had my social work salary our family would have suffered more. For years I sent money home to help with family expenses."

Deer's father worked at the tribal lumber mill and managed to hang onto his job although the new manager hired by the tribe reduced employment to make the mill more efficient. Deer described "an immediate clash of culture" with the arrival of the white manager from the Pacific Northwest timber industry. Before termination the tribe had operated the mill partly to provide members with jobs. After termination, faced with the necessity to pay taxes and make a profit, the new manager dismissed workers, often for things that previously had been overlooked. The mill's efficiency increased, but so did unemployment.[7]

The profit motive had other effects. Before termination, most people on the reservation had electricity from the nonprofit tribal utility. The tribal business entity sold the utility to a private company, which charged market rates. A number of people were unable to pay their bills and lost electric service. Some, unable to pay the taxes that came with the loss of tribal status, lost their homes.[8]

In addition, Deer said, "Termination brought a terrible identity crisis to our people. I remember one gentleman telling me he was mystified—one day he's an Indian; the next day he's not. In my estimation termination was a deep psychic blow to the individual and the tribe. We are still overcoming some of the damage. . . . It just gave them a blow to the stomach."[9]

Looking back half a century later, an observer is inclined to ask two questions: If the Menominees were so unable to cope with termination, why was the tribe selected as one of the first to lose federal protection? And couldn't the problems have been foreseen? The answer to the second question is yes. The answer to the first is more complicated.

On the surface the Menominee Tribe was wealthy. It owned one of the most productive pine forests in the country; its timber was valued at $36 million. Tribal logging and mill operations provided enough money that the tribe paid almost entirely for its own services, including the salaries of five dozen federal employees who managed the reservation. In 1953 the federal government paid only $95,000 for roads, blister rust control, and maintenance of federal buildings and $50,000 for education under the Johnson-O'Malley Act, which provides federal payments to school districts that educate reservation children. The tribe itself paid $56,745 for operation of two schools on the reservation. In all, the tribe budgeted $2.86 million for operating the BIA agency, the mill and forest, health care, welfare, and law and order.[10] Watkins and others looked at the tribal operations and saw a thriving business and no reason for government supervision. They needed to look further.

"The Menominee are tribally wealthy and culturally assimilated," anthropologist Rachel Reese Sady wrote in 1947. "Individually, they were poor and socially disorganized." Their housing, health and education were below national norms.[11] Writing nearly two decades later, Princeton political scientist Gary Orfield said, "Termination was based on a series of false assumptions and the policy cannot achieve the goals so convincingly set forth in the subcommittee hearing room."[12]

Two years before the Menominee termination bill was introduced in Congress the Wisconsin Human Rights Commission described the tribe as "a prosperous people" second only to the oil-rich Oklahoma tribes in wealth. But the report added a couple of troubling notes: a reservation survey showed less than 5 percent of the children had an adequate diet, and the community hospital had been condemned with an estimate that it would require $100,000 to bring it up to state standards.[13]

Among other problems that Congress overlooked or brushed aside was the fact that few Menominee tribal members had been involved in management of the tribal enterprises. Those functions were handled by BIA personnel, few of whom were Indians and even fewer were Menominees. The Interior Department, however, in its report to Congress on the proposed legislation sloughed off its own agency's role as "one of advising the tribe." However, few tribal members had the educational background to assume management of a large business such as the forest and mill. Of 1,226 adult tribal members polled, 889 had finished the eighth grade, 328 had graduated from high school, and 9 had finished college. Twenty-two tribal members neither spoke nor understood English.[14] Nor was the tribe organized for effective self-government. Most decisions were made by the General Council, composed of all adult tribal members. An advisory council handled business between General Council meetings, but it had no administrative functions or staff. It had won the right to approve the budget for tribal operations in 1934 and used that power to influence—and sometimes remove—BIA managers. In the dozen years after the advisory council won budget authority the reservation had two superintendents, four mill managers, and two combination superintendents/mill managers. Half a dozen of those managers left as a result of antagonism and conflict over the budget.[15]

Tribal homes had been built on lots assigned by the tribe. Homeowners did not own the land or pay taxes on either land or houses. Jobs outside the mill were scarce and generally low paying, but many tribal members maintained family food supplies through hunting and fishing on the reservation lands that were open to all tribal members.

If all these concerns failed to impress Congress, Assistant Secretary of the Interior John A. Carver Jr. put the issue in stark economic terms only a few days before termination went into effect. "The basic premise," he told a congressional hearing, "has come to be a question of whether the lumber industry as presently constituted on the reservation is big enough to support the Indians." Carver called the tribal enterprise "a very attractive operation." He added, "But there is a basic difficulty in translating a single industry operation into all the ramifications and complexity of community and government activities. Furthermore, we don't really have any way to make a direct conversion of one sawmill operation, which is customarily carried out as a private proposition, into full support of an American community . . . the proceeds of the mill won't reach all of the needs which will follow on termination."[16] Congress ignored Carver too.

The tribe sought delays in hopes that a more sympathetic Congress and administration might be elected.[17] However, despite the warnings scattered over the seven-year period from initial termination legislation to the actual severing of federal ties, the tribe was pushed out of the federal family of Indian nations April 30, 1961. Senator Gaylord Nelson (D-WI) said later that in 1960, when termination could have been halted, he went to Washington as governor of Wisconsin and "made all the same predictions of exactly what was going to happen," adding, "So it really was an unnecessary tragedy because we had enough information then to know that the policy of termination would not work."[18]

Before Nelson became governor in 1959, the state's record on the Menominee termination was more mixed. The state tax commissioner, Harry Harder, told Watkins in the 1954 hearing, "The governor [then Walter J. Kohler Jr.] is not opposed to termination. . . .

He would like it done in more orderly fashion." After that the state, although trying to help the tribe prepare for the transition, mostly supported the Menominees' requests to delay termination.[19]

Verna Fowler was in the fifth grade when the inexorable march toward termination began in 1953. Like many tribal children, she accompanied her parents to meetings of the General Council through her grade and high school years. She didn't remember much about the discussions, she said in a 2001 interview in her office at the College of the Menominee Nation, where she was president. She did remember "leaving General Council meeting and seeing people leaving crying." Of termination, she said, "it's a foreboding word, not a good thing for people."[20] The word "termination" had been adopted as less threatening than "liquidation," the initial designation of the program.[21]

Whatever term was used, Fowler said, "People never felt they had any say. It was pushed on them. . . . They did not know what they were voting on; they never understood." Many tribal members said later they thought they were voting only on approval of the per capita payment from tribal funds. Others said they felt they had to approve the idea of termination to get Congress to give them their money.

When termination finally took effect, Fowler said, "we were told we were not Indian. I remember being in Chicago and told I was not an Indian. I was numb. It was like I had lost my identity. . . . It was hard to cope with . . . Once I was told I was not Indian, I had to ask 'who am I?' 'what am I if not Indian?'"[22]

Watkins asked numerous Indian witnesses in his hearings how they defined themselves as Indian, mostly in what appeared to be an effort to show that there were few "real" Indians. He asked Indian witnesses what percentage of their heritage was tribal. He asked how many tribal members were full-blooded Indians. He told a spokesman for the Menominees at a 1954 hearing: "The Menominee can either be U.S. citizens [giving up their tribal status] or renounce their citizenship and be foreigners. There is nothing else."[23] When Laird raised issues related to the government's treaty with the Menominees, Watkins dismissed them as irrelevant. The Administration was equally cavalier. H. Rex Lee, assistant secretary of the interior, told Laird there was no conflict between the Menominee treaty and the termination bill. "The tribal attorney told us no rights are affected," he said.

Watkins was in a hurry to get termination carried out. As the Menominees, Wisconsin state officials, and the tribe's supporters in Congress argued for more time to develop plans for independent tribal and forest operations, Watkins insisted on shorter periods. After a June 1953 meeting with the tribe, Laird suggested a five-year period of preparation. Watkins responded that the Eisenhower administration would be out of office in four years—1957—and it was necessary to have the tribe terminated by then.[24] It seems odd that Watkins, a Republican, would believe that Eisenhower, whose GOP administration was only six months old, would not be re-elected in 1956.

After ambushing the Menominees with his 1953 substitution, Watkins accepted the tribe's invitation to visit the reservation. He spent two or three days traveling around the 233,902-acre reservation in north central Wisconsin and met with the General Council for about forty-five to fifty minutes on June 20, 1953. Antoine Waupochick, then the tribal chairman, described the visit for a congressional hearing twenty years later: "I took him around the plant and I escorted him all over. We took him around. We showed him all our old buildings, all our old dilapidated homes, and I showed him what termination would do. I said those homes are only worth $10, and they wouldn't bring in much tax money. . . . I took him around the mill and one of the things he wanted was, he wanted the Menominees to run their own affairs . . . during my walk with him he asked me, Tony, he said, 'I always see white people in these positions, these boss positions.' 'Well, I said, they don't trust the Menominee. They hire white people to run our affairs and that's the way we have to take it. We don't have much to say,' I said. We took him up to Zoar and showed him the old burial grounds. We showed him some of our old homes, and, like I said, even in Washington it appeared to me that he—that all the statements we made opposing termination, he just said, 'well you're good boys,' and that is it."[25]

After Watkins left the reservation, the General Council, composed of all adult tribal members, discussed the issue for several hours and "adopted a resolution approving withdrawal in principle." The vote was 169 to 5, a small portion of the adult members of the tribe. Opponents of termination said later that most tribal members "chose to be absent" to express their negative reaction to termination. Many authorities have noted that Indians' failure to vote generally means opposition. Even so, tribal attorney Ernest Wilkinson, testifying at the 1954 hearing, said, "I and the council felt that [the vote] represented a substantial commitment to Senator Watkins's desire." However, when the tribal delegates again met with the senator in Washington, there was "a failure of meeting of minds." The delegates returned to Wisconsin. "He [Watkins] wanted this legislation wrapped up during the present administration. We needed further instructions." The tribe took another vote in July and told its delegates to give up the per capita payment rather than accept Watkins's bill.[26]

Watkins told witnesses at the 1954 hearing, where he was presiding, "If we don't begin to set deadlines and get termination dates, it will go again and again and again. The U.S. has already lost $9.5 million because of alleged failure as guardians. There is the prospect of another suit. . . . This tribe is probably better prepared than any other tribe in the U.S. It sort of sets the pattern. If it gets 10 to 15 years other tribes will want five times that and this generation won't see termination."[27] Later, he said he blamed Congress for the

Indians' continued lack of independence from government because Congress sets policy, and it vacillates. Faced with Watkins's insistence that termination was inevitable, the Menominees tried to delay, winning a deadline of four and a half years instead of the three years Watkins favored.[28]

Although committee hearings are ostensibly held to provide Congress with information on which to base legislation, Watkins devoted much time to giving witnesses his opinions. In the 1954 hearing, for instance, he ridiculed the idea that the government should obtain tribal consent for termination. Indians vote on imposing taxes on whites, he said, "but they will not consent to paying taxes. And it is something we have found is the main question when you really get down to the kernel of things."[29] Many Indians, on the other hand, argued that exemption from property taxes was one of the promises the government made in taking most of their land. It was another example of the difference in viewpoint between Indians and whites such as Watkins. To the Indians the treaties were permanent promises; to Watkins they were outdated documents and irrelevant.[30] In the same 1954 hearing, he said he thought termination was "in the best interests of the Indians." He added, "Even though they don't like it, I think it is better for them to have more and more control of their properties . . . see what the colored people have done without reservations or properties. . . . They had been taught to work in the white man's way . . . they take care of themselves. Matter of getting down to basic principles involved in growth of peoples." Watkins's other frame of reference for Indians was the post–World War II refugee camps of Europe and the Near East, which he described as similar to his visit to the Menominee Reservation. The senator argued that federal supervision was destructive to Indians.

In response, Jonathan M. Steere, testifying on behalf of the Indian Rights Association, argued, "There is no advance if Indian assets are dissipated and they are reduced to dependency." He quoted

Indian Commissioner Glenn L. Emmons in a speech earlier that year, "What is holding the Indians back is ill health, lack of full education opportunity and poverty. By attacking at the root we can hasten federal withdrawal." Watkins's response was to return to his theme that Indians just didn't want to pay taxes.[31]

James Caldwell, who was logging superintendent for Menominee Indian Mills, outlined some of the problems associated with moving the lumber mill from tribal status to full commercial operation, including the necessity of using much of the mill's net income of $200,000 a year for taxes. "Employment will have to be scaled down," Caldwell said. That would cause disruption in tribal and individual economies. "We have to do studies to find out how to shift surplus labor," Caldwell said.

Watkins scoffed, "One way to protect them is tell them to work or else." Caldwell said it would be no different from potato growers and other farmers getting subsidies. Watkins said he favored taking away as many subsidies as possible, although subsidies for defense were all right if they were necessary. As for those farm subsidies, they could be justified by the country's need for food. He said the Indians, however, needed to get stimulated "with a little ambition and necessity."[32]

The June 1953 tribal resolution called for selection of a planning officer. The council met September 14 to elect a person to that new position, but the BIA did not approve the selection, and the job was not filled. The council met again September 30 and voted 156 to 0 to create a planning commission to draft a proposed bill. Working with state officials and others in Wisconsin, the commission presented its proposal to the General Council at two meetings in December. "There was much discussion but no action," Weso, the tribal delegate, said. The commission took its plan to smaller groups of tribal members throughout the reservation in a series of December meetings. In a session January 6, which continued January 7, the General

Council approved the planning commission bill with two amendments. Senator Joseph McCarthy (R-WI) introduced the measure in the Senate, and Laird introduced it in the House.[33] It was those bills that were the subject of the March 1954 hearing.

The two bills provided for the per capita payment the tribe desperately wanted. They also authorized withdrawal of federal supervision over the tribe, with a deadline for tribal takeover in five years. The process contained in the bills required the tribe to submit a plan for withdrawal and for managing tribal assets and government. The bills allowed the tribe to hire management specialists to assist in drawing up the plan. Workers at the tribal lumber mill would keep their federal job benefits for ten years. Tribal members would keep their hunting, fishing, trapping, and harvest rights. The tribe would retain title to the lakes and streams on the reservation. The BIA recommended passage.[34]

Congressman Byrnes told the 1954 hearing he favored releasing the Menominees from federal supervision, and he believed the tribe favored that action. "The tribe has demonstrated . . . it should be relieved from wardship," Byrnes said. He added, however, that there was a "serious question whether the older people of the tribe have the ability to be on their own."

Byrnes was at least equally concerned about the fate of the Menominee forest, which he described as big business, an important aspect for the general economy of Wisconsin. "It would be a frightful thing to the state as a whole if something should dissipate this or it got tied up in a confused state," he said, adding, "There has to be some mechanism to protect individual tribal members." Then Byrnes said the obvious, which others ignored: "This is in a sense a pilot operation. It is an area of first experiment."[35]

There were many problems getting the experiment started. The first misstep was the failure of both the BIA and the Congress to let Wisconsin state officials know that the Menominee people and property were about to be dumped into state jurisdiction. After Watkins's meeting with the tribe and the passage of the tribal resolution approving the principle of termination, there was no opportunity to confer with the state, explained Lee of the Department of the Interior. There was only a "short time until amendments were drafted and the bill introduced."[36] Harder, the Wisconsin director of taxation, complained, "I find it peculiar, the federal government had these Indians for 100 years. Now the state is supposed to get everything done in a couple of years." Replied Watkins, "We assumed the state was working on it." He had never met with any state officials to discuss the issue. Harder and Congressman Laird found it difficult to make Watkins understand some problems the state faced, beginning with the necessity of assessing reservation property for tax purposes.

Couldn't the state just use the federal appraisal of the forest? Watkins demanded. Laird explained that the BIA evaluation was merely a timber cruise, assessing the market value of the tribal timber, not an evaluation of all property for state taxing purposes. And, said Harder, the BIA took five years just to do the timber cruise. The state would need time to obtain an appropriation from its legislature, to hire additional appraisers, and then to evaluate more than two hundred thousand acres of timber, farm, residential, and business property. "The federal government is slower than anybody else," snapped Watkins. "The state will be more efficient. That is one of the reasons for termination."[37]

Watkins also dismissed a warning comment from Lloyd Andrews, a local attorney for the tribe. "Leaders of the tribe have a terrific problem of education to get many of these people to understand what they should be doing logically here," Andrews said. Replied the senator: "They'll have a lot of expert help like I do. They have resources to do it. They can understand they own stock and there will be dividends."[38] This, remember, was the mid-1950s, when few people outside the wealthy owned stocks and probably fewer understood them even outside the isolated world of an Indian reservation.

Gordon Dickie, a member of the tribal advisory council and a logging contractor on the reservation, said it would be two to four years before the mill operation realized all the benefits from planned improvements. Only in the past few years had the tribe made real progress toward finding and solving its problems, he said. It also would take time to develop a plan for agricultural land and to develop other businesses to provide jobs for tribal members. "It's not your job to try to furnish work for all," Watkins said, revealing again his lack of understanding of Indian culture.[39] In fact, the tribal authorities were at least as committed to providing jobs for tribal members as to making a profit.

The process leading to termination sharply divided the tribe, which had never been politically cohesive. Tribal delegates to Washington were trapped between their members, who wanted delays and changes in the legislation, and Congress, whose members wanted rapid termination. In the midst of negotiations the General Council censured and replaced its delegation to Congress. The BIA was no help to the tribe. Its officials in Washington gave little weight to objections from its own area director in Minneapolis, who opposed rapid Menominee termination.

Despite pleas from the Menominees and Wisconsin officials, Congress passed the termination bill in 1954, mostly unaware that the tribal vote for termination came after Watkins threatened to prevent the tribe from getting its settlement funds and that the General Council had unanimously reversed its vote a short time later. In signing the measure June 17, 1954, President Eisenhower commended the tribal members for "the impressive progress they have achieved." He added, "In a real sense they have opened a new era in Indian affairs—an era of growing self reliance." Eisenhower conceded that the Menominee bill did not solve all the problems of federal withdrawal from Indian affairs but added, "I am sure that it will provide useful and sound guide lines for authorizing other Tribes to realize their full potentialities."[40]

The measure gave the tribe until 1958 to develop a plan for the tribe's future and submit it to the secretary of the interior for approval. The Indians had four choices for their reservation: convert it into a national forest; convert it into a state forest; give residential parcels of land to tribal members and split the reservation between adjoining Shawano and Oconto counties to govern; or convert the reservation into a separate county.

Faced with such a monstrous change in everything they had known, the Indians delayed. Many did not understand what "termination" meant. Some who did understand could not believe their treaties no longer would protect them. Others just didn't know what to do. Tribal members agreed on only thing—they wanted to keep Menominee land intact. Members chose the fourth alternative—a separate county despite estimates that it would be more costly than annexing to an adjoining county.[41]

The state eventually did the real work of helping the Menominees make the transition. In 1955 the Wisconsin Legislature appointed a Menominee Indian Study Committee to determine the problems the tribe and state would face in making the transition. This high-level group, with University of Wisconsin faculty members doing most of the research, accumulated the detailed information about potential costs to the tribe of managing health care and welfare. Committee members, however, expressed fear that the Menominees were so divided they could not agree on a workable plan to administer the community or their economic affairs.[42]

Just when the Menominees really needed the BIA's help, the agency cut the number of its people on the reservation by half.[43] Even when the tribe asked BIA for help with an analysis of the tribe's money in the U.S. Treasury, it had to wait months for the data. In 1960, as termination was approaching, BIA transferred the long-time mill manager to Minneapolis and replaced him with a man with no familiarity with the Menominee operation. By that time the tribal economy had declined to the point it needed federal help, and it was becoming increasingly evident that operating a county would require more money than the tribe had paid for the BIA operations on the reservation.

Converting a tribally owned reservation that had been under federal trust for a century was no easy task even with the help of state officials and the vast amount of information compiled by the state study committee. The state committee labored under several false assumptions—that termination resulted from agreement between the tribe and federal government, that there was a working political democracy on the reservation, and that the General Council, made up of all adult tribal members, could make extraordinarily complex governmental decisions in a limited period of time. Rather than offer recommendations for developing county government and tribal business, the committee offered options. When its subcommittee reports came in between 1956 and 1958, they were twenty pages each, outlining the current situation and several broad options for the future. "They essentially put into writing what everybody already knew," said tribal leader George Kenote.[44] After the final report—listing seven options for ownership and management of tribal assets—the state committee bowed out.

Although the study committee endorsed the tribe's plan to convert the reservation into a county, it warned that tribal members might not be ready for self-government. The committee noted an apathy toward politics, with domination of tribal government by a small clique, and said that a century of government paternalism had left its mark. With the termination date only two years away, the Wisconsin Legislature sent a memorial to Congress asking that the federal trust be continued indefinitely on grounds that termination "was seriously premature."[45]

Meanwhile, as the tribe struggled to design a government and business structure, it won the requested delay in the termination date. In 1957 the Tribal Council appointed a four-member Coordinating and Negotiating Committee to work out a plan, and with a 1958 deadline for submitting its plan approaching, the council endorsed, 139–2, a plea to the BIA to send Kenote, a longtime BIA employee, back to Wisconsin to help lay out the tribe's future. Kenote went to a large Milwaukee law firm for advice. The result was a complicated corporate structure governed by trusts that, in effect, put the management of the Indian corporation in non-Indian hands. The Wisconsin Legislature quickly approved the committee's recommendation that the tribal forest be taxed at 40 percent of its value if the woods were to be clear-cut instead of managed for sustained yield. There was more delay over the tribal business plan, with approval coming only after the tribe agreed that its property could not be mortgaged or sold without state approval. That action removed the last vestige of tribal control.[46]

While the Menominees were struggling to plan for termination, Interior Secretary Fred A. Seaton declared on September 18, 1958, there would be no more terminations without tribal approval.[47] But no one stopped the Menominees' reluctant march toward severing the tribe's government ties. The termination law was in effect, and there was no move to reverse it. Most tribal members did not understand the Kenote plan; they had been told if they did not approve a plan, the government would impose one and go ahead with termination. The tribe, again with only a small portion of its members voting, approved the plan for county and company 91 to 16 on January 17, 1959. On July 3 of that year Gaylord Nelson, then governor, signed a law making Menominee the state's seventy-second county. It also was the least populated, at 3,700 residents, and soon the state's poorest county, almost entirely dependent on a single taxpayer—the tribal timber business. The law would not take effect until April 30, 1961, at the same time the federal government's ties to the tribe were to be formally dissolved.[48]

Meanwhile the tribe faced the details of setting up a county government, in which no tribal members were experienced, and restructuring its forest and mill operations. Few members went to the meetings held to provide them with information about the new government, hoping that if they did not attend, termination would not happen. The directors of the new Menominee Enterprises Inc. struggled to bring the operation into compliance with state industrial standards, implement workers' compensation, and create a new accounting system. In 1960, as state officials became increasingly concerned that the tribe would still be unprepared when termination arrived, the state study committee returned to the issue, sending a member of the attorney general's staff to help implement the business plan.[49]

Both the state and tribe had reasons for concern. Kenote reported that by the end of 1962 the tribal corporation would have reserves totaling only $835,000, less than half the sum required for annual operation. At the same time, the BIA decided it would not make the final stumpage payment, an annual sum paid tribal members as a share of tribal mill profits. That left individuals scrambling for money to pay their debts to the mill store in the time remaining before they received termination-related money.

The termination bill provided for the $1,500 per capita payments the tribe had begun seeking in 1952. That took almost $5 million of the tribe's $10 million in capital. About the same time the BIA discovered that it had underpaid tribal members' annual dividends from the timber operation for several years and distributed $2 million from the tribal funds to make up for that oversight. Costs related to the termination cut more deeply into the reserve fund. In addition, the lumber market had begun a downward trend in 1958 just as the Menominees were preparing to depend entirely on that market for their existence. Even an increase in the annual amount of timber that could be cut to take advantage of markets for pulp and other additional products did not provide the needed revenue. By 1960, the year before termination went into effect, the once profit-making tribe was operating with a $250,000 annual deficit.

Six weeks before termination the financial situation forced the mill to lay off one-third of the workforce. That action caused an immediate jump in the county's welfare rolls before the county officially existed. Ironically, the tribe that had been costing the government $144,000 a year under federal supervision received $2.357 million in its final year as a recognized tribe for the expenses related to termination.[50]

After the federal ties were severed April 30, 1961, things got worse for the Menominees. To manage the timber business, the tribe hired an experienced industry manager from the Pacific Northwest, where lumbering practices were very different from the Upper Midwest. He bought new logging trucks, too big and heavy for the existing forest roads. One fully loaded truck sank in mud. The new manager changed the method of measuring logs, bringing in material the mill could not process. Workmen, who once felt part of a family business, feared for their jobs if they criticized management. By February 1962 the company reserves were down to $300,000. Two months later Congress enacted a package of financial assistance.[51]

The new county faced as many problems as the timber business. The added welfare load resulting from mill layoffs was only the beginning. The tribal hospital was forced to close because it did not meet state standards, and there was not enough money to make the required improvements. That left the county with no full-time medical care. Almost simultaneous with termination, there was an outbreak of tuberculosis among residents of the new county. With the hospital closed and no access to the federal Indian health program, the Indians faced severe suffering, and the county faced a $75,000 bill. In all, the state and new county spent nearly $200,000 to control the outbreak. The county planners learned belatedly that the county would be required to pay $50,000 for care of delinquents. Upgrading the sewer system to state standards cost several hundred thousand dollars. The planners had projected a $380,000 budget. The added costs boosted the figure to $600,000. The mill, which accounted, for 90 percent of the county tax base, was expected to earn only $240,000.[52]

The faltering lumber market collapsed in 1963, and the mill closed for six weeks for major repairs in 1964. On termination, title to all reservation real estate was transferred to the new corporate entity, Menominee Enterprises Inc. (MEI). Home owners were forced to buy the land under their houses from the corporation. For most, the only money they had was their share of the corporate stock, which they had received in the form of income bonds. Within three years six hundred families had traded their bonds for the property.[53]

The next few years were full of anecdotal evidence that termination had created more problems than it solved. A fire seriously damaged the mill when the county's fire engine wouldn't start, and when the truck belatedly reached the scene, the rotten hoses were ineffective. Some tribal members, unaccustomed to having any source of cash, bought unneeded cars or appliances with their per capita payment or MEI bonds. The largest payment tribal members had received previously was $150 each. Within a few years, 46 percent of the county's families were on welfare. Average per capita income in Menominee County was $881 compared to a state average of $2,404. Wives and mothers complained that paying for the formerly free electricity, fuel, and water cut further into family funds. One woman said she had to haul water from three miles away. By 1962 more than three hundred families had not paid the new property tax, and at least a thousand of the payment bonds had been assigned to buy home lots or obtain welfare assistance. Verna Fowler recalled that her family was unable to pay the taxes on her mother's land, and "we don't have it now." Water and electricity had been cut off to some customers for nonpayment. Despite the congressional rhetoric about freedom for the Indians, the Menominee people had far less control over their lives and property than before termination.[54]

The Menominees' problems drew much attention from newspapers, both in Wisconsin and nationally. Among the new county's problems cited by the *Green Bay Press Gazette* were a birthrate more than two-thirds higher than the state average, substandard housing and education, tuberculosis, diabetes, poor infant health, and dependence on welfare. Only one-fourth of adult Menominees had gone beyond the eighth grade, and only 50 of the 2,606 adults had gone beyond high school. One-third of pregnant women got no medical supervision. The infant death rate was 63.1 per thousand compared to 20.4 for the state as a whole. Writer Ray Pagel found 113 problem drinkers among 496 families. He added, however, that drinking was less serious than before termination because tribal members could have a few drinks in a bar rather than buying a bottle illegally and drinking the entire contents. The Federal Housing Authority reported that less than one-third of tribal homes were in sound condition while one-third were classified as deteriorated, old, unpainted, and sagging. About 55 percent of county residents had running water, and 44 percent had indoor plumbing. There was a brighter side. Thirty six tribal members had taken advantage of their new eligibility for FHA loans, and a dozen senior citizens obtained $1,000 grants to improve their houses.[55]

Both the *Green Bay Press Gazette* series and a *New York Times* article the same year concluded the Indians still needed federal help but ended on optimistic notes. The *Times*, however, quoted tribal member Mrs. Jerome Sanapaw as saying the loss of fishing and hunting rights (later won back) meant her family sometimes went hungry. She could not afford milk at 23 cents a quart, she said.[56]

James Ridgeway, writing in the *New Republic*, was less sanguine than the other writers. He noted that a dental survey showed 809 of 865 children needed dental work and that hospitals and clinics at Shawano, neighboring the new county, held $200,000 in unpaid Menominee medical bills. Ridgeway concluded, "The tribe is likely to be slowly extinguished, the Indians either moving down to the cities or dying in the woods."[57]

Recognizing a crisis, Governor John Reynolds called a meeting in July 1964 that outlined a dozen potential areas of state action but provided no solutions for the county's basic problems. One concrete action came out of the meeting: funds for a county nurse. By 1965 the Wisconsin Legislative Council's summary report described the Menominees as "demoralized as any poverty stricken people anywhere."[58] That year, with signatures of one-fifth of its members, the tribe petitioned Congress to reverse termination. Congress took no action. The state then stepped in with aid, which was what Watkins and other termination proponents in Congress seemed to have in mind all along.

However, it was the federal War on Poverty that rescued the impoverished county. The Economic Opportunity Act provided money for several projects, including some basic county services labeled "pilot projects." The county's plight got the attention of Congress later that year when Laird introduced a bill for a multimillion-dollar package of aid. Providing justification for the measure, Wisconsin state senator Reuben La Fave, chairman of the Menominee Indian Study Committee, said, "The lack of adequate preparation by the federal government is the determining factor of the financial crisis now being faced by Menominee County."[59]

Orfield, the Princeton social scientist, summed up the situation: "A policy designed for rapid integration of a successful Indian community into Wisconsin has virtually destroyed the community while confronting the state with massive problems with which it is totally unable to cope."[60]

3 Klamaths

Disaster

Disaster was both predictable and predicted. Over a period of more than two decades, various people told congressional committees that removing the federal government's ties to the Klamath Tribes of Oregon would bring trouble. "Traditions built on land occupied for thousands of years do not end in a day," L. S. Cressman, head of the University of Oregon Anthropology Department, pointed out in 1956. He said the Indians faced an emotional crisis moving from federal wardship into mainstream society.[1] The termination steamroller rolled on, however, and Cressman's predictions proved correct.

Like the Menominees, the Klamath, Modoc, and Yahooskin band of Snake Indians owned vast stands of pine forests. Like the Menominees, the tribes of the Klamath Reservation in southern Oregon were considered rich and capable. Like the Menominees, the Klamath Tribes paid for most of their own administration and programs, costing the government little. Also like the Menominees, the Klamath Tribes had won a multimillion-dollar claim against the government, the Klamaths for land losses and the Menominees for mismanaging the tribe's timber. Congress levered the Indians' attempts to collect their money into removing both from federal protection.

Unlike the Menominees, however, the Klamath Tribes sold their forest. Their tangled story is even more tragic than that of the Wisconsin tribe.

The three neighboring tribes that made up the Klamath Tribes were gathered onto a reservation created on Klamath land under an 1864 treaty that gave the U.S. government title to vast areas of southeastern Oregon and northeastern California.[2] By the mid-twentieth century the tribes had been complaining for years about the Bureau of Indian Affairs management of their lives and resources. Tribal delegates appeared more than a dozen times before congressional committees beginning in 1916. There were aborted moves in the 1920s and in the 1930s to give the Indians control of their reservation. Each time the judgment was made that the tribes were "not ready" to manage their own affairs.

After World War II, the general movement to "free the Indians" from government supervision and assistance converged with other factors to create another push in 1947 to "liquidate the estate" of the Klamath Indians:

- The tribe sought payments to each tribal member from their 1939 claims settlement for land illegally taken from the Klamath Reservation.
- The BIA listed the Klamaths among tribes most ready to be "freed" from government ties.
- County governments throughout the West began an effort to put Indian property on the tax rolls, and officials of the two counties in which the Klamath Reservation was located persuaded Oregon's senators to introduce a bill to achieve that.
- A Klamath Indian who had once been the reservation's superintendent for the BIA won the ear of Congress.

Wade Crawford, who had been removed as superintendent in the mid-1930s at the request of tribal leaders, led a faction of Klamath

Indians, most of whom lived off the reservation, in seeking their individual pieces of the tribal assets. The leaders on the reservation also chafed under the heavy hand of BIA administration but wanted to keep the tribe and reservation intact with more Indian voice in the management. They saw a need for more education for tribal members and for experience in managing their very profitable business enterprise before eliminating federal supervision.

Crawford engaged in a long and bitter battle with Boyd Jackson, a reservation elder who was a member of both the tribal executive board and the new tribal loan board. Jackson spent years representing the tribe in Washington DC and continued to work for tribal interests after termination until his death at age ninety. He claimed that giving all Klamath tribal members equal shares of reservation assets would be unfair because some, such as Crawford, had earlier received allotments, which they sold.

Despite his removal as superintendent, in the 1940s and 1950s Crawford was several times elected a tribal delegate to Washington DC. He and his wife, Ida, railed at tribal government as a communist entity with no place in America. At the height of the Cold War, some members of Congress used this same argument to end treaty obligations to Indian tribes.[3]

Klamath tribal members were inclined to blame timber interests for the push to end the tribe's federal status. However, records in the National Archives contain evidence that counties, guided by Forrest Cooper, a Lakeview, Oregon, attorney, were much more involved in the issue than timber companies. Cooper, a onetime aide to the House Indian Affairs Subcommittee, was counsel to the National Association of Counties when that organization asked that Indian land be transferred to local tax rolls. As counsel for the Interstate Association of Public Lands Counties, Cooper drafted a proposed "emancipation" bill for the Klamath Tribes at the request of the Klamath Falls Chamber of Commerce. That effort brought cries of outrage from tribal leaders who said they knew "nothing of this abominable scheme."[4]

Between 1947 and 1953, the future of the Klamath Tribes was almost constantly before the Congress. Jackson's papers, archived in the University of Oregon Library's Special Collections, record efforts to write a Klamath bill and reflect the Indians' fears of being terminated on the government's terms rather than their own. The reservation superintendent, the tribe's attorney, and the General Council all made different approaches toward termination in those years.[5]

Both the Subcommittee on Territorial and Insular Possessions of the House Public Lands Committee and the Indian Affairs Subcommittee of the Senate Public Lands Committee held hearings on Klamath bills in 1947. The House hearing was on a bill providing for payment of $1,000 to each tribal member, with an additional $200 to each member who had served in the armed forces during World War II. The money would come from the $5.3 million settlement the tribe had won in 1939.

The Department of the Interior opposed the distribution on grounds the payment, totaling about $1.5 million, would seriously deplete the tribe's capital fund.[6] Oscar Chapman, undersecretary of the interior, said the money should be used instead for tribal economic development and for a loan fund that would allow tribal members to establish businesses.

The Senate measure provided for removing restrictions on individual Indians' land and money, selling the tribally owned lands, dividing the proceeds, and granting tribal members "full citizenship rights."

Jackson reluctantly testified in favor of the payment bill because the per capita payment "is the only way we can get that benefit paid over to us." He said, "I believe we should keep an estate for a rainy day," but Congress had ignored earlier tribal requests for development funds. He said he believed his people did not have enough experience handling large sums of money to invest in a sound business.[7]

Crawford, favoring the per capita payment, said the Indians did not get the benefit of their $2 million or more in the U.S. Treasury. "It goes for the personnel and for the supervision of the Indian Service," he said. The next month the Klamath General Council removed Crawford as delegate. In supporting the Senate measure, Crawford claimed that under the BIA's ten-year management plan for the reservation the tribe would be $25,209 in debt by 1955. He said 275 adult tribal members had petitioned for passage of the bill.[8]

Jackson, in his testimony, viewed the Senate bill as a land and water grab by non-Indians. He pointed out that tribal members had lost 106,000 acres of the reservation's best hay and grain land in the early 1900s when the allotment act gave land to individuals and allowed them to sell it. According to Jackson, tribal cattle ranchers, who utilized their allotted lands and the tribal grazing land, would need time to learn to compete with the non-Indian ranchers in the area. He said he favored a study looking toward an eventual end to federal supervision.[9]

In the Senate hearing Utah Republican Arthur Watkins presided in his typical fashion. He let Crawford go with only perfunctory questioning. He frequently interrupted Jackson before the tribal leader could finish an answer. The senator badgered Jackson until he got agreement that the Indians should "take the lead and stand on their own feet and become full-fledged American citizens." He called Jackson by his first name while addressing other witnesses, including Crawford, as "mister."[10]

Even as Congress insisted the Klamath Tribes were ready to manage their own business, it continued to micro-manage tribal spending—although it was almost entirely Indian-earned money, not taxpayer dollars. The Senate's Interior Appropriations Subcommittee, for example, refused to approve the tribe's budget request for $50,000 to reopen the tribal hospital.[11]

In December 1951 the Klamath General Council voted to explore the possibility of transferring the tribal trust to the state, and Oregon governor Douglas McKay, a year before becoming secretary of the interior, named a high-level committee to work with the tribe. Like earlier proposals, that one came to nothing.[12] Still, in 1953 the House Interior Appropriations Committee report for fiscal 1954 noted, "Obviously, the Klamath Tribe in Oregon is also ready for complete separation."[13]

As soon as termination became congressional policy with passage of House Resolution 108 that same year, the BIA began writing a bill in Washington DC to end its supervision of the Klamath Tribes. Also, Cooper, then counsel to the Public Lands Committee of the Association of Oregon Counties, was again in Washington urging speed in getting Klamath lands onto state tax rolls. He apparently remained involved, at least peripherally, through the termination period.[14] When Erastus J. Diehl, the Klamath reservation superintendent, took the finished termination proposal back to the reservation, it carried a notation, signed only DF, stating the bill "does not go far enough to fully protect the interests of the Klamath Indians or the general public."[15] Area BIA director E. Morgan Pryse noted an "inherent weakness" in the proposed bill: abrupt termination would make impossible continued "wise management" of the Klamath forest as directed by President Eisenhower's policies on conservation.[16]

Diehl told a congressional committee the state was concerned about preserving the sustained yield management of the Klamath timber lands so that the economy of the area would not be upset and that the Indians would not become state welfare charges.[17]

The tribal executive committee rejected the bill with little discussion. The committee said it first wanted to accumulate data, lay groundwork for deciding what to do with tribal assets, and then draft a bill based on their findings.[18]

In 1954 the congressional Indian committees conducted a series of joint hearings on termination for several tribes, including the Klamaths. In the first session Jonathan M. Steere, representing the Indian Rights Association, a nonprofit organization devoted to Indian issues, testified that the Klamath Tribes were "less well prepared to assume responsibilities" than the Menominees. He also expressed concern about the possibility that "premature removal of restrictions and division into individual holdings will result in dissipation of their assets, leaving the Indians poverty stricken and dependent."[19]

Throughout the 1954 hearings Watkins demonstrated his scorn for treaties with tribes. Discussing the hunting and fishing rights that tribes had insisted on in their treaties, Watkins said, "I would suggest that possibly it might be a good idea for the United States to buy out that so-called right, pay them off, because then you would not have difficulty with the white people in those areas."[20]

Watkins also scoffed at Jackson's fears the Indians would not be able to hold onto their property if it were removed from trust. But Jackson said the loss of allotted lands around 1917 showed the Indians "lacked guts" to say no to people seeking to buy their land. Jackson, however, mostly pleaded for delay, saying that the tribe would need time to set up a viable livestock operation to supplement its lucrative timber business after the cutting of virgin forest was completed under the sustained yield program. "Three years is not going to cover it," Jackson said.

Watkins kept insisting that because the tribe paid the BIA employees, and the executive committee or General Council approved the budget and programs, the Indians had plenty of management experience to take charge of their multimillion-dollar business. Jackson said, however, that "the planning of the budget was done by the officials of his (superintendent's) staff."[21]

The BIA employment records in 1947 showed only 44 Klamath

tribal members among the 139 employees on the reservation. Nineteen of the tribal members were seasonal or intermittent employees; just 2 had supervisory jobs, a road maintenance foreman and a seasonal fire crew boss. Only the members of the new tribal loan board could be considered as having actual business experience, and Jackson, a board member, said on several occasions that he had neither training nor experience for managing a business. Stanford Research Institute, later hired to study the tribe's situation before termination, concluded, "The fact of the matter is that the Klamaths have never managed their own affairs as a group since the establishment of the reservation and there is a large group of the Klamaths whose members do not manage their own affairs as individuals." At the time the termination measure was passed, nearly half the adult tribal members living on the reservation were considered incompetent to handle their personal funds.[22]

There is every indication, from interviews with tribal members and from tribal records, that the Klamath Indians did not really understand what was happening to them. A paper prepared for the American Indian Policy Review Commission in 1976 reported, "Evidence suggests the vast majority of Indians neither understood nor participated in the termination process."[23] There was never a tribal vote on the issue of whether to accept termination of federal supervision, only votes on one plan or another.

Tribal member Phil (Bill) Tupper was in his mid-twenties in 1954. He worked on his father-in-law's reservation cattle ranch when he wasn't competing in rodeos as a saddle bronc rider. "Termination was just a word," Tupper said. "First time I heard it, I was building fence—man from Stanford came up and asked me, 'how much do you think your tribal rights are worth?' I didn't understand it. It kept coming up . . . We'd vote it down . . . I don't think at that time people could comprehend what termination was . . . I don't think they understood."[24]

His view was confirmed by Theodore A. Crume, also a tribal cattle rancher, who was in his early thirties in 1954 and had served on the tribal executive committee. "We never knew the full story until it was completed," Crume said. "Even today we are learning about things that were done that shouldn't have been done." He added, "The government used language Indians didn't understand. They had no concept of losing land."[25]

The Klamath measure was similar to the Menominee termination bill in that both provided for creation of a tribal entity to manage the Indians' resources. However, at the last minute the Klamath bill was amended to allow individual tribal members to withdraw from the tribe. With the help of the Indian commissioner, Wade Crawford, who sought the withdrawal provision, had worked his way into negotiations with the BIA and the House.[26] It was the provision for withdrawal that destroyed the Klamath Tribes.

The bill provided that the secretary of the interior appoint three people from outside the tribe to develop a management plan and oversee an appraisal of the reservation. The appraisal would tell the Indians how much each individual's share would be if he withdrew from the tribe. The management plan would tell those remaining what sort of income they could expect from the remaining tribal assets. Each adult Indian would then decide whether to take the money and go or to remain in a tribal organization. Parents would decide for their minor children. Everything was to be done and the federal government was to be out of the Klamath picture by August 13, 1958.

The next few years were chaotic and contentious. Questions about the law cropped up almost immediately after it was signed. A former chief of the U.S. Forest Service, Lyle F. Watts, warned that the law contained no provision for continued sustained yield management of the tribal timber. "The future economy of the Klamath Basin demands sustained yield management," he said. He recommended that the federal government buy the forest and add it to the national forest system.[27] Within months the timber industry also was raising concerns. The *Timberman*, an industry publication, editorialized that dumping four billion board feet of timber "can only be harmful." It concluded, "What happens to the Klamath Reservation is important to all western lumbermen, not only as a market factor but as a pattern for the coming liquidation of other reservations."[28] Interior Secretary McKay also was concerned that allowing the timber to be "disposed of indiscriminately . . . would be bad for the economy of Oregon and the nation."[29]

When the issue arose as the planning for termination got under way, some tribal members objected to requiring continued sustained yield management. Tribal advisory committee member Laurence Witt told forester Earle Wilcox it wasn't fair to force sustained yield, which would benefit the community at the expense of the Indians, because the land would be sold for less.[30]

In spite of his public statements that the Klamath Tribes were ready to shed federal protections, McKay said privately the Klamath termination represented a major challenge. He also sought to keep an illusion that the Indians were involved in the process.[31]

However, throughout the period the government paid little heed to tribal requests, drawing objections for making funds available to the management specialists without providing itemized statements and allowing the specialists to hire a forestry adviser whom the tribe's General Council had voted to have fired from the BIA's Klamath agency.

McKay selected as the specialists three of his personal friends who were unknown to the tribe: Thomas B. Watters, a retired real estate dealer and former mayor of Klamath Falls; Eugene G. Favell, a land developer and manager from Lakeview in Lake County in which much of the Klamath Reservation was located; and W. L. Phillips, an auto dealer from Salem, the state capital, which also was McKay's home.

In the first months of 1955 the tribe appointed a committee to work with the management specialists. Throughout the period before termination went into effect tribal members also met; they discussed the looming threat and often quarreled over how to deal with the specialists, timber sales, inheritances, water rights, education, hunting and fishing, law enforcement, the tribal loan board, whether to fire the tribal attorneys, and whether there were enough members present to make decisions. Later, arguments turned to the size of land units to be appraised and the time frame for termination-related actions.

Through the turmoil of the termination years, the Klamaths lacked a BIA adviser whom they knew well. B. G. Courtright, who served as Klamath Agency superintendent for ten years, was removed soon after he testified in 1947 that the Klamath people were not ready to take over management of their reservation.[32] There were five more superintendents before termination became final in August 1961. McKay ignored a plea in 1954 from six senior tribal officials who asked to keep Diehl because "we should have a voice in who will aid us during this termination period." Also that year Don C. Foster replaced Pryse as area BIA director in the Pacific Northwest.

In addition, the Klamaths were hampered by an organization that was not equipped to deal with complex issues. Most decisions were made by the General Council, all adult members of the tribe. A ten-member executive committee existed but had not operated between February 1950 and August 1952, when the General Council delegated wide powers to act.

One of the management specialists' first actions was to arrange for a survey of the reservation and its people, something Boyd Jackson later pointed out should have been done before the law was passed. The other initial action was arranging for a comprehensive appraisal of the land and timber.

To survey tribal members, the specialists selected the highly re-
spected Stanford Research Institute (SRI). Its findings put into sta-
tistical form Watters's early judgment that the tribe was not prepared to lose federal assistance and almost every warning Boyd
Jackson had issued in his appearances before congressional committees over the years.

SRI's report concluded, "It will be several years, even under a
stepped-up educational program, before many of the Klamath people will be qualified to manage their resources successfully without
continued assistance. . . . Also, there is little reason to think that
earned income of individuals (or family units) can be increased,
within the next few years at least, to the extent necessary to provide
for their living requirements should per capita payments cease."
For withdrawing members there would be "a very difficult period
of readjustment" once they had spent their payments.

SRI also noted that in the 1953–54 school year 40 percent of the
Klamath tribal children in Klamath County public schools, where
most tribal students were enrolled, were not doing well enough to
be promoted. Between 1934 and 1947 only ten tribal members had
graduated from public high schools. Although income for Klamath
families was close to the median level for the surrounding county
SRI pointed out that much of the Indian income was from the per
capita payments from tribal timber, not from jobs, and their effective
income was extended by their ability to hunt, fish, and gather berries
and roots from the abundant resources of the reservation.[33]

Eighteen months of study convinced the management specialists that the bill would not work for the Indians. In a July 1956 letter to Watkins signed by Watters, the specialists asked for amendments to "safeguard the interests of the Klamath Indians and their
resources."[34]

The specialists also had to arrange guardianships to manage fi-
nances for the 1,166 tribal members who were minors and deter-

mine the competency of many adults to manage their own money. There was the problem of informing tribal members about the process. Watters told Indian Commissioner Emmons in a January 1956 letter, "unless a stepped up information and education program is inaugurated they will not know what they are voting on." The tribal executive committee added its voice to the plea for more education and information.[35] Congress had appropriated one million dollars for education programs for the Menominees, Klamaths, and other affected tribes. The program included vocational education for tribal members without job skills and training in language, non-Indian customs, and basic hygiene, sanitation, and housekeeping.

The state of Oregon managed the education program for the Klamath people, setting up an office in Chiloquin, the heart of the reservation. The office arranged education opportunities, conducted community information meetings and classes on such things as money management, and published a monthly newspaper with information about the progress toward termination and stories about tribal members successfully attending various schools to learn trades. Despite those efforts, about a third of tribal members apparently believed they could receive their share of the tribal assets and at the same time remain a member of the tribal group that would form a corporate enterprise. Klamath students enrolled in classes on barbering, radio and TV, X-rays, business, accounting, diesel mechanics, medicine, and education. Of 118 who entered technical and business schools, 75 had dropped out by midway through the second year. Nine had graduated, and 34 remained in their courses. Ten of the 28 who entered college had dropped out.[36]

Other troubles were piling up for tribal members. Area hospitals and doctors refused to accept assignments and orders for Indian patients on grounds the Indian agency would no longer pay. Many members urgently needed care and had no money to pay medical bills, which had always been covered by the tribal budget. The executive committee and then the General Council in January 1957 quickly approved a $75,000 loan fund to help members pay medical bills with amounts borrowed to be repaid from the member's share of tribal assets when they withdrew from the tribe.

The specialists ran into their own problems. Beginning in August 1956, Watters wrote three times to the new interior secretary, Fred A. Seaton, asking him the scope and amount of detail to be included in the proposed management plan. With no reply by December, Watters said he could not meet the deadline for writing the plan.[37] Watters also warned that some of the possible social implications of termination could create a public reaction that "might well 'terminate' the whole termination program."[38] The specialists' work also was stymied by the months-long appraisal of tribal land. Both the tribal vote and the management plan would be based on the appraisal.

In September 1956, more than two years after the Klamath Termination Act was approved, Indian Commissioner Emmons, other BIA officials, the management specialists, tribal officers, and attorneys gathered in Portland to discuss whether the law should be amended. In a two-hour meeting, Jackson told Emmons the tribal delegates had been promised a chance to amend the bill later. Now was that later time, he said. The tribal attorney, Ernest Wilkinson, told the gathering, "I now feel I made a tragic mistake" in accepting the withdrawal amendment. Emmons conceded that the law probably should be amended although he was not sure how.[39]

The management specialists also sought a delay in the final termination date and began urging federal purchase of the Klamath Forest as timber prices tumbled. The Indians—more specifically, their forest—found a champion in Senator Richard Neuberger, a Democrat and strong environmentalist who won election to the Senate from Oregon in 1954, after the termination law was passed. The push toward termination already was slowing, but it was too late to save the Klamaths. Neuberger, concerned about the economy and about the potential for clear-cutting the magnificent pine forest, introduced a bill calling for the federal government to buy the Klamath timber lands. The management specialists, issuing their recommendations in February 1957, concurred with Neuberger. The Eisenhower administration opposed federal purchase. However, state officials, many of them Republicans, and George Weyerhaeuser, head of the giant lumber company that bore his name, all warned that the sale as planned would destroy the economy of the Klamath Basin.

The congressional hearing on a bill to require any buyer of the Klamath Forest to retain sustained yield management ranged into related topics, including the Indians' vulnerability to fraud. Watkins rejected the notion that the tribal members might easily be defrauded of their anticipated huge lump sum payments. "I do not believe that anyone will deliberately try to cheat them, except possibly someone who might want to do the same thing to non-Indian people," he said. He added that help would be available or those who wanted it.[40]

At the same time, the Interior Department was investigating the higher-than-normal fees the Klamath County Bar had set for attorneys handling guardianships for Indian children and incompetents. The SRI report also warned that there would be efforts to exploit the newly rich Indians.[41]

Meanwhile the Oregon Legislature weighed in with concerns that liquidating the Klamath Forest "would deal serious injury to a watershed upon which the people of Southern Oregon and Northern California are vitally dependent." The state also feared that private purchase of the forest would deprive the counties of the income they would receive as a share of timber sale receipts under federal ownership.[42]

In September 1957 the management specialists published their proposed management plan for the portion of forest and other assets that would be held by the remaining tribal entity. The first section of the plan refuted every presumption on which Congress had based its decision to remove the Klamath people from the federal roll of tribes. "After studying the background which these people have in business experience and education," the document stated, "the management specialists have concluded that it would be unwise to allow the members who participate in the management program to operate an unrestricted corporation." The specialists said all but one of 118 adult members who had expressed an opinion on that subject agreed.

The specialists recommended that the management "be placed in the hands of a qualified trustee." The trust would continue through the lifetime of the enrolled tribal members who were beneficiaries—that is, those born before the termination law was signed.[43]

The appraisal ordered by the termination law was completed in February 1958 while the fate of the forest was still being debated by Congress. The professional appraisers placed a total value on the land of $121,659,649.10 and then listed values on individual blocks of land. Tribal members complained that the blocks were too large for them to bid on and that each block contained both grazing and timber lands. The Indians wanted the grazing lands, but the inclusion of timber put the price out of their reach. Watters relayed their complaints to Seaton, but no changes were made.[44]

So, with doubts that they would be able to buy any of their own land if they withdrew and facing an uncertain, complex management plan if they stayed, members of the Klamath Tribes began a month-long vote March 22, 1958. Only 80 of the 2,133 enrolled members voted to stay with the tribe. An additional 378 members did not vote and so automatically remained. However 1,659 members—77 percent—voted to withdraw.[45]

Later, Jackson and J. L. Kirk wrote that many tribal members did not vote because they did not believe the appraisal assigned a fair market value to the reservation. They said some failed to vote because the remaining land would be too small to be viable.[46]

Some families hedged what they considered a bad situation no matter what they decided. Charles Kimbol, later a tribal administrator and chairman, withdrew. His wife and three children remained. His individual share gave the family a nest egg while his wife and children received the continuing per capita payments, providing income in addition to Kimbol's pay as a lumber mill and timber worker.[47]

Seaton, who had replaced McKay as secretary of the interior, had set a deadline of July 28, 1958, for comments on the plan from tribal members. Instead of submitting individual written comments, the tribe held a meeting in July and asked Congress to repeal the termination law. Tribal members listed some serious complaints, including failure to retain fishing and hunting rights and mineral rights and the lack of water for the land they would keep. None of the three reservation rivers touched their portion. The Indians also contended that the termination law required that they give positive approval—not just lack of comment—and the new amendments gave them until February 1961 to prepare a plan. The remaining tribal members elected an executive committee with Seldon Kirk as chairman.

In August 1958—when termination originally had been scheduled to become final—Congress and President Eisenhower reached a compromise on the future of the Klamath Forest. The sustained yield requirement would be retained, and the forest would first be offered in large blocks to private operators. Sales would be delayed until April 1959 for a "review of the appraisal" because of falling lumber prices. The federal government would buy the 15,961-acre Klamath Marsh, a vast wetland used by migrating waterfowl and the source of the wocus plant, a major food source for tribal members. Any blocks of timber and grazing land not sold would be purchased by the federal government for the national forest system. The management specialists, by challenging the original law, saved the economy of the Klamath Basin and a magnificent forest, if not the people who owned the forest.

Passage of the amendment was the cause of celebration in Klamath County. The Klamath Falls Chamber of Commerce staged a civic dinner to honor Neuberger for pushing the measure through Congress. The long list of invited guests did not include a single Indian.

Sales of so-called fringe units—smaller parcels of land containing timber of marginal commercial value and grazing land—began in November 1958. Four non-tribal members bought 5,058 acres of the fringe units, and three dozen tribal members or tribal partnerships purchased 51,663 acres. In addition, 27,283 acres that initially brought no bids went to twenty-two tribal individuals or groups.[48]

The reappraisal was finished in January 1959. With market prices for ponderosa pine down 15 percent from the time of the original appraisal, the tribal timber was worth some $30 million less than the earlier estimate. Tribal members passed a unanimous resolution protesting the lower figure.

The Klamath County Court decided to place the Indian lands on the county tax rolls for the 1960 tax year. The U.S. Public Health Service, which was supplanting the Indian Health Service, took over the medical clinic at Klamath Agency. Tribal funds would no longer pay the costs of the clinic; medicines were restricted, and some medical supplies were discontinued. The clinic at Beatty on the east side of the reservation was closed.

Nearly a year after the tribe divided itself into withdrawing and remaining members, U.S. National Bank of Oregon won the bidding to take over management of the remaining members' 144,690 acres of timber and 8,000 acres of marsh, farm, and range land.

The bank also acquired responsibility for 434 head of cattle under contracts to tribal members, the tribal cattle herd, tribal loan accounts, and an assortment of feed grains and hay. The trust agreement between the bank and the federal government was put into effect March 3, 1959. Where the BIA staff had included four tribal members working full-time, the bank's only tribal employee was a seasonal log scaler.[49] The Indians still had no voice in managing the lands. The first of the sustained yield forest units and the tribe's other property—vehicles, farm equipment, furniture, and tools—went on sale in March 1959.

There were indications that the transition to life outside the tribe was not going to be easy for many Klamath people. The Interior Department stepped in to remove 980 trust accounts from a Portland attorney who eventually was found guilty of misconduct and suspended from law practice for two years. In September both withdrawing and remaining members suffered a financial blow when the largest single fire in reservation history swept across 14,000 acres of forest. The blaze killed three-quarters of the trees within the fire area.

One private buyer, Crown Zellerbach, paid $1.64 million for one sustained yield forest unit of 91,541 acres. The federal government bought 525,680 forest acres for $68.71 million and 14,641 acres of the Klamath Marsh for $476,401. In April of 1961 proceeds of those sales plus the sale of "fringe units" and other property were divided among the 1,659 withdrawing members of the Klamath Tribes. Each individual got $43,124.71.[50] Of those members, 744 were minors whose payments went directly into guardianships or trust funds, as did the money for 274 adults living on or near the reservation who had been judged unable to manage their own sudden wealth. Slightly more than 400 adults lived outside Klamath County, and there is no evidence of their immediate response to acquiring a large sum of money.

There are varying reports about the fate of the funds of the 226 adults living in Klamath County who had no restrictions on their spending. Word-of-mouth accounts, nearly all unsubstantiated, told of Indians who bought multiple cars, wrecking one after another, and of drunken Indians toting paper bags filled with currency.

However, the *Klamath Falls Herald and News*, the daily newspaper in the community where most of the legendary spending supposedly took place, told a different story at the end of the payout week. "This community . . . found itself agreeably surprised by the manner in which tribal members handled themselves and their money," wrote reporter Floyd L. Wynne in a front-page article on April 21, 1961. Wynne quoted the local managers of U.S. National Bank and First National Bank as reporting that most of the Indians were putting their money in checking and savings accounts, with few taking cash. In addition a number of the former tribal members opened new accounts at First Federal Savings and Loan. All the managers reported Indians paying bills, contracting for new cars and household goods, and inquiring about buying real estate.[51]

But four years later—by September 1965—nearly 40 percent had none of the money left. One-fifth still had $20,000 or more, and almost half had $10,000 or less. A study showed that most of the money went to living and medical expenses, cars, home improvements, household furnishings, and housing. An unknown amount of the money was saved.[52]

The statistics tell only a part of the story. A dozen years after the payments the federal government looked into allegations that Indians had been frequently cheated in 1961. The staff of the Northwest Region of the Federal Trade Commission documented numerous cases in which Indians were denied sale prices, charged more than non-Indians for the same item, or tricked into signing fraudulent documents that either allowed their property to be sold without their knowledge or forced them to pay unnecessary interest.

One elderly Klamath man authorized a real estate dealer to sell 160 acres of land for him. The dealer obtained the Indian's signature on a blank paper he described as authorization to advertise the property and then sold it for half its $40,000 value without telling the Indian owner. An all-white jury ruled fraud and awarded the Indian seller $2,500 in addition to the real estate agent's $20,000 sale price. A car dealer quoted a Klamath woman $3,663 as the price for a 1972 automobile. The dealer offered the same car to a Caucasian woman the same day for $2,900.[53]

Allen Foreman, chairman of the restored Klamath Tribes, saw such incidents firsthand. He said, "It was get what you can while the getting's good. . . . That was pretty much the case across the entire consumer economy."[54] That attitude created deep distrust between tribal and nontribal people that persisted into the twenty-first century, Foreman noted. The FTC piled up considerable evidence that the merchants, real estate dealers, and lawyers made every effort to get as much of the Indians' money as possible. In the introduction to its report, the FTC said the unfair practices ranged from over-priced appliances peddled by door-to-door salesmen to race-based pricing on homes.[55] Large quantities of money vanished from trusts and guardianships. One attorney went to prison; two others were disbarred. But the Indians didn't get their money back.

Gail Chehak, a founder of Indian Art Northwest, an organization promoting Native artists, was three years old when termination occurred. Her family had voted to withdraw, and her $43,000 payment was placed in a trust fund with a bank. When she turned eighteen and asked for her money, only $20,000 was left. She asked the bank for records showing where the money had gone. The bank said she would have to pay for the records and would have to buy all of them, not just those for a year or two. The cost was so high that she faced a choice between spending most of the remaining money to find the missing funds or take what she had left and give up. She took the money.

Chehak's family was severely disrupted by termination. Her parents' marriage, one of the last arranged marriages in the tribe, ended soon after the termination payment. The money gave Chehak's mother the independence to leave her drinking husband. "Termination destroyed a lot of homes that way," Chehak said. Her mother eventually also turned to alcohol and lost her children to state custody.[56]

Being cheated, losing money, and being poor were not the things that Klamath Indians said hurt them most, however. The deepest scars were psychological and came from losing their identity as Indians and from losing the land they believed their ancestors assured them forever. Those deep psychological scars of a people lost manifested themselves in what cultural anthropologist Patrick Haynal described as "sociocultural disintegration," which affected the tribe half a century later and after the restoration of its federal recognition.[57]

Talking to almost any tribal member brought out stories of heartbreak and loss traceable to termination. Elwood Miller, the tribe's natural resources director, kept a picture of his first-grade class in the Chiloquin grade school, taken in 1959 or 1960. There were thirty students in the picture, most of them Indians. In 2002, Miller said only he and two others among the Indians from that class were alive. "It's the same with others around my age. We lost a generation," he said. He was forty-nine years old.[58]

In 1961 the median age at death for Klamath tribal members was 46; by 1971 it had dropped to 39.5. That compared to the overall figure for Oregon in 1971 of 72.1. Many of the premature deaths resulted from alcoholism, which exploded with the dislocations of termination. By 1977 the Klamath Alcohol and Drug Abuse Council said three-quarters of the Indian deaths were alcohol or drug related.[59] Alcoholism also was considered responsible for other social problems the Klamaths experienced: children taken from alcoholic parents, parents and siblings in prison, school dropouts—wasted lives. Even those with stable lives, who survived with their sense of identity and their marriages and families intact, talk of the loss—of their land, their place in the family of Indian nations, their culture.

Miller's family stayed in the tribe, but Miller remembered when the others got their 1961 payments. He said before termination most tribal members had jobs. When they received the sale money they bought homes and cars, but then were no longer able to get jobs. "People didn't want to hire people who just got lots of money," he said. "They just wanted to get their money."

Like most young tribal members, Miller saw little hope for his future. He dropped out of school after tenth grade and "drank for a decade." Then he got married, mostly quit drinking, and got a job. By 2002 he supervised a staff of fifteen in the tribe's Natural Resources Department and dealt with thirty-five entities involved in managing the water, game, and fish of the former reservation. He also had served as chairman of the Inter-Tribal Fish and Water Commission, which includes three California tribes and the Klamaths.

Miller said the people who remained with the tribe, such as his family, wanted to manage their share of tribal assets themselves. "We were betrayed by the government," he said. "I don't think they wanted Indians to be prosperous."

Gordon Bettles, former cultural director for the tribe who later formed a consulting business, said Klamath tribal members found themselves in a kind of limbo in which legally they were no longer Indians, but white society did not accept them as equals—in "no man's land, not Indian, not white . . . a nonbeing."[60] Some Indians also rejected the Klamaths. Bettles recalled that when he was a student at Eastern Oregon College, hundreds of miles from the Klamath Reservation, students from other tribes "could get very mean and nasty" about the Klamath Tribes, who they considered had sold their birthright. One night, five Indian male students—all apparently drunk and one a Marine veteran of the Vietnam War—entered his dormitory room and beat him up, calling him a "sell-out." Romance suffered too. The father of one girl he was interested in told her to stay away from Bettles because he was from a terminated tribe.

Bettles did make it despite some rough times. His 2001 interview was conducted at Eugene, Oregon, where he was working on his master's degree in linguistics, archeology, and indigenous culture at the University of Oregon.

Termination brought more divisions within the tribe as well, between the suddenly wealthy withdrawing members and the mostly still poor remaining members. Bettles's conclusion: "There's not one good thing I can say about termination."

Studies back him up. Haynal in his doctoral dissertation at the University of Oregon recited a litany of losses in addition to the psychological trauma. By 1975 more than one-third of the Indians in the Klamath Basin were below the poverty level.[61] With termination, they had lost the health, education, and economic development assistance that came with being a recognized tribe, services paid for with tribal earnings from their forest. Those forest revenues now went to the federal treasury. Tribal members who did not have allotments lost their right to select a residential site—for free—on the reservation. Tribal members who did own land lost thousands of acres to taxes, especially inheritance taxes then in effect. After living in a largely noncash economy in which there were no taxes on their land, many Indians were caught unaware.

Tupper, the rodeo cowboy–rancher, was one of those. He and his wife, Rachel, and her parents were successful cattle ranchers at the time of termination. With the vote looming whether to remain within the tribe or take a share of tribal assets, the Tuppers learned they could use their withdrawal payment to buy pieces of the reservation land. "That inspired Rachel and I to bid on a couple or three pieces that adjoined our ranch," he said. "We went in with partners, with other tribal people, and bought more. Some [land] had timber. That's how Rachel and I took most of our money—in land. We kept our allotment land." With pride and sadness, he said, "During and after termination Rachel's family and mine were the largest landowners on the reservation—6,000 acres." But it was all lost to taxes in ways he did not want to discuss because he was still trying to regain his ranch. He added, "The few dollars we got was nowhere near the worth of our heritage." Although his family suffered through tough economic times as a result of termination, the Tuppers avoided the other social disruptions that plagued so many tribal members.[62]

In the period of termination, both the federal and state governments imposed inheritance taxes. The state-operated education program for the Klamaths included material on taxes but focused on property and income taxes.

Foreman, the tribal chairman, and his uncle, Theodore Crume, stayed on their Sprague River ranch for fourteen years after termination, but they finally gave up, sold out, and moved to Nevada to work as cowboys. What had been a profitable three-hundred-head operation under the Indian system could not survive against competition from larger ranches. When Indian ranchers were able to graze their cattle on tribal lands, they could grow hay and feed for the winter on much of their own land and maintain a small herd. After termination, the Indians had to apply to the Bureau of Land Management for grazing permits on public land—and all the permits had gone to white ranchers. With that grazing land gone, Foreman said, "most ranches are not profitable." Indian ranchers said the BIA never explained that aspect of termination.

As Foreman drove the road through the ranch land that once belonged to his family, he noted the changes in the landscape. As a boy he had to search for places where he and his horse could ford the Sprague River. Now, the water level was so low a horseback rider could cross anywhere. New water rights, mostly for crop irrigation that were issued after the tribe's termination, lowered the level of the water and raised its temperature. Where Foreman caught trout more than a foot long, only a few chub and catfish lurked in the warm sluggish water. The water contained the chemical fertilizers and pesticides used on crops. The timbered land was cut over. The remaining trees were small. The wetland had been drained for crop and pasture. "It hurts to see how the old ranch is not cared for," he said.[63]

Other Klamaths also mourned the changes. The sustained yield timber cutting that kept much of the reservation forested gave way to the Forest Service's more extensive logging. Elwood Miller noted that with state management and non-Indian hunting there had been a decline in deer, elk, and other wildlife that kept Klamath tribal members fed for generations. Wetlands, where people gathered the wocus plant, had been drained and planted with irrigated crops.

Financially, the members who remained within the tribe fared somewhat better under bank management than they had under the government. Their annual payments from timber sales totaled about $200 more than the $1,100 they averaged in the final years under the BIA. However, they had no more voice in management of their lands than they had before. Five years after termination, the remaining members voted to continue the bank trust. Five years later, however, in 1969, their vote ended the trust, resulting in sale of their remaining lands in 1974 and giving them each a check for $103,000 — except for Edison Chiloquin, a crusty twice-wounded World War II veteran. The government bought the land for $49 million and added it to the Winema and Fremont National Forests.

Chiloquin, however, staked his claim to 580 acres around the site of his ancestral village on the bank of the Sprague River. There, he settled down in a tepee, refused to accept the money, and stood off the government for a decade. Congress finally gave in and granted him the land for his lifetime. In a 2000 interview, looking back on his long battle, Chiloquin said he was glad he held out. "No amount of money is enough," he said. "The land is more important."[64]

4 Western Oregon

Invisible

If saving money was the purpose of terminating government ties to tribes, as some members of Congress said, there was scarcely any reason to bother with the western Oregon Indians. The five dozen tribes and bands scattered the length of Oregon west of the Cascade Mountains cost the government $22,226 for 1950—$10.68 per Indian.[1] The Bureau of Indian Affairs agencies at Grand Ronde and Siletz had long been closed, and the bureau's few dealings with the tribes were conducted out of the area office in Portland. Only a few of the tribal children went to the Chemawa Indian School. An occasional patient was admitted to the Indian hospital in Tacoma, Washington. A physician saw Indian patients at Siletz on a part-time basis and made once-a-month visits to Coos Bay to see members of southern coastal tribes, mostly to administer vaccinations.

"We were invisible people so far as the BIA was concerned," said Sharon Parrish, director of tribal records management and tribal member services for the restored Coquille Indian Tribe. Farther north, at the Confederated Tribes of the Grande Ronde Reservation of Oregon, June Olson, the director of tribal cultural resources, said, "There was no real government—just Indian people living on Indian land. The culture was . . . all stamped out. People were fighting to survive." For the Confederated Tribes of Siletz Indians of Oregon, largest of the terminated western Oregon tribes, "I don't recall any services we had before termination," said Bensell Breon, a cattle rancher in central Oregon.[2] A former public school teacher, he also was a former member of the restored Tribal Council. At the time of termination he was twelve and lived at the town of Siletz, a mixed white and Indian community adjacent to the tribal headquarters. Even the BIA, in a document supporting a 1950 plan to terminate the western Oregon tribes, noted that the number of its employees "has diminished to such an extent that adequate services are impossible."[3]

Members of the Siletz and Grand Ronde tribes tend to blame the Oregon terminations on either timber companies that wanted their tribal forests or on former Oregon governor Douglas McKay, who became interior secretary in 1953 and enthusiastically endorsed the policy nationwide. Before that, in 1950 McKay as governor created an Oregon Indian Council composed of tribal and state officials with the key policy to "advocate, support and promote progressive measures to integrate the Indians into the rest of our population"[4]—in other words, end their separate tribal identity. Harvey Wright, the governor's representative to the council, said he would not recommend immediate termination of tribal entities but warned, "The time is coming when all Indian reservations will be dissolved." The council actively supported removal of discriminatory laws—such as banning liquor sales to Indians and barring marriage between Indians and non-Indians. It also kept proposed termination programs for some of the western Oregon tribes on its agenda and called for a long-range goal "to progressively end federal wardship." McKay's executive assistant, Tom McCall (a later Oregon governor), invited the Association of Oregon Counties, which was an early supporter of Klamath termination, to join the committee. McKay himself told the BIA that the federal termination effort "is in line" with state policy.[5]

At the same time, E. Morgan Pryse, the Portland Area BIA director, was eagerly trying to terminate Oregon tribes several years before

Congress adopted the national termination mandate. He worked with the governor's committee and threw himself into the program diligently. By 1948 he was presenting western Oregon tribes with termination proposals. In August 1951 he reported to the Interior Department's Northwest Field Committee that "definite progress is being made toward the ultimate withdrawal of federal supervision of all Coastal tribes." The next month he told Commissioner Dillon S. Myer, "I believe the commissioner would be justified in starting action without formal resolutions [by tribal governments] since not one Indian has objected." Pryse also lost no chance to tell his superiors in the BIA or interested members of Congress how hard he worked. He referred to "the herculean job" of preparing for termination, part of which apparently was figuring out how many tribes there were to be terminated. "We keep finding more tribes and groups all the time scattered throughout Western Oregon," he said. Pryse also solicited support for termination from officials in the counties where the Grand Ronde and Siletz reservations were located. Officials of all three counties gave enthusiastic endorsements, saying it would be good for the Indians. And in a December 7, 1953, letter accompanying his report to BIA headquarters on progress by various tribes toward termination, he said, "I have spent much of my own time Saturdays and Sundays from 1948 to the present in meeting with various groups." When Senator Arthur V. Watkins, the Utah Republican leading the drive for termination, congratulated Pryse on an excellent report, Pryse allowed, "I did a lot on my own time and at my own expense."[6]

White settlers began moving onto western Oregon tribal land before the United States had settled its claim to the territory with either England or the Indians. After England and the United States agreed on the forty-ninth parallel as the international boundary in 1846, the number of settlers grew, and later the discovery of gold in southern Oregon accelerated the influx of whites. Clashes were inevitable as the Indians tried to cling to their homelands. In the 1850s Indian agent Joel Palmer signed treaties with dozens of tribes and bands west of the Cascade Mountains. The Senate ratified seven of these treaties covering two dozen groups. It did not ratify treaties covering other small bands and the Coos, Lower Umpqua, and Siuslaw Tribe. Nevertheless, the government attempted to corral all the Indians of the Willamette Valley and Oregon Coast on reservations at Siletz on the central Oregon Coast and inland at Grande Ronde sixty miles southwest of Portland. Some from the southern coast were taken by ship. Others from the far southern reaches of the territory were forced to walk more than a hundred miles in a West Coast version of the Trail of Tears. The Cow Creek band of the Umpqua Tribe of Indians sent a young scout to look at the band's designated reservation before tribal members began to move. He reported deplorable conditions, and most members of the band decided to remain in their homeland near the present-day inland city of Canyonville. Many members of the southern coast tribes remained in the Coos Bay area. Other Coos tribal members drifted back to their homelands after the government opened their reservation sections to white settlement.

The tribal members who went to the two reservations formed governments as the Confederated Tribes of Siletz Indians and Confederated Tribes of the Grand Ronde Community. Indian agents were assigned to both reservations for a time. Later, there was a single agency at Siletz. Later still, both reservations were administered from Portland. As with most reservations, the government reduced their size over the years and eventually allotted much of the remaining land to individuals.[7] A century after the tribes agreed to settle on reservations totaling 1.7 million acres, the Siletz tribes owned a little more than 2,500 acres of timber land and 44 acres at the tribal headquarters. The Grand Rondes had 60 acres of timber land, a half-acre government site, and a cemetery. The only other remaining tribal property was 6.12 donated acres near Coos Bay where the Civilian Conservation Corps had built a tribal hall for the Coos and Coquille people in 1941. Nearly 15,000 acres in 157 individual allotments remained in trust. That included a number of allotments the southern coastal people had obtained in the public domain. These were focal points for the tribal members who had either refused to go to the reservations or who had escaped and returned.

When Congress in August 1953 finally approved the resolution establishing termination as the newest government policy to solve the "Indian problem" once and for all, Pryse was ready with his recommendations for western Oregon tribes. There appears to have been some differences of opinion about termination among members of all the affected tribes, but it probably didn't matter. The little tribes were put on the fast track for "independence" almost immediately. After all, Pryse's letters and reports cited only positive reaction toward termination from both Indians and local communities.

Tribal members tell a different story. Coos tribal member Sherman Waters told the American Indian Policy Review Commission in 1975 that during early discussions of termination in the late 1940s about forty members of the Coos Tribe went to a meeting of many western Oregon tribes at Siletz but were locked out and not allowed to vote.[8] Sharon Parrish of the Coquilles remembered that her mother "was dead against termination," even writing articles for the local newspaper opposing it. "In her eyes, the tribe was never terminated," Parrish said. When the Coos, Lower Umpqua, and Siuslaw Tribe sought restoration of their federal status, the House report on the bill noted, "The tribe vigorously opposed termination." Some members of the tribes either weren't informed or didn't understand what was happening.[9] "We were angry when we found out we'd been terminated," said Leon Tom, a Grand Ronde tribal elder and former council member. "We were not paying attention." One Siletz tribal elder recalled that termination came "without much input from our people." The woman said a lot of people had moved away as part of the government program to relocate Indians to cities that was occurring at the same time as termination. She called relocation "a setup to promote dissolution of the tribe."[10]

Records in the National Archives and Records Administration in Seattle show that the Siletz Tribe voted in 1951 to authorize the BIA to sell the tribal lands. Three years earlier in a meeting in which a termination proposal was discussed, tribal members voted 13–2 (out of 35 members present) to accept the plan on condition of some amendments. There is no record the amendments were made or that another vote was taken. Four members of the Grand Ronde council voted in 1951 to accept a proposed termination measure if it was amended to retain their hunting and fishing rights. Again there is no record such a change was made or new vote taken before Congress acted.[11] In 1953 the Grand Rondes voted 20–0 to demand payment of money owed the tribe for a land claim judgment—"then we will talk about withdrawal."[12] The BIA presented these resolutions in making its case to Congress in 1954 that western Oregon tribes had approved termination.

As the termination program gained momentum, Glenn L. Emmons commenced his duties as commissioner of Indian Affairs under President Eisenhower by traveling around the country to discuss issues with Indian leaders. Siletz chairman Elmer Logan described the session held in Portland on October 11, 1953, when the Oregon tribes were targeted for termination. The Siletz and Grand Ronde delegates got ten minutes each to report, he said. That was the only "discussion."[13]

But by February 1954 a bill had been drawn up to terminate the federal ties with all tribes in Oregon west of the Cascade Mountains, with total membership listed at 2,081. The list was at best imprecise. It named sixty tribes, including the Grand Ronde and Siletz confederations, that counted individually listed tribes among their members. The Indian Affairs Subcommittees of the House and Senate Interior and Insular Affairs Committees held a hearing on February 17. The session lasted one hour and ten minutes. Three officials from the BIA testified. The House and Senate members heard only the BIA version of Indian opinion. Not a single Indian testified.[14]

"We had no money," recalled Kathryn Harrison, former chairman of the Grand Ronde Tribal Council. She said the council's attitude was, "It was going to happen anyway. We might as well go along. We could not even think of going to Washington."[15]

The American Indian Policy Review Commission, in its 1977 report on the status of Indians in the United States, found: "The Klamath and Western Oregon Indians were not involved in the termination process to any significant degree nor did they have a basic understanding of the implications of termination. President Eisenhower promised full consultation with the Indians, but it didn't happen in termination."[16]

Some members of the tribes say they accepted termination as unwanted but inevitable. Some thought it might make life better for them by ending the state ban against white-Indian marriages, removing them from the federal ban on liquor purchases by Indians, and perhaps erasing white prejudice based on Indian hunting and fishing rights and the belief that Indians did not pay taxes. The BIA pushed that perception, said Wilfred C. Wasson, a one-time chairman of the Coquille Tribal Council. He told a congressional committee in 1989, "The Bureau of Indian Affairs officials had told us they were going to remove all the special liabilities and limitations of being Indian and thereafter we would be just like white people. This, of course, did not happen. Employers, teachers and government officials still treated us like Indians. We still felt like and thought of ourselves as Indians. The only difference was that we no longer had health services, we no longer had education benefits and we could now pay property taxes just like non-Indians."

For the Grand Ronde and Siletz tribal members there also was the matter of money; each one would get a share of the proceeds from sale of tribal property. "The second class citizen status was the major thing causing Indian support for the idea [termination]," said Michael Darcy, former Siletz Tribal Council member and retired principal of the Siletz public school. "Getting money also got to the Indians. Money is a big incentive for poor people."[17]

Some tribal members said those who approved termination did not fully understand its implications, and almost all resent what they consider the lack of consideration of Indian viewpoints in the process. Many tribal members said they did not vote on termination although they were old enough at the time. Some said those who opposed the plan did not attend meetings to vote. Members of other tribes said they weren't consulted.

Although there is no evidence of direct threats that money from claims settlements would be withheld if the tribes did not agree to termination (as occurred with the Menominees and Klamaths), many tribal members believed that there was at least the suggestion that the money would be paid more quickly if they agreed to termination. The payments had been delayed for years, and the Indians were growing impatient. For example, the Coquilles, one of twenty-eight tribes with substantial claims judgments unpaid, had been waiting since 1945 for payment of a judgment in the tribe's favor. In response to a question at the 1954 subcommittees hearing, Pryse, the area BIA director, denied that pressure involving claims payments had been applied. Representative E. Y. Berry (R-SD), asked, "Were they told at any time they would not get their money until this passed?" Responded Pryse, "It was explained that the money had to be appropriated and rolls made up first." Berry: "That meant that this would pass before they get their money?" Pryse: "Oh, no." Berry: "At no time?" Pryse. "No." However, the BIA's report on the proposed termination legislation outlined a "schedule for withdrawal" that clearly tied the timing for paying the claims judgments to that legislation by suggesting that funds for preparing tribal rolls and making the distribution be part of the termination law. Without that legislation to accelerate the process, "it will take six or seven years to distribute" the money, the report stated.[18]

The bill terminating the western Oregon tribes' relationship to the federal government sailed through Congress with little or no discussion and became law in August 1954 along with the Menominee and Klamath measures. Because the western Oregon Indians were considered so ready to be "freed," their termination date was set for two years in the future instead of the four years granted the two larger tribes.[19]

The state legislature had repealed the ban on marriages between Indians and Caucasians before the first termination legislation.[20] Tribal members also could belly up to the bar. But, for many, prejudice did not seem to go away. Billie Lewis, a Coos tribal member, traveled from Washington State each year for tribal ceremonies. Light skinned, blue eyed, Lewis remembered stopping at the same coastal restaurant each trip for forty years. She remembered good food, good service, and pleasant conversation—until the trip on which she wore her tribal regalia. The service became perfunctory. "The waitress took my money, but she told another person, 'I can't deal with these people.'" Lewis and her family quit patronizing the restaurant.[21]

Others from the western Oregon tribes did not recall prejudice, or at least not much. Darcy, the former school principal, said before termination there was no racial tension in the town of Siletz, occupied by both Indian and white families. "Siletz had six hundred people," Darcy said. "There were not enough to fight with each other." For teenage boys sports often provided entry into the larger society. Leon Tom, in his seventies, said he was "probably made fun of" in grade school, but playing football and basketball at Willamina High School helped. At least two non-Indian athletes at the school became lifelong friends of his. Coaches and the principal urged him to accept an athletic scholarship at one of the several colleges that contacted him. "Instead," he said, "I went into the woods for forty-five years."[22]

Darcy's experience bears out the BIA's assessment in the 1950 document detailing tribal assets and social situation: "Almost every employable male is employed—logging, fishing, mills, own business, offices, teachers in public school."[23]

In the years just after World War II jobs as loggers and lumber mill workers were plentiful on the Oregon Coast, and many Indian men worked in the timber industry. However, James I. Metcalf, former Coquille chairman, recalled: "A lot of Indians didn't want to admit they were Indian. It was a lot easier to get a job if you weren't. Indians were the last hired and first fired." The reluctance to admit to being Indian might also have explained the 1950 document's pronouncement that "Indian culture has almost entirely disappeared in Western Oregon except for an occasional basket. Tanning deer hides and making moccasins are almost lost arts."[24]

This was an era when many tribal members either did not talk about being Indian or tried to hide their heritage. Pictures of earlier generations of Indian women show faces covered with white powder to lighten their skin. One of the reasons federal officials frequently cited for removing federal ties to the western Oregon Indians was that they dressed, lived, and worked the way their white neighbors did. In 1952, as the forces for termination grew stronger, the state's largest newspaper, the *Oregonian* of Portland, published a picture page quoting half a dozen western Oregon Indians on the "impending emancipation." Three approved, and three expressed no opinion. The author of the accompanying article, James Stuart, outlined a history of the tribes and noted, "It must be remembered too that the coast Indians meet none of the requirements of quaintness or backwardness sometimes associated unfairly with their race."[25]

Wilfred C. Wasson, then chairman of the Coquille Tribal Council, explained to a 1989 congressional hearing why coastal Indians appeared to have adopted white ways so completely: "As time went by our people found that by giving the outward appearance of being like white people they would be left alone. They wore white [style] clothing, cut their hair, spoke English and patterned tribal government after white organizations. It soon became second nature not to use Indian languages when white people were present and never to allow whites to see any portion of Indian religious practices."[26] So successful were the south coast Indians at blending in that Don C. Foster, who replaced Pryse as area BIA director in 1954, complained that it was "impossible to identify individuals as belonging to any specific tribe."[27]

Longtime Coos tribal leader Bill Brainard recalled that some of his contemporaries "were not going to be Indian." He said, "For me, it was easier to get in a fight." Dark-skinned and rugged, Brainard remained ready for verbal battles with all comers. He served in the National Guard when it was activated during the Korean War, worked thirty years for the local power company—retiring as stores manager—and served on the Coos County Planning Commission, a controversy-filled post. Throughout, he devoted considerable time to tribal affairs, ensuring the tribe's recovery of its tribal hall and working for restoration of federal recognition.

In addition to the second-class citizenship and money issues, many tribal members saw termination as just the most recent in the string of broken promises that went back to the 1850s. Brainard remembered tribal meetings the second Sunday of every month in the 1940s when he was still too young to participate. He recalled seventy-five to a hundred women gathering in the meeting hall at the little community of Empire outside the town of Coos Bay (then Marshfield): "They all had big black purses. Every month they would put the bags down on the floor, pull out a folded brown paper sack and sit with it on their laps. Every month they would say, 'the BIA promised us a sack of money. We came for our money.'" Needless to say, they never got any money. When the tribal meetings started, Brainard's father, Henry, would call him from play. "He told me to listen—I was going to need that information some day," Brainard said.[28]

Despite the BIA's insistence that all the employable men of the tribes had jobs, the agency in late 1954 approved a program of education and vocational training for members of tribes being terminated. It was designed, according to acting Indian commissioner W. Barton Greenwood in a letter to Area Director Foster, "for appropriate vocational training away from the reservation for those Indians who wish to settle and secure employment away from the reservation." Tribal members considered the program another effort to make sure that no tribal organizations survived—along with the specific prohibition on federal payment for any "communal" property or organization. The BIA also emphasized that the government would not pay for a return trip home for any tribal member who signed up for the program. In the same report Martin Holm told Foster that the education branch of the BIA in Washington was emphasizing that agents should not promise Indians specific training in a specific field but "encourage them to arrive at the relocation center with an open mind." The report was written in April 1955, just sixteen months before the termination date.[29]

Joe Thomas remembered the relocation program well. He had just finished high school and was working in a sawmill. The promise of a year in college looked like an opportunity he had never been able to consider. The government gave him a choice of six locations—San Francisco, Los Angeles, Phoenix, Denver, Philadelphia, or Boston—all at least 500 miles away. He had once been a little over 300 miles from home as a patient in the Indian hospital in Tacoma, Washington, when he had meningitis at the age of six. Otherwise, he had been no farther from Coos Bay than Crescent City, California, 130 miles down the Pacific Coast, and had never been east of the Cascade Mountains. Any of the six cities he could choose would be like another world. He picked Denver—1,200 miles away, with a population of 416,000. At the time, Coos Bay and neighboring North Bend, the largest cities in Thomas's area, had a combined population of less than 15,000.

The BIA gave him a bus ticket. As he neared Denver, he "realized it was one way," he said. "I could not go back. I would have to stay." He did stay, but his memories of those first days remain vivid. "It was a strange environment. The culture was foreign. I had been right here [in the Coos Bay area] all my life." He was used to the Oregon Coast, which is wet, mild, and lush with evergreens. In Denver, "even the seasons are different," Thomas said. "The trees are smaller. One of the things that bothered me was in the fall trees were naked." The move from sea level to mile-high Denver left him gasping for breath in the thinner air. "I spent three days in the hotel room before I went out," he said. When he did go out he met with the BIA to get enrolled in the University of Denver. Because it was still summer the university's dormitories were not open. He found a room in a private home. For a young man who grew up in an extended family and had rarely been away from home, it was a lonely time. "The BIA sent checks once a month and came around sometimes to check on me," he recalled.

The end of the school year was the end of BIA help, but Thomas wanted to finish college. "I didn't know how to get the rest," he said, but he went back to Denver after a summer at home. "I learned to do a lot of things on my own." He sold cosmetics and other items door to door. He played in a dance band. He earned a bachelor of arts degree in music. He came home three times in his four years at Denver, spending his vacations working in the woods. Where did he find the incentive to keep going for four years? He laughed. "Did you ever work a year in a sawmill?" he replied.

He returned to his home territory and taught in public schools for eighteen years, was a deputy sheriff for sixteen years, and then became chief of security for CEDCO, the development arm of the restored Coquille Tribe. Of the relocation he said, "It was a helping hand. It was good. But for most it was bad, not good. Most of those who were relocated would last three or four weeks, then give up and go home," he said.[30]

Roy Gilkey, who was in military service at the time of termination, said the government, in effect, told the relocated tribal members "to get out of town and don't come back." He added, referring to the wholesale removal of people of Japanese descent during World War II, "Even the Japanese were allowed to stay with their families and neighbors and keep their culture. Our people were destroyed, our culture trashed and degraded." Gilkey later went to San Francisco long enough to take a carpentry course; then he served as tribal chief when the tribe officially did not exist between termination and restoration.[31]

With termination less than a year away, some tribal members became apprehensive. A BIA program officer who signed his memo only "H. Dushane" told Area Director Foster that a prominent Siletz tribal leader, Coquelle Thompson, had expressed fear about how the interests of the old people and minors would be protected. "This seems general among those I have talked with," Dushane wrote.[32] They had reason to worry.

The good times for logging along the Oregon Coast were coming to an end as the termination policy was being put into effect. The trees and the jobs were gone. "After logging pretty much ended here . . . kids had to look other places," Darcy, the former school principal, said. While the jobs lasted, tribal leaders such as Darcy tried to little avail to persuade youngsters to graduate from high school. "The only jobs were in the woods. . . . They could make good money. They'd say, 'Why go to school? We can make as much as a teacher.'"

Then for two decades, with no tribal help available, there were no tribal youngsters going to college, and many families and young people left in search of work.[33]

The Coos-Coquille tribal hall and six acres were turned over to the city of Empire with the provision that if the city ever was abolished, the land would revert to the Indians. The other little bands, which owned no property, took their claims settlements and all but disappeared as entities. The Siletz Tribe sold its forest land and turned over the tribal cemetery and adjacent administrative area, about forty-four acres, to the city of Siletz. Each tribal member got about $792 in two distributions. The Grand Rondes sold all but their six-acre cemetery, which had a small caretaker's tool shed on the property. The price worked out to $35 per member.[34] Kathryn Harrison, later Grand Ronde tribal chairman, recalled that only four of her ten children were eligible for the payment. One bought a bicycle; another bought school clothes. "That part [the money] was good," Harrison said. She added, "We didn't realize the full impact then."

With her then-husband not working, Harrison discussed the possibility of relocation for vocational training. "A man came around and asked if I was interested, but when he found out I had ten kids he told me I was better off here." She later attended college and became a licensed practical nurse.

She said some tribal members accepted the offer of training, stayed away from the area, and are sorry. "It's almost like they can't come home," she said. "You can hear the longing. They did not return until they were elders and wished they'd never left." Others would return home two or three times a year.[35] Some who left made successful lives elsewhere. Violet Zimbrick, newly married at the time of termination, remained in the area with her family, but she said a cousin's family went to Los Angeles and never came back, and other family members scattered around the country. Nearly a dozen members relinquished their membership in the Grand Ronde Tribe and enrolled in the Yakama or Umatilla tribes.

The only thing Zimbrick remembered the tribe losing was its cannery, where women of the tribe canned fruit and vegetables for their families every year.[36] It was part of the property sold, although H. Rex Lee, assistant secretary of the interior, told the congressional committees the department felt losing community buildings such as the cannery would disrupt community life.[37]

After termination, the Siletz also scattered from their coastal homeland, some as far as Alaska, and others to the Oregon cities of Portland, Eugene, and Salem. Others stayed because they had nowhere else to go. As timber jobs declined, tribal unemployment and alcoholism grew. "There was no way for the tribe to help them," said Darcy, the retired school principal. "They were no longer Indians; so they were not eligible for aid."[38]

But being a federally recognized tribe is more than government services, more than tax exemptions on property, more than treaty rights to hunt and fish on their traditional lands. It is also the intangible matter of being Indian, of pride in the tribal culture, of being part of a recognized entity and part of the family of Indian nations. To many in the western Oregon tribes that intangible loss was the most severe blow wrought by termination. To Billie Lewis, the Coos tribal member who lived with her Indian mother, non-Indian father, and little sister in Washington's Columbia Basin, "it was like something died in our house, in our life. . . . We knew something had changed in our life forever."[39]

To some, termination was actually good. "In ways it was a positive thing," said Darcy. "People stood together" and were forced to work for their own survival.[40] However, Darcy and others cite ill effects from termination. The scattering of tribal members was one. The perceived loss of hunting and fishing rights, which brought either disputes with state law enforcement officers or the loss of food sources, was another. The economic status of many tribal members declined, as did their level of medical and dental care.

Twenty-five years after termination one-third of Grand Ronde tribal members were unemployed, and more than two-thirds lived below the poverty level. Twenty-nine percent of Coquille families with children younger than eighteen also were below the poverty level, six times the proportion in Oregon as a whole. Twenty years after termination 93 percent of western Oregon Indians polled by the American Indian Policy Review Commission said they would advise other tribes not to vote for termination.[41]

5 Alabama-Coushattas of Texas and Catawbas of South Carolina

Entangled

The Alabama-Coushatta Tribe of Texas wanted someone to manage its forest. Instead, the tribe wound up managed by the state of Texas. The Catawba Tribe of South Carolina bargained with the British for its first reservation in 1763 before there was a United States, got defrauded in a mid-nineteenth-century land deal with the state of South Carolina, and was misled by the federal government into accepting termination in the mid-twentieth century.

Despite the fact that tribal status is almost exclusively within the jurisdiction of the federal government, these two tribes became entangled with state governments, and both fell victim to the federal government's termination policy. Neither seems to have benefited.

Their stories are quite different although both tribes historically had won the gratitude of their states' residents. The Coushatta Tribe helped Texas win its independence from Mexico. The Catawbas fought on the side of the colonists in the Revolutionary War.

In 1954 the 450-member Texas tribe was too poor to send a representative to Washington to plead its own case when Congress tossed it off the list of recognized tribes. The South Carolina tribe, left in poverty, clung to its traditions and art as it fought to persuade the federal government to help it gain its long-promised land.

Like many other Eastern Indian tribes, the Alabamas and Coushattas, both members of the Upper Creek Confederacy, were forced from their aboriginal lands as the descendants of Europeans overran their homelands. The Alabamas migrated west from Alabama and Mississippi in 1763. In 1854 Texas bought 1,210 acres of heavily wooded land in the Big Thicket area near present-day Woodville in southeastern Texas for the Alabamas. An effort to move them four years later was thwarted, and the tribe remained in Texas. The Coushattas, meanwhile, were compelled to move frequently after 1763 and finally settled on the Alabama land grant, joining the two tribes. The federal government in 1928 bought 3,181 acres adjacent to the state-granted land and set it aside for the two tribes. At the time of the land purchase the covering of timber had been cut, and the land was considered practically worthless.[1]

Arnold Battise, an attorney and tribal member, in 1986 described the Alabama-Coushatta situation: the state was in a trust position for the tribes concurrent with the federal government until 1954, "but the state was more active."[2] The federal trust seems to have been mostly in name only. The Alabama-Coushatta Tribe was the only federally recognized tribe in Texas. By the 1950s the Bureau of Indian Affairs did not have a single employee in Texas and administered the tribe through the BIA area office at Anadarko, Oklahoma, four hundred miles to the northwest. However, federal administration was almost non-existent; the reservation superintendent was a Texas state employee, as were the three carpenters and the nurse and cook at the twelve-bed hospital. Administratively, the reservation was considered a part of the Department of Texas State Hospitals and Special Schools.[3]

A little over twenty years after the tribes acquired the cut-over forest land, the trees had grown back, and the tribes wanted to create some income with a managed program of logging. The BIA, which managed vast timberlands for big tribes such as the Menominees and Klamaths in other areas, said the Texas tribes were too far from any BIA foresters to make management of the Texas Indian forest practical. The Texas Department of Forestry, on the other hand, was located just down the road—seventeen miles away. The tribes petitioned the federal government to let Texas manage its forest. Texas was willing. The BIA and some members of Congress, in the midst of termination enthusiasm, were eager to go even further and let Texas take all responsibility for the tribe.[4]

So the Alabama-Coushatta Tribe became part of the marathon series of termination hearings held by Senator Arthur Watkins and Representative E. Y. Berry in 1954. Financially unable to send anyone to the hearing, the tribe asked the congressman from its area, Democrat John Dowdy, to speak for it. Dowdy did so, acting as a forceful and able advocate for the Indians. He scolded the BIA for going beyond the tribe's proposal for forest management and succeeded in winning at least a couple of amendments to the measure.

Dowdy said he became involved in the issue after tribal members saw the proposed legislation and told him, "This isn't what we had in mind."[5] The Interior Department told Congress that the tribe had voted in favor of termination. The transcript of the meeting in which state and federal representatives discussed the forest management show that the Indians thought timber was all that was being considered.

The tribal members approved a resolution asking that the state of Texas be authorized to "assume full responsibility for the management, protection and conservation of our forest resources." The resolution also stated that no timber sales were to be made without a contract with the tribe, that cutting was to be on a sustained yield basis, and that employment preference would go to tribal members.

William Wade Head, the area BIA director from Anadarko—introduced to the tribe as "the No. 1 man with the federal government regarding tribal affairs"—told the Tribal Council, "It seems to me that a management plan for your forest should be started and that the State of Texas and the Alabama-Coushatta Indians could work together and develop this plan. . . . Some of the timber when the time comes should be sold and you can save this money which will be deposited in the United States Treasury and later buy additional land."[6] Termination, of course, precluded any tribal money from being deposited with the federal Treasury.

Dowdy called attention to the conflicting views of the various parties regarding an agreement. The Indians said they wanted the state to manage their timber. The state said it would take over the land and assets and manage them. In fact, state officials had first suggested a pilot program to manage two tracts of the Indian forest. The Texas Legislature voted approval. The BIA said it wanted nothing more to do with the Indians.[7]

The 426 tribal members living on or near the reservation included 108 children who were attending public school just off the reservation. In those days of racial segregation, Texas had a white school and a colored school in the district; the Indians attended the white school. The federal government was paying the local school district for the Indians, as it did in other communities where Indians attended the public schools. However, until the district built two schools near the reservation in 1946, few tribal children attended school. Many of the adults, feeling more comfortable in their own tongue, either did not speak English or refused to do so, and some pretended not to understand English. The tribal chairman, Andrew Battise, was a college graduate and a draftsman for the state highway department. Three tribal members were carpenters on the reservation. A few were teachers or logging contractors. Most, however, worked as laborers. Family income averaged $1,400 a year, about

$400 less than for white families in the surrounding area. The tribe already had used timber from its land to build sixty-five homes, with the state paying for construction. There was no explanation in the record why sixty-five homes were built while the number of tribal families was listed at sixty-nine.[8]

At the request of his Indian constituents, Dowdy pressed for a provision allowing tribal members to continue using Indian hospitals and trade schools. "Those are far away," Watkins said. "If they can get equal services from someplace else why would there be any dissatisfaction?" Dowdy said there was no equivalent elsewhere. Watkins said he assumed Texas had vocational education schools. Dowdy said if it did, he didn't know where. He said tribal elders were suspicious of white doctors, and if they could not go to an Indian service hospital, they would "use medicine men." The tribal members looked on themselves as Indians, Dowdy said. "They just feel they are being deprived of something if they are not given the right to attend Indian schools and Indian hospitals. All they want is to use them as long as they last." In fact, the tribal members made little use of the Kiowa Indian Hospital. In the previous year nine tribal members had spent a total of 130 days in the facility. None had used the tuberculosis hospital at Shawnee.[9]

Perhaps because he was dealing with a member of Congress and not an Indian, Watkins was more conciliatory about tribal wishes and situations than he was in other hearings. He did, however, show his usual lack of understanding about Indian ties to Indian institutions. He asked Dowdy, "If they have no property except timber and go to Texas schools, use Texas roads and whatever the Texas civilization gives to them I cannot understand why there should be any serious objection on their part" to losing their federal trust status. But as the committee discussed the tribe's status, Watkins said, "I realize these Indians are too poor to come here. I'd like to work out something agreeable to them." And when Representative

J. G. Donovan of New York asked, "Why treat these people any differently than those in yesterday's bill?" Watkins responded, "Their conditions are different. Tribes are at different stages. We try to adjust to fit these situations. We cannot draft a universal bill."

Nevertheless, Watkins appeared to continue to hope for the possibility that the tribe could simply manage on its own. He asked Dowdy, "Do you think they are prepared to manage their own affairs?" "No," Dowdy replied. "If the land is turned over to them by tomorrow night they would not have it."

"They would dispose of it?"

"Yes, and would not get 10 acres apiece, which would be the down payment on a bunch of second hand cars."

He said the tribe then had no income and was probably among the most primitive in the country.

Dowdy tried to appeal to the committee's sense of justice. Discussing the school and hospital issue, he said, it is a small thing, but it is a matter of keeping faith with the Indians, and the state of Texas has no Indian hospital and it has no trade schools for them to attend. If the federal government set the tribe entirely adrift, he said, the Indians would feel betrayed.[10]

However, the Alabama-Coushatta Bill was approved with the only concession giving tribal members the right to attend Indian schools and use Indian hospitals. The bill that Congress approved turned the Indian reservation over to Texas effective in 1955 with the understanding that it be placed in trust similar to the federal trust—that is, the land would be exempt from property taxes. The state trust was to continue until the tribe and the state agreed to dissolve it. The federal government agreed to cancel the tribe's debt to the federal treasury—approximately $39,278, much of it the sum the government had paid for the three thousand acres it added to the reservation in 1929. Members of Congress conceded that the tribe had no money to repay the debt and would have had to the sell the land, worth an estimated $3 to $5 an acre.[11]

A little over a year after the bill passed, Orme Lewis, assistant secretary of the interior, in a speech to the Phoenix, Arizona, Press Club, pointed proudly to the termination program. He said the Alabama-Coushattas had become the "first tribal group to achieve full independence from Federal supervision since 1909." He didn't mention the state trust.

Lewis also stated, "It is fully realized that tribal groups who have failed to demonstrate capacity for managing their own affairs must continue to receive federal assistance for a great many years to come."[12] He also didn't mention Dowdy's assessment of the effect of giving the Alabama-Coushattas "full independence." Texas agreed to accept the trust so that, unlike other terminated tribes, the Alabama-Coushattas retained the tax-free status of their land. At first Texas paid the salaries of administrators and other administrative and maintenance costs of the reservation, but there was no state money for service programs. However, beginning in 1959, the state allowed the tribe to lease mineral rights on its land, and income from those leases, timber, and grants paid for education, health, education, housing, and employment programs, with an emphasis on education for young tribal members. The state also used the tribal money to pay the state employees on the reservation.[13]

Despite those programs, thirty years after termination 90 percent of the fifty students enrolled in the Alabama-Coushatta tribal Head Start program came from families at or below the poverty level. The other 10 percent were from families in which both parents had jobs, pushing total family earnings just above the poverty level. One-fourth of the youngsters were diagnosed as handicapped—visually or speech impaired, physically handicapped, or mentally retarded. One-fifth needed extensive dental work. A community assessment showed 12 percent of homes housed more than one family. There was a need for transportation services so families could get to better medical care on a regular basis. Most families did not have enough income to buy and maintain a car. Most of the tribal senior citizens had to rely on friends or relatives for transportation.[14]

Unlike the Alabama-Coushattas, the Catawba Tribe of South Carolina was never pushed out of its home territory even though it lost its lands and spent more than two centuries trying to win them back or get compensation. The Catawbas felt one effect of termination that no other tribe suffered—the law appeared to blot out the tribe's nearly two-hundred-year-old land claim, contrary to representations made by the Bureau of Indian Affairs. The Catawba claim dated back to its treaty with British-governed South Carolina in 1763. The Catawbas were mostly farmers who raised corn, squash, and beans, but by the mid-1700s, they controlled much of the trade between the area's tribes and the European traders from Virginia and South Carolina. After South Carolina emerged the victor in rivalry between the two colonies, South Carolina gained control of the Catawbas through debt. The colonial government then used that leverage to persuade the tribe to cede vast areas of North and South Carolina and settle on 144,000 acres in the north central section of the colony. However, whites already had settled on some of the Catawba land, and the government wasn't about to remove them.

By the first decade of the 1800s there was little land whites had not claimed in the Catawba territory. So in 1840, half a century after the matter of relations with Indian tribes devolved to the U.S. government, South Carolina made another treaty with the Catawbas. This time the state promised to buy a new reservation in exchange for land the tribe then occupied. The state sold the Catawba land but never purchased the property it had promised the Indians. In fact, after a brief move to North Carolina, the tribe returned to its home area and acquired 660 acres from the state in 1850. By the time of the Civil War, the tribal area was less than 100 acres. The state did make the annual payments it had promised for education, medical care, and welfare, but this amounted to little. During this period the tribe's unique 4,500-year-old pottery art became more important as a source of income. From time to time, beginning in 1782, the tribe pleaded to the national government for help but was ignored.[15]

In the 1930s BIA official D'Arcy McNickle described the Catawba situation: "The economic situation under which these Indians exist are about as hopeless as they could possibly be. This pocket size reservation is infertile, rough, for the most part uncultivated and unfit for cultivation. There is not enough equipment even for the few patches which could be farmed. There are only two scrub mules, one with a bad foot. When it is worked it needs an extra man to pick him up when he falls. There are no hogs, chickens or other stock. Day labor provides a little income." McNickle recommended that the federal government negotiate with the state so that the tribe could "benefit from BIA field personnel."[16] Finally, in 1943 the federal government agreed to provide services to the Catawbas that it provided to other tribes. The state bought 3,434 acres and placed it in federal trust for the tribe, but the federal government did not provide the promised services.[17]

During World War II employment opportunities increased for tribal members, especially in the local cotton mills. Some moved from the reservation to other federal lands. Most worked in local industry. The children were in public schools; there was a school, part of the state public system, on the reservation. On the surface, everything was fine.[18] Then, when the termination policy came along, the BIA listed the Catawbas as among the most ready to cut the federal ties.

The Catawbas weren't happy with their situation. Tribal Chief Gilbert Blue told the House Interior Committee many years later that tribal members accepted termination because they were unable to develop their land without either federal help or the ability to get credit, and they had been unable to secure either. Federal

officials played on the dissatisfaction to win support for termination. They said they were unable to provide the additional services
the tribe wanted, but they could help remove federal restrictions
so the tribal members could improve their farms and homes. BIA
agent Raymond Bitney went door to door urging each family to accept termination. His reports show that several tribal leaders were
concerned about the effect of termination on the tribe's land claim,
which it had continued to pursue. Blue said most of the tribal leaders at the time, including his uncle, then Chief Samuel Blue, could
not read or write and, without an attorney, accepted Bitney's assur-
ances that the termination law would protect their right to pursue
their claim.[19]

Bitney drafted the tribal resolution approving termination on
the condition that it not affect the land claim.[20] After several tribal
meetings and two votes, tribal members approved the resolution in
1959. Bitney included the tribe's insistence on retaining the right
to pursue its claim in his report to the BIA. However, the agency
drafted the termination legislation leaving out the condition. Assistant Commissioner Thomas H. Reid wrote Bitney that headquarters had revised his report. "For your information, we have deleted
any controversial statements with the idea that in the event they
are called for by the committee, a clean report free of controversial
issues will be available for them," Reid wrote. "We are retaining
your draft copies in our confidential file." In other words, Congress
might not approve termination if members knew the tribe was still
pursuing a land claim. However, Representative Robert Hemphill
(D-SC), who introduced the Catawba "division of assets" measure
that ended any federal services to the tribe, certainly knew that the
tribal vote was conditional on the ability to continue pursuing its
land claim. After all, he had helped negotiate the termination agreement with the tribe in 1958 and 1959.[21] But a congressional report
in 1993 said the tribe's concern about the claim was "never relayed

to Congress" at large.[22] So when the tribe tried to press its claim in court, it found that termination had dropped the claims issue into state jurisdiction. The state's statute of limitations took effect, giving those occupying the former Indian lands title to the property. The tribe appealed to the federal government for help, but Attorney General Griffin B. Bell refused to support the tribe's claim because the affected landowners were innocent of wrongdoing.[23]

The termination measure passed in 1959 gave tribal members the right to buy the land that had been assigned to them for homes and farms on the reservation and provided that the remaining land would be divided among them. The division of the 3,400 acres of federal reservation took place in 1962. The state of South Carolina continued to hold a 630-acre reservation for the tribe.

Although there were some in the tribe who favored termination as a step toward assimilation in the larger society, there was still a strong element among the tribal members that was not ready to abandon the spiritual and cultural traditions, including devotion to community and to their ancient pottery art. There was little, if any, consideration of the effect of termination on individual tribal members who suddenly possessed land or several hundred dollars. As at Klamath, the merchants and speculators were waiting.[24]

Soon after termination, one woman who wanted to hold onto her land wrote in Cherokee (some Catawba tribal members had at one time moved to join the Cherokee and had learned that language, which was then handed down within the Catawba Tribe) seeking cash to buy school clothes for her children. She said some tribal members already had sold their land and had cash. Another sought money to move from one military base to another. Another traded his land for a car, which broke down in less than a year. Some gave their land away. One woman who sold her land said she had not realized she could have cut down the trees on the property to build herself a house. The woman and her children had enough land for a farm, but they sold it and soon had nothing. Some returned to the 630 acres of state-purchased land that remained in tribal ownership. By 1979 that land was crowded with framework houses and trailers.[25]

Despite their problems, many of the Catawbas maintained their tribal ties, and in 1993 fifty traditional potters continued their craft. Private owners held the lands where the Indians' unique clay and tempering agent were located, but for many years these owners generally granted access for the tribal potters. The *Charlotte Observer* reported in 1977 that only 5–10 percent of the 1,200 tribal members lived on the state reservation and that the reservation "does not differ conspicuously from other rural neighborhoods in South Carolina."[26] Through all the rebuffs, deceptions, and changing government relations the Catawbas maintained their claim to the 140,000 acres they had agreed to accept two centuries before. They asked only that another government keep its side of the bargain.

6 Utah Paiute Bands

Helpless

"For Congress to terminate the Paiute bands was the equivalent of giving a lame, jobless man and his family a new house, then looking the other way when the mortgage came due."

That is how one Utah congressman described the termination of four small bands of Paiute Indians twenty-two years later. "It simply wasn't fair. It wasn't right," said Representative Dan Marriott, a Republican from the southwestern Utah area that was home to the Shivwits, Kanosh, Koosharem, and Indian Peaks bands of Paiutes.[1] A fifth little band in the same area, Cedar Band, wasn't mentioned in the 1954 termination legislation, but the Bureau of Indian Affairs apparently forgot it was there and discontinued its minimal services also.

The Utah Paiutes were among the poorest and least educated Indian groups in the United States. They met none of the criteria set by Congress and the BIA for tribes being terminated, but they were part of the first round of tribes to lose their federal recognition and federal assistance. Afterward they sank deeper into poverty, lost much of their land, and came close to losing their culture. The bands had not asked to be terminated. They didn't have enough money to send a delegate to Washington to testify on the bill that took away their meager federal assistance. And there is evidence that Senator Arthur Watkins, the leading congressional proponent of

termination, persuaded them to accept the action by making promises that were not in the termination bill and were not kept. Bruce
Parry, director of the Utah Division of Indian Affairs in the 1970s,
speculated that because Watkins was from Utah "he felt the Utah
tribes should probably be an example for the rest of the country."
Judge Reid Blondquist of the Sevier County, Utah, Justice Court,
said he felt the termination "was a political maneuver on the part
of certain congress people at that time for political influence."[2] Historian R. Warren Metcalf confirms that view in *Termination's Legacy:
The Discarded Indians of Utah*. Watkins's first target, Metcalf wrote,
was the Ute Tribe, but when that large tribe did not resolve differences over tribal assets quickly, Watkins turned to the tiny and poor
Paiute bands "because he needed a quick example for his Indian
program."[3] At the time Oliver LaFarge, executive director of the Association on American Indian Affairs, said the termination was an
effort for non-Indians to get the minerals on Paiute land.[4]

   Before Euro-Americans arrived in the Southwest, the Utah Paiutes lived along the Virgin, Santa Clara, and Muddy rivers and in
more arid areas around springs. They raised small irrigated crops
of corn, squash, melons, gourds, and sunflowers but foraged for
most of their food. The arrival of the Mormons in the 1850s dis-
placed the Paiutes from their foraging and camping areas, and their
numbers dropped sharply as a result of starvation and disease. In
1865 the bands signed a treaty with the federal government, but
the Senate did not ratify it, and the Paiutes had no land until 1891
when the federal government created the Shivwits Reservation near
St. George. The government established other small Paiute reservations, for the Indian Peaks band in 1915, Koosharem band in 1928,
and Kanosh band in 1929. The Cedar Band lived on land donated
by the Mormon Church.[5]

   The group of so-called mixed-blood Utes, about one-fourth of the
Ute Tribe of the Uintah and Ouray Reservation, also was terminated

in 1954. The Utes took a different path from the Menominees, who retained their tribal organization and organized their former reservation into a county, and from the Klamath, who let individuals take their shares of the tribal assets while a remaining nucleus tried to hold onto the rest of the land. The two groups of Utes appeared—in the records, at least—to have been more amicable in their dealings with each other than were the various Klamath factions. Under the legislation, which the Interior Department said in a report to Congress had been worked out by the Indians, the two groups divided the $15.8 million in tribal money and their 980,000 acres in proportion to their numbers. Of the 1,765 members, 439 were listed as mixed-blood. The two groups arranged to jointly own and manage their extensive oil, gas, and mineral rights. The mixed-bloods' termination became effective in 1961, but they formed an independent organization called Affiliated Ute Citizens. The full-bloods (actually those who were 50 percent or more Indian) remained under federal jurisdiction as the Ute Tribe of the Uintah and Ouray Reservation. In early 1958 the two groups finalized an agreement on distributing the cash, about $64,000 to each mixed-blood and $69,000 to each full-blood. The mixed-bloods worked out one deal as they departed federal protection—an exemption from property taxes on the distributed land for seven years so long as the property remained in the hands of the original Indian owner.[6]

Metcalf says, however, the notion of a voluntary severing of the tribe was "a convenient argument to absolve" a variety of interests that pushed the tribe into dividing itself. The division was "developed as a ploy to thwart termination," he wrote. Instead, the government acted on it. Several Utah bands of Shoshone Indians also were targeted for termination but were dropped from the legislation after they hired lawyers and raised objections.[7]

The little Paiute bands, meanwhile, were being persuaded, apparently by Senator Watkins, to approve termination in exchange for adding several provisions to the law. Only one of those, cancellation of government loans and mortgages to tribal members, was written into the law and carried out. The loans and mortgages were for construction of irrigation systems; there was a serious question whether the Indians ever approved the construction, although they were being charged for the projects. The Indians thought that in meetings with Watkins in December 1953 and February 1954 they had won agreement also that the marriages, divorces, and adoptions performed by Indian customs would be recognized as legal, that oil and mineral rights on their lands would be released to them immediately after termination was approved, and that restrictions on their crops would be removed for five years. (During the termination era the federal program covering basic crops such as wheat included limits on the acreage that individual farmers could plant.)[8] Watkins said during the February 1954 hearing on the Utah bill that he did not think it would hurt the wheat market if the small number of Indian farmers were allowed to grow an unlimited amount of wheat.[9] However, neither that provision nor the other two were in the termination bill, nor were they implemented. In addition, later congressional testimony indicated that the Indians thought Watkins had told them taxes on their land "would be taken care of." They weren't.[10]

The day after the Indians' second meeting with Watkins, Utah oilman Charles H. Harrington wrote the senator thanking him on behalf of the four bands for meeting with them. Harrington said the meeting provided the Indians with a better understanding of the bill, "and they are more enthusiastic than ever and their wish is that the bill will be passed as soon as possible." According to testimony at the congressional hearing, Harrington had been at odds with the BIA over his efforts to bypass the normal bidding procedure to acquire oil leases on Indian land and was serving as a "counselor" to some of the tribal people.[11]

The four little bands were never unanimous in supporting termination. At one point one tribal official sent a telegram to the congressional committee stating that his band objected to ending its ties to the federal government. That was followed almost immediately by a second telegram from two other officers stating that the tribe did support termination.[12]

The termination bill called for an education and training program to prepare the Indians for getting jobs and managing their own affairs. The records are not clear whether that program was carried out. Assistant Secretary of the Interior John A. Carver Jr. told a Utah congressman in 1962 that vocational training had been offered, and "a number" of Shivwits band members took part. However, in 1979 a top BIA official, Ralph Reeser, told a congressional hearing he was not aware that any such program had existed. He said some individuals may have been served with other programs. In 1955 the BIA said forty-five Utah Indians had applied for relocation, the program that moved Indians from reservations throughout the country to several major cities for job training and work. The agency did not say how many were from the small remote bands being terminated.[13]

Congress and the BIA listed four criteria to determine whether a tribe was ready for termination.[14] The first criterion was the degree of acculturation to white society. About 20 percent of the 180 members of the four Paiute bands could neither read nor write English. There had been virtually no intermarriage with non-Indians, and there was no evidence that tribal members took part in the wider communities where they lived.

The second criterion was the tribe's economic condition. In 1954 the bands owned more than 40,000 acres of land, most of it considered not even suitable for grazing livestock. Their income was estimated at one-third to one-half that of neighboring non-Indians. Even Senator Watkins noted that "many of these Indians live in the depths of poverty."[15] Some of the Koosharem band members lived in tents located on the outskirts of Richfield, Utah. A majority of the families received welfare or assistance from the Mormon Church. There was little permanent employment in the areas where the tribes lived; those who worked had mostly seasonal jobs harvesting sugar beets and potatoes or doing other farm labor.[16]

The third criterion was the attitude of the tribe toward termination. The bands did agree to be terminated but only because of promises that were not kept.

The only one of the four criteria that was met by the Paiute bands was the one not related to tribal status—the attitude of state and local officials; those officials favored the termination. (State and local governments tended to support termination of Indian tribes because they wanted Indian land on local tax rolls.) The Utah bands also met only one of five criteria that Indian Commissioner Dillon S. Myer had set in 1952: they received only nominal services from the government. Myer's other criteria divided tribes into those in which substantial numbers had sought termination, those with substantial assets, relocated tribes, and those considered ready for termination.[17]

A quarter century later, Senator Daniel Inouye of Hawaii asked Dr. Emery A. Johnson, director of the Indian Health Service, whether anyone in the agencies spoke up against terminating those bands they knew were not qualified to leave federal assistance. Johnson replied: "The position of the Administration and Congress was that termination was the way to go. Those of us who were in this program were required to carry out laws and policies."[18]

So the bands' termination went into effect in 1957. Little changed for the Paiutes except that life got even more difficult. Lacking health care and income, tribal members died at increased rates during the next twenty-five years. The Kanosh, Koosharem, and Indian Peaks bands lost nearly all their land. The Shivwits placed their 26,680 acres in trust with the Walker Bank and Trust Company of Salt Lake City, which leased most of it to non-Indians for grazing fees just high enough to cover the property taxes on the land. The BIA also had leased Paiute grazing land, but Metcalf says the agency never told the tribes there was income from their land.[19] At one time the bank put the property up for sale, but band members who formerly lived there saw the sale advertisement and objected. The band then formed a corporation and took over the management. The Kanosh band parceled out its 4,280 acres to its five dozen members, who lost all but 80 acres either by sale to pay taxes or for unpaid taxes. The Koosharem band lost its 400 acres to unpaid property taxes. The Indian Peaks band sold its 8,960 acres to the state for wildlife management despite objections from some members. The Cedar Band never owned any land; Congress appropriated money to buy land for the band in 1910, but the Indian Service never made the purchase, and the money reverted to the Treasury.[20]

In less than ten years after termination, Carver, the assistant secretary of interior, wrote, "It is apparent that not only are living conditions poor but there is considerable family breakdown and demoralization."[21] More than twenty years after termination, the average adult tribal member had an eighth-grade education. Unemployment stood at 30 percent, rising to 60 percent in winter. Just one-third of family heads had full-time employment, and an additional one-third had part-time jobs, all at low wages. The remaining third were considered unemployable.[22]

There was one bright spot in the termination years. In 1965 the tribe's attorneys negotiated a settlement for the 26 million acres the Indians lost to white settlement. The $7.25 million—minus $697,000 in attorneys fees' and costs—amounted to 27 cents an acre. The money allowed the bands to begin to build their communities. Ironically, Watkins, who had been defeated in his bid for reelection in 1958, was the head of the Indian Claims Commission that approved the settlement.[23]

In 1979 Senator Inouye questioned BIA officials about the near sale of Shivwits land, demanding whether BIA retained oversight after naming the private trustee. Reeser, the director of BIA's legislative affairs office, said the whole point of termination was to end any federal involvement with the tribes.

"Once termination occurred the law was not concerned with the Indians?" Inouye asked.

"I'm afraid that's right," Reeser said.

"So if they were conned it was their hard luck?"

"Unfortunately, I guess that's the way it went."

Inouye also questioned Reeser about whether the terminations would be legal if the government did not carry out all the requirements of the act, such as education programs. "Other tribes took us to court," Reeser said, noting that termination of a number of California rancherias was voided because the government failed to take promised actions. "It could be the case here," he said. "Because there has been no contact since termination, information is sketchy. Of all the groups that went through termination these people were the least ready and perhaps suffered the most."[24]

The Cedar Band was not listed in the termination law, but in 1979 the Indian Health Service said in written testimony to Congress that IHS had been created about the same time as the Utah terminations and had never served any of the Paiutes, including Cedar Band. Because officials "believed Cedar Band was terminated they may have been denied services or members may have thought they were terminated and not asked," the IHS stated.[25]

For all the bands, housing remained derelict until 1975, when the Paiutes formed the Utah Paiute Tribal Housing Authority and obtained funding from the U.S. Department of Housing and Urban Development to build low-rent and self-help housing units. The housing authority was able to use some land that had remained in Indian hands and some Indian-occupied land provided by a local church.

About the same time, running water and electricity were made available to some Paiute homes for the first time. Many, however, continued to live in homes without hot or cold running water or indoor toilets. In fact, 81 of 110 families had poor housing conditions. Parry, the Utah Indian affairs official who cited the housing numbers, said he couldn't say if the conditions had deteriorated since termination "because they were about as low as you can get."[26]

Chairman Travis Benioh of the Cedar Band, speaking on behalf of all five southern Utah Paiute bands, said the Paiutes had a hard time "trying to develop themselves into white society." Loans and credit were hard to come by for Indians, he added. "It seemed like the senator at that time in the 1950s wanted termination, but the respective communities won't give the Indians a chance, and today they still don't." He said discrimination in the schools helped create a very high dropout rate among Indians. "Most give up and go into the Job Corps or just bum around town working at a few jobs that generally don't last a week." Lack of education kept them from better jobs, he said. And he said the bands had made no progress in education at any level in the two decades since termination. He added that the Paiute "are slowly losing their culture and pride," while recognized tribes are retaining their heritage.[27]

Beverly Snow, chairman of the Shivwits band, said that at the time of termination the band's elders did not understand English well and did not understand termination at all. "People that came to them gave them a good story and they fell for it," Snow said. She added that since then "my people haven't progressed much. Land lies covered with weeds. The rest is leased for grazing cattle and some by the cattle association to relatives for gardens." The money made from those leases was used to pay taxes, she said. "In that way we are able to retain the old reservation." Band members who hold jobs made just enough to make them ineligible for welfare "so we do without doctors."[28]

Tribes had a misunderstanding of the termination bill, said McKay Pikyavit, chairman of the Utah Paiute Tribal Corporation. "The Paiute have really suffered in a lot of ways. I didn't really understand termination. Since termination we have gone down." He added, "It is hard for an Indian with no background to try to step into white society within a few months and try to make a living." He said the Paiutes tried to get a school for their bands, but it did not go through. When Indians attempted to get loans or grants for education or business, the federal government said they were not Indians, to go to the state. The state then said they did not qualify.[29]

Pikyavit's view was supported by S. D. Aberle, executive director of the Commission on Rights, Liberties and Responsibilities of the American Indian. She met with about a third of the members of the four officially terminated bands about a year after termination. "One crucial problem," she said, "is that terminated Indians do not automatically become average non-Indian citizens with birth certificates, Social Security numbers, recorded land deeds and a command of English and know-how which allows them to operate in white society. They have difficulty in knowing how to register to vote, how to comply with government regulations for a fishing or hunting license, how to obtain a Farmers Home loan or Soil Conservation Service assistance or other benefits the Federal or State government offers its citizens. So termination actually puts them in the class something like the newly-arrived peasant immigrants."

Therefore, the Congressional policy statement to make Indians subject to the same laws and entitled to same privileges as other citizens "from any realistic evaluation is not accomplished by the legislation" to end their relationship with the federal government. Although no records make the analogy, it appears that the Indians' understanding of termination was similar to earlier Indian generations' understanding of treaties. The European concept of land ownership was incomprehensible to the generations of Indians who signed treaties. The concept of termination made no sense to the mid-twentieth-century Indians.[30]

The mixed-blood Utes, who filed a lawsuit seeking to restore them to tribal status, also claimed they suffered from loss of their tribal identity and the loss to non-Indians of most of the land and money they received when tribal assets were divided.[31]

The Kanosh band summed up the effects of termination in a letter to the Senate Indian Affairs Subcommittee in 1979: "After we were terminated it was not like they said it would be like. They promised that everything we want will be much easier, like getting a bank loan—which was not true. We could not get a bank loan because we did not have the right kind of a deed. We couldn't buy farm equipment or seed grain and we were given a small wheat allotment that wouldn't support us. Before we could do anything land taxes were on us. We had to sell some property to pay taxes until all was gone."[32]

Patrick Charles, chairman of the Koosharem band, listed similar problems. He added, "We want our children and descendants to have opportunities to grow and excel."[33]

7 California

Scattered

No one seemed to know how many Indians or how many Indian tribes were in California in the late 1940s and early 1950s as the termination movement gathered strength. By 1954 the best guess appeared to be that there were 117 reservations and rancherias in the state and around 31,000 Indians, about a third of them living on Indian or government land.[1] Even then, the population of two rancherias was listed as unknown in the legislation that terminated them. Those Indians and tribes or bands that could be identified disagreed sharply about losing federal protection. As he did elsewhere, Senator Arthur Watkins turned the divisions to his advantage, excoriating as "selfish" Indians who opposed termination and giving wider voice to those who approved. In the end, of course, Watkins won most of what he was after, removal of federal government responsibilities toward some of the least educated and poorest people in one of the country's wealthiest states.

The Indians of California suffered two waves of genocide, the first between 1769 and 1834 at the hands of Spaniards who held thousands in slavery at twenty-one Franciscan missions between Baja California and San Francisco. The Indian population dropped by half in that period.[2] Miners and soldiers engaged in the second wave of genocide during the Gold Rush years after the United States acquired California from Mexico. Thousands more Indians died from disease, starvation, psychological stress, and intentional killing in northern California during that period.[3] Before the arrival of the Spanish, the California Indians lived in bands of 50 to 100 people and found abundant food sources in the animals, birds and fish, wild plants and nuts without engaging in agriculture. The population may have been as great as 300,000.

U.S. government records show that in 1846, two years before the United States wrested California from Mexico, an estimated 200 tribes and bands with more than 100,000 people occupied about 75 million acres in California. The rush of gold-hungry prospectors into the state drove many of the Indians from their lands, turning them into refugees, sometimes with a $200 bounty for each dead Native. The state condoned indentured service (tantamount to slavery) for Indian women and children and took no action against slaughter of individuals and groups of Indians. In 1852, after California became a state, the federal government negotiated eighteen treaties with California Indians, promising that they could keep 8.5 million acres. The California Legislature, however, asked Congress not to ratify the agreements, and the treaties were shelved, leaving the Indians scattered, practically—if not legally—landless. In the 1860s the federal government began a series of executive orders, land withdrawals, homestead designations, and purchases that eventually gave the 17,000 Indians surviving in 1890 the use of 687,000 acres of land, mostly bits and pieces that no one else wanted, scattered from the Mexican border to Oregon. However, two of the larger pieces contained valuable timber, and one desert bit was in the middle of what became the city of Palm Springs.[4]

In 1928 the Court of Claims awarded the Indians $17 million for the California land taken without compensation. The government deducted $12 million for services since 1850 and the cost of land it had acquired for the tribal people.[5] Nineteen years later, the Indians were still waiting for the remaining $5 million. By that time so many people covered in the claim had died and so many more Indians had been born that the government sought authority from Congress to conduct a census to determine who was entitled to the money.[6] The census, the prospect of finally paying the claims settlement, Indian objections to the heavy hand of the Bureau of Indian Affairs, and the country's general "free the Indians" sentiment combined to put the Indians of California near the top of the list for termination.

The first plan, contained in the 1947 bill authorizing the tribal census, was to turn the Indians over to the state. That plan would have given the Indians no more independence than they had, substituting probably less sympathetic state authority for federal law and the BIA. That agency seems to have drawn some especially intense opposition from its charges in California. Nor were state officials enthusiastic about taking over services to Indians. The California Assembly adopted a resolution early that year urging release of the state's Indians "from the virtual political and economic slavery in which vast numbers of them are now held." In addition to calling for "full personal, political and economic rights" for tribal members, the resolution urged that their lands be sold and proceeds distributed to individual Indians.[7] The plan was not enacted.

In 1949 the BIA drew up a program to terminate federal ties with all the California Indians. That proposal called for contracting health, welfare, law enforcement, and road maintenance to state agencies. It also called for developing a sustained yield plan for the tribal timber lands, completing irrigation and domestic water supply projects, rehabilitating the road system, and then turning all those lands and projects over to the Indians. And the BIA recommended that the Indians finally get the 1928 judgment fund—$150 per person plus a $1 million loan fund.[8] This plan also was met with only lukewarm support from the Indians.

Haggling continued through the last years of the 1940s and first half of the 1950s, with the BIA pushing the Indians to accept removal of government programs and government protections for their land. The California Legislature sent a formal memorial to Congress in 1951 calling for immediate termination.[9] Again, as elsewhere, some of the conflict arose because of different attitudes about time by Indians and government agents. As Robert Lovato, chairman of the Pala Indian Reservation Council, explained during a panel discussion at a Conference on California Indians in late 1956: "The majority of California Indians have not asked for termination because they do not understand what it means or what problems will come up. . . . They have not had enough opportunity to study the proposed bills. . . . Federal and state governments should not hurry the process. . . . We Indians like to go slow."[10]

The government kept pushing one step at a time. By 1950, the BIA had sold 300 of the 1,100 individual public domain Indian allotments, meaning that the Indian allottees had received money for their property but no longer had the use of the land. In 1954 only 466 of the public domain allotments remained, covering 42,237 acres. There also were 3,280 allotments of reservation land totaling 67,962 acres. Most of the land occupied by California Indians, however, was not owned by the tribes or individual Indians but had been purchased by the government, which retained title. Indians occupied the land by assignment. Most of the areas were small, and the land, located in mountains and deserts, generally was too poor to support any type of farming. A few families, however, did produce grapes, tree fruits, garden crops, and livestock on sixteen of the rancherias. Most California Indians worked for wages, generally in seasonal farm jobs and some in logging.[11] By the early 1950s mechanization was beginning to reduce the number of farm jobs.

In 1952 the commissioner of Indian Affairs directed that no more California Indians be admitted to Indian boarding schools and that as rapidly as possible all California Indian children be enrolled in public schools. By that time most Indian children in California al-

ready were attending public schools under contracts between the
BIA and school districts. The BIA also had ended welfare aid to Indians and thrust the responsibility on the state and counties.[12] Training and relocation programs offered to members of other tribes
were not open to most of the California Indians, although one of
the major relocation centers was San Francisco.[13]

As it was for other tribes, the concerted push toward terminating California tribes was the 1953 resolution making termination
official congressional policy. That resolution named the California
tribes among those ready to give up government aid. Also, as with
other tribes, the termination bills provided that the expenses of cutting the Indians free would be paid from tribal funds although most
of the California tribal groups had little or no money. In a 1954 letter transmitting the proposed California termination legislation to
Congress, Orme Lewis, assistant secretary of the interior, said of the
Indians, "as a group they are poor and the majority fall in the lowest income group in the state." He said few of the tribes and bands
had responded to the department's request for comment on the
proposed legislation. However, he acknowledged, "Comments by
the Indians were limited in number because of the limited time for
consultation, the reluctance of the Indians to put their thoughts in
writing and apparently general lack of interest." He did not note the
instances in which groups of Indians left meetings before a vote was
taken or the tendency of Indians to decline to attend a session rather
than vote no.[14] As noted elsewhere, Indians' failure to participate
generally meant disapproval of the proposal at hand.

The House and Senate subcommittees on Indian Affairs heard
two long days of testimony on California tribes in March 1954 as
part of its marathon sessions on the first wave of termination legislation. The California sessions followed the familiar pattern: Senator
Watkins, chairman of the Senate subcommittee, and Representative
E. Y. Berry, chairman of the House subcommittee, were merciless in

questioning opponents of termination and lavished praise on the supporters. Three other members of Congress were present, two of them from California—Republican senator Thomas Kuchel and Democratic representative Clair Engle. The third was Republican senator Henry Dworshak of Idaho. The hearing also highlighted a number of issues involved in termination:

- Situations of tribes and bands varied. The size of tribes or bands ranged from a handful of families to several hundred individuals. A few had income from timber sales or leases, providing some money for tribal programs. Others had unproductive land and no source of tribal income.
- Federal programs, such as irrigation projects or loans to finance cattle raising, had been started but then halted before completion.
- Many Indians had no understanding of the termination proposals, and neither the BIA nor Congress was prepared to give them time to fully comprehend the government plans or develop plans of their own.
- Indians disagreed about the entire idea of termination. Some wanted no changes in their status; some wanted to get rid of the BIA but retain government trust protection for their property; some wanted to get rid of government connections altogether.
- Committee members, to a large extent, considered the Indians "selfish" and "greedy," wanting to retain their government ties only to avoid paying taxes.
- Committee members also tended to consider as Indians only those whose families had never intermarried with whites, regardless of whether they had spent their entire lives in a tribal culture.
- Committee members and BIA officials tended to blame "out-

side influences," such as the National Congress of American Indians (NCAI) and the American Friends Service Committee, for any tribal opposition to termination.

The Indians remained largely skeptical. A Los Coyotes Rancheria committee appointed by the members listed reasons the rancheria opposed the current bill. "We are uneducated and not equipped to take on full responsibilities upon such short notice," the committee statement began. "We are not ready and did not request termination." Noting that the band was "still waiting for treaty ratification," the committee said the Indians feared a "repeat 1851–52" when they were driven from their homes. Also, the committee stated, "Our land is unproductive." In addition, the former area director of the BIA, James Stewart, had promised that roads, homes, and irrigation systems would be developed before termination. "None of that has been done."[15]

Representatives from two tribes that eventually escaped termination provided descriptions of programs the BIA had started but failed to complete, thwarting Indian efforts to make economic progress. Their complaints were typical of tribal frustrations. Erin Forrest of the Pit River Tribe near Alturas in northern California described the plight of a group of tribal members who started a cattle ranch under a federal program only to have the program closed just as it was on the verge of becoming profitable. The government purchased the land, and eleven tribal members formed the Pit River Home and Agricultural Cooperative Association. "We had to borrow $11,000 to buy equipment to farm," Forrest told the committee. "That was all we had. . . . The first few years we sold hay and grain. We paid ourselves $40 a month, sometimes $2.50 a day during the summer. Most of us had been getting $10 to $15 day outside. Later, we got cattle under the Indian Bureau repayment program. In a few years we paid back the cattle and paid off the loan. But we were never fully stocked. We were about half stocked when the program was cancelled. So we were never built up to economic units. The government got the cattle in the 1930s for as little as $5 a head. When it shut off the replacement program we had to pay as high as $190 a head. Almost immediately after we bought the XL, the Indian Bureau started an irrigation project without consulting us. The dams they built were not adequate and we had to pay several thousand dollars to repair them. . . . In five years we will have to pay taxes [under the termination bill] and we will have nothing."

Watkins was less than sympathetic. "Then you won't have to pay taxes" [if you have nothing], he said.

Forrest: If the land is given to us we'll have to pay taxes.

Watkins: You said you'd have nothing.

Forrest: I meant money for cattle, which is the source of income.

Watkins said cattlemen in Utah were doing just fine with feeder operations. Forrest explained that getting into feeding operations required capital, which the Indians didn't have. The Indians were raising cattle, which they sold at low prices to feeder operations, which then got high prices for the ready-to-market cattle. Watkins suggested a loan from the Farmers Home Administration. Forrest said he already had been turned down there because he was an Indian.

Forrest also described the educational level of four hundred members of his tribe: there were no college graduates, twelve high school graduates, and only forty elementary school graduates. Most tribal members spoke English, he said, but only half could read and write.[16]

Elsie Gardner Rickels, representing the Hoopa Tribe of northern California, explained to Watkins the failure of an irrigation system in her area: "Well, I think in some cases moneys were appropriated for a certain project, and they were begun, and before the completion the moneys were not forthcoming. So they were left in a state of incompleteness, and naturally with the passage of time and weather, et cetera the whole thing just fell apart. And then some of the projects that were set up were not of a permanent nature so that they also deteriorated to the extent that they were nonfunctional, or very poor and offered very poor service. And, of course, I will say that some of them probably just were not properly maintained, either by the Bureau or by the Indians themselves. I am not absolving ourselves of any blame, but, anyway, all of these factors have combined to make this situation where we do not have" an adequate water system.

Watkins said he was happy to find someone willing to accept part of the blame for things that had gone wrong. Rickels, in addition to insisting the water system should be improved, said, "We make one last final plea to retain hunting and fishing rights practiced in conjunction with religious customs." Watkins said he was baffled by the relationship between hunting and fishing and religion.

Rickels acknowledged that she usually had to explain that to non-Indians. "To most people, hunting and fishing is a sport," she said. "To the American Indian it is part of a religious custom. The American Indians are . . . a very religious people. We did not believe in church just one day; we believed in a church every day of the week and in every act that we did. And we have continued with that belief. Therefore, even the taking of food was a religious sacrament in a way, particularly to the hunting of deer."

Watkins thought that was just fine but questioned Mrs. Rickels closely on whether the rights should extend only to people who were full-blood Indians, or perhaps half-blood. Watkins also used Mrs. Rickels as a foil for one his favorite themes—treaties with Indian tribes were now meaningless because Indians had become citizens of the United States "and have taken advantage of its opportunities."[17]

Watkins could be relentless when he didn't get the answer he wanted. Virgil R. Lawson, delegate from the Cabazon, Augustine, and Torres-Martinez Indian Reservation, tried to explain the Indians' fear of losing their land if it was removed from trust status. Watkins insisted that Lawson speak only for himself as an individual. Lawson, a thirty-six-year-old graduate of Riverside Junior College who worked as an aircraft engine specialist in an aircraft factory, conceded that he was not afraid that he would be unable to resist would-be buyers of his twenty acres of farmland. But he finally got a chance to tell Watkins that he was the only one among the 300 tribal members who had attended college and that only half a dozen were high school graduates. "Possibly 20 percent" had completed elementary school, he said.

The senator bored in on Lawson: "Isn't the main reason why you are opposed to this bill because you do not want your land placed on the tax rolls?"

Lawson conceded, "That is one reason."

Watkins: And that is the big reason is it not?

Lawson: Yes, sir, and we could lose our lands under that reason.

Watkins: Certainly and the white man can too if he does not pay his taxes. . . . If he does not get out and work and take care of himself he can lose a lot of things, including the ability to take care of himself.

Lawson responded, "It is my understanding that you want me to imply that there is some merit in this proposal, which I will not do."

Involved in the dispute between Watkins and Lawson was an irrigation project then under construction. Watkins said it was being built to benefit both Indians and non-Indians. Lawson said that was not true. Lawson explained, "We have had a special act passed whereby we could come under that canal and it has not been materialized. . . . One reason is that there is a shortage of water in the canal and the local water district is not anxious to give us water to supply us. The other reason is that the Indian Bureau has stopped negotiations."

That led to another argument between the senator and the Indian over whether the prospective taxes and payments would be an undue hardship on the Indian landowners. "We do not object to a reasonable payment, but it would be too expensive for the poverty-stricken Indians to afford," Lawson said. Watkins suggested that the Indians could rent their land to others for many times the taxes and water charges. Lawson noted that whites too had lost developing lands to taxes.

Watkins scoffed, "I have not seen a more prosperous area in the United States than they have down there, or any better farming." Lawson said the increasing value of the land was another reason his tribe opposed termination: "it will take some years before we can receive the full value for our properties; whereas if we were to be terminated within the next 10 years we would have to sell out cheap." He reminded Watkins that the government had promised to guarantee water for the Indian lands and allow the Indian owners to "pay as we went along." He said he felt it was the government's responsibility to see that the Indians got water before terminating the tribe.

Watkins snapped, "I don't care to argue any further with you" and once more accused him of wanting to keep land in trust only so he would not have to pay taxes. He had not responded when Lawson said he had traded his own reservation (trust) land for land outside the reservation on which, presumably, he had to pay taxes. Lawson also challenged Watkins's assertion that the reservation land was worth $1,000 an acre, saying $200 was more like it.

Later, Berry joined in badgering Lawson for "having more privileges [than other landowners]. You do not have to pay taxes. You get the same thing that we get only you do not have to pay for it."

Watkins concluded by accusing Lawson of "getting away with" voting without being taxed.[18]

Watkins similarly badgered Billy P. Salgado, the delegate from the Cahuella band of the Cahuella Reservation and the Catholic Progressive Society of the Pechanga Tribe of the Pechanga Reservation in Riverside County. Salgado, a high school graduate who worked as foreman of a firefighting crew for the California Division of Forestry and Natural Resources, said his groups opposed the termination bills because they saw no advantage to the Indians. Watkins asked why they did not want "to be like other citizens." Salgado replied, "because the United States government made that promise to us." Watkins said that was when the tribes were foreign nations, not citizens. Watkins said the Indians opposed termination only because they didn't want to pay taxes. Salgado said, "Only because that is the price the government gave us" [for their land and the treaties]. Watkins said he didn't think the Indians had any rights under the treaties because the treaties were never ratified by the Senate. "We feel that all the lands that were taken have more than paid our share of taxes," Salgado said.

Watkins pointed out the court judgment and added, "You have not given up everything and this country nothing. We have developed civilization. You have a wonderful country out there in California that was not very much until the white people took it over and started to develop it and you are getting the advantage of that. . . . Really you have to pay a little something."

Under attack from Representative Engle for insisting the Indians should keep their "advantages," Salgado responded, "You call it selfishness. Go back to when our treaties were made, how the government treated our people, how we kept our part of the bargain, how our people were treated. We were supposed to forget that? That is not easy to forget. And it will never be forgotten, no more than the attack the Japanese made on Pearl Harbor will ever be forgotten by this Government."

Engle: Do you think that has any pertinency to this legislation?
Salgado: I do. Yes, I do.

Engle said the two issues were separate matters and launched into a rambling discourse on his own sponsorship of removing discrimination against Indians in the purchase of alcohol.[19]

Criz Siva from Los Coyotes Indian Reservation near Warner Hot Springs made the case for delaying termination, calling his "the forgotten Indian reservation." His tribe, left with unproductive land, believed it had paid with land in the 1800s for any benefits the tribe was receiving. The nearest town, Hemet, then a tiny desert community, was fifty to sixty miles away. Reservation children had no way of attending school until 1930, and most of the fifty-five tribal members living on the reservation were uneducated. From 1930 on, children were sent to boarding schools, but as elsewhere, many of them ran away to return home. With their lack of education, most tribal members were unable to make a living. Some found seasonal jobs; a few raised cattle, but the range was poor. "We are trying to send our kids to school," he said. "We need more time." He said the tribe was depending on the generation then going to school.

Siva said Mission Federation, an organization of tribes in the Southern California mission area, had caused a split among tribal members. He said proposals from Los Coyotes for projects to benefit that reservation had been vetoed by the federation.[20]

"We are beginning to believe termination is inevitable," stated Lovato, the Pala Reservation chairman. But he warned that "blanket termination will not work" because of different conditions on the dozens of reservations.

There were other problems. Lovato asked why a well on his reservation had not been finished although work on it had been started two or three years earlier. Leonard Hill, the BIA area director for California, admitted, "no good reason." There was a power line that had not been finished. Someone discovered an 1890 water rights agreement "that is still being studied." He said he believed the Pala people, who already had paid for part of the project, would get the well eventually. But, he said, the water table in the area had been lowered by development, and they probably would not get additional water from the well.

Lovato asked two things of the government before it terminated its relationship with the tribe. First, the tribe wanted assurance that it could keep the 9,000-acre Morgan Hill Reserve, used by the tribe for gathering food, basket fibers, and medicinal herbs. The reserve was set aside for the Indians in 1903, but Lovato said the land had become nearly inaccessible. The Indians had to cross private land to reach their reserve, and the land owners were requiring right-of-way permits. In 1953 the BIA said unless the Indians proved they were using the reserve, the BIA would turn the land over to the Forest Service. Second, the tribe wanted the government to bring the homes, roads, and water system up to standard. Lovato said when Warner Springs, San Felipe, and Paiute bands were moved from their homelands around Warner Springs to the Pala Reservation in the early 1900s, they were promised good homes. "Those were never provided." He said about 160 of Pala's 11,016 acres were irrigable, with most families among the three hundred members having something less than 2 acres of irrigable land.[21]

While the Warner Springs and Pala Indians said they would accept termination with some delays and some conditions, Max C. Mazzetti, delegate from the Rincon Indian Reservation, said his tribe opposed it entirely. Adding to his tribe's problems, Mazzetti said a man named Purl Willis, acting as counselor for the Mission Indian Federation but without the knowledge of any individual tribes, had gone to Washington in 1950 seeking termination of all mission tribes. Mazzetti said a number of issues remained to be resolved before termination could be considered, including surveys of reservation lines, water rights, homes that might not meet state and local building standards, mineral rights, liens (generally for irrigation) that were so high that the Indians would be unable to pay. And Mazzetti complained that when Indian Commissioner Glenn C. Emmons came to California he promised to listen to the Indians "but didn't."[22]

Fifteen tribal councils went on record opposing the termination plan. A number of the Indian delegates endorsed a nine-point program proposed by the Association on American Indian Affairs (AAIA) in a letter to the Appropriations Committee. Its outline covered the issues raised by Mazzetti.[23]

In contrast to the poor bands with little arable land in the desert, the Agua Caliente Tribe was doing quite well, according to Vyola Olinger, who represented the tribe at the hearing. Its land included two acres in downtown Palm Springs, valued at $5 million to $6 million. The tribe's other land, located a two-hour drive from Los Angeles, "with proper development could be something to be proud of," she said. The limitation of leases to five years was holding back development, but she said given five years and some education in business, the tribe would be ready to run its own operations. It already was supporting its own Indian agency with income from a bathhouse and canyons. The bill proposed by Commissioner Emmons, she said, "would push the Indian into social and economic slavery."[24]

A non-Indian organization, Indian Land Development Inc., made up of people developing Indian property under permit, supported the tribe's opposition to termination. In a letter submitted to the committee, the organization said it had invested $100,000 in new buildings on Indian land in the past two years, believing that the status quo would continue. However, the city of Palm Springs enthusiastically supported termination, at least partly because it wanted the additional taxes from the Indian land within its limits. City Councilman Earle C. Strebe said terminating the federal trust over the Indian lands would end the five-year lease restriction "which has stunted the growth of important and substantial areas of our city." He added, "When it is recalled that Palm Springs is a resort city, relying not only on its unsurpassed climate but enviable beauty, one can see why the city is so anxious to rid itself of the plight of an economic blight thrust upon a portion of its population, namely the Indian suffering from a lengthy and uncompromising wardship." Carefully led by Berry and Watkins, Strebe told the committee that the Indian property generated only 2.6 percent of the city's tax revenue but required 20 to 30 percent of the police and fire departments' time.[25]

Further support for termination came from Purl Willis, the self-described counselor to the Mission Indian Federation of California mentioned by the Rincon Indian Reservation's Mazzetti. Like Mazzetti, Willis opposed the bill then under consideration. "The Mission Indian Federation of California wants immediate freedom from federal authority and funds," Willis said. Willis, a non-Indian and not an attorney, described himself as an adviser to the federation of forty-six little bands. He urged a plan in which each band would work out the fate of its own lands with an advisory committee with members named by the secretary of the interior, the state, San Diego County, and the Indians. "Don't the Indians know now what they want done?" Watkins demanded. "Tell us what they want." Willis wound up his testimony with a diatribe against former Indian commissioner John Collier, who, he said, "was the voice of Russian communism" and "part of a conspiracy to communize America." He also castigated the National Congress of American Indians as an "undesirable influence" on the Indians. The organization was largely responsible for opposition to termination, he said.[26]

Willis's testimony covered fourteen pages (at least half an hour), not including a supplemental statement he submitted. Helen Peterson, the executive director of NCAI, whose membership included

California tribes with five thousand members, was given two minutes. She said the tribal leaders opposed the present bill but were willing to help draft termination legislation providing that certain government services were guaranteed. In fact, they had agreed to meet to develop some proposals for legislation. Watkins responded, "We appreciate that statement and we will be very glad to hear from the people, but they will have to get their proposals in right away because we are going to act on this legislation."[27]

One last plea against abrupt termination came from Bethine Stewart, the delegate from Indians of California, the tribal group that had won the land claims settlement. "Many, especially the older people, do not understand taxation," she said. "We have tried to educate them because we knew termination was coming. They laugh at you. They have not the slightest understanding of the word. They are still living on the land as their ancestors did." Stewart asked that a provision for education about taxes be included in the bill.[28]

There was not as much reason to hurry as Watkins indicated to Peterson. Not until several years later did Congress enact three California termination bills—one in 1956 for the Lower Lake Rancheria, another in 1957 for the Coyote Valley Rancheria, and a third in 1958 for thirty-two rancherias. The last group had 1,100 people, but even when the bills were passed, Congress didn't know how many people were in the Lower Lake and Coyote Valley tribes. Those two terminations went into effect the year they passed. The others became effective over several years, beginning in 1961.[29]

Cheryl Seidner, chairman of Table Bluff Rancheria, the Wiyot Tribe of Loleta, California, said the Wiyots agreed to termination believing they had done well. "But they didn't," she said. "They got the land deeds, but the government didn't do what it promised: bring houses up to code, build a safe water supply, bring the sewer system in. They never did any of it." Her sister, Leona Wilkinson, a member of the Tribal Council, added, "The only reason tribal members signed was they were promised so many things."

At the beginning of termination only one tribal member lost his land to taxes. The owner, faced with losing the land, sold it for $100 to a non-Indian. "The Indians were not happy about that," Seidner said. "Militants burned the house in the 1970s." "All the tribal members had jobs," she said, and some farmed. Her father was a logger who was "always looking for work in the off season." He was killed in a logging accident in 1966.

A major loss as a result of termination was help toward higher education, although Seidner conceded, "Our problem was not getting tribal members into college—it was getting them out of high school. Alcohol was a big problem in high school." She was one of two tribal members who graduated from high school from the half dozen in school together. The others dropped out at the legal age of sixteen. Seidner graduated from Heald College Business School and later worked for Humboldt State College at Eureka, twenty minutes from the Wiyot Reservation.[30]

Don Arnold, chairman of the Scotts Valley Rancheria, did not grow up on the reservation, but he recalled that those tribal members who did live there were on welfare because there were no jobs except for seasonal work in pear orchards. Cousins who lived on the reservation did not have shoes until they were eight or ten years old, he said. Arnold, who retired from the San Francisco Bay Area Rapid Transit (BART) system in 1998, blamed termination for the death of a sister. She was one of his family members sent to San Francisco for job training as part of the termination program and was killed in a traffic accident there. He said his mother lost her allotment land to taxes "and other events" after termination.[31]

Viola Pack, former chairwoman of the LaJolla band of Mission Indians, recalled that ten families in her small tribe lost their land to taxes after termination.[32]

Even tribes that were not terminated felt the impact of the termination policy, said Sue Masten, chairwoman of the Yurok Tribe and former president of NCAI. Land problems went unresolved because of reduced staffing of the BIA. Termination left a generational anger that led to welfare, alcohol, and drugs, she said.[33]

Keith Pike, a member of the Guidiville Rancheria at Talmage, California, and business manager of the neighboring Pomo band at Big Valley Rancheria, was twelve when termination came. "All I knew was they took our playground away from us," he recalled. As he later learned, the tribe lost more than the playground. In two years the tribe lost 95 percent of its real estate, he said. There was 60 to 70 percent unemployment, and those with jobs were mostly part-time farm workers. By the third year after termination, the land was being foreclosed. People sold their land to survive. "The devastation was incredible," Pike said. There was a high cost in human terms. Families disintegrated, and many had to separate. People moved to cities in search of work. Most were unskilled and did manual labor. Alcoholism increased. "There were all the ills of extreme poverty," Pike said. "The worst thing that happened was the destruction of hope."[34]

8 Oklahoma Tribes and Poncas of Nebraska

Afterthoughts

When Congress passed the resolution setting termination of Indian tribes as national policy, it included the oil-rich Osage Tribe of Oklahoma among the ten tribes considered ready for independence immediately.

The Osages never lost their ties to the federal government, but three smaller, poorer tribes not listed as ready were subjected to termination legislation just as congressional sentiment was turning against the policy. A fourth group, the Modocs, who never had been recognized as separate from the Oregon Modocs, lost federal recognition in the Klamath Termination Act.

There were no hearings for the Oklahoma tribes except for the Osages, who lined up the entire Oklahoma congressional delegation to oppose their termination bill. Representatives of the Wyandotte, Peoria, and Ottawa tribes said later that their leaders agreed to accept termination in exchange for promises made by the BIA, few of which were kept. The Wyandotte, however, got a clause inserted stating that termination would not go into effect until its property, including a cemetery in Kansas, was sold under terms acceptable to the tribe. The tribe could find no one who would buy and maintain the cemetery, and so the tribe technically stayed within the federal family although it lost most federal services.[1]

Two decades later a Senate committee report said the record did not indicate why these small tribes with populations totaling fewer than 2,500 were selected from among the Oklahoma Indian population of more than 75,000 in approximately forty tribes. The report added, "The current position of the Department of the Interior is that they were politically weaker and unable to resist."[2] A Wyandotte tribal history stated that "things seemed to be falling apart" for the tribe in the 1950s with loss of the traditional language and culture and a continuing battle between the Oklahoma tribe and the so-called Absentee Wyandotte over a tribal cemetery. "Because of these reasons and others," a tribal history stated, the government terminated the tribe in 1956.[3]

The four terminated tribes arrived in Oklahoma at different times by various routes, none of them entirely voluntary. The smallest group was the Modoc Tribe, whose forty-six members were the direct descendants of tribal members exiled to Oklahoma in 1873 after the Modoc War in southern Oregon and northern California. Many Modocs eventually were allowed to return to Oregon, where they were placed on the Klamath Reservation and joined in the confederation of the Klamath, Modoc, and Yahooskin band of Snake Indians, one of the first tribes Congress ordered terminated in a 1954 bill. That termination, which included the Oklahoma Modocs, did not go into effect until 1961.

The largest of the four tribes, the Wyandottes, with nearly a thousand members, lived near the Great Lakes and St. Lawrence River when Europeans first entered the region. Fleeing west in the wake of tribal wars, remnants of two tribes from the once-powerful Huron Confederacy united to become the Wyandotte in 1650 and settled in what is now the Upper Peninsula of Michigan. The combined tribe spread through Michigan and into the Ohio Valley and took part in the French and Indian War on the side of the French, the American Revolution and War of 1812 on the side of the British, and in Indian coalition battles against the Americans. The Treaty of 1842 forced the tribe across the Mississippi River and into what became Kansas. In 1855 a large number of Wyandottes relinquished their tribal ties and accepted U.S. citizenship, but a small band refused the treaty and moved to Oklahoma and back to Kansas before achieving recognition of their tribal status and a permanent home in northeastern Oklahoma through the treaty of 1867.

The Peoria Tribe, with 640 members at the time of termination, also originated in the Great Lakes area, scattered through Illinois, Michigan, Ohio, and Missouri. A confederation of Peoria, Kaskaskia, Piankesaw, and Wea tribes, the Peorias were relocated first to Missouri, then to Kansas, and finally to Oklahoma near the Wyandottes. The Ottawa Tribe, too, came from the Great Lakes area, occupying land near Georgian Bay on Lake Huron. It also was removed from its homelands, first to Iowa and Kansas, and finally to Oklahoma near the other three tribes. When termination came, the tribe had 600 members.[4]

The 1950s did not mark the federal government's first attempt to terminate some of the Oklahoma tribes. The Wyandottes, for example, were considered to have relinquished tribal status under the treaty of 1850. However, five years later, the government assembled the tribe again to sign a new treaty, which again presumably extinguished the tribal status. The government continued to treat the Wyandottes as a recognized tribe, however, until 1935. That year Congress passed legislation to distribute tribal funds to individual members and considered that action would effectively end the Wyandotte Tribe's federal status. But two years later the Wyandottes organized under the Oklahoma Indian Welfare Act, and the federal government again recognized its existence. The tribe's status then remained unchallenged until the 1956 termination act. The tribal organization by that time had nearly ceased to function. The law's requirement that the tribe prepare a roll of members and finalize its business revitalized the tribal government. Instead of extinguishing the tribe, the termination act indirectly led to its renewal.[5]

Information furnished to Congress by the BIA at the time of termination indicated that the Wyandotte, Ottawa, and Peoria people "are almost completely integrated into the non-Indian community." Their median family incomes were comparable to their non-Indian neighbors. The children were in the public school. The majority of tribal adults were self-supporting with employment off their reservations in occupations such as electrician, plumber, or carpenter; some held public office. None were listed as receiving welfare under BIA programs.

The only remaining tribal land was the Wyandotte's 94 acres, and much of the allotted land had passed out of Indian hands. However, a few Wyandottes still made a living as farmers. Ottawa tribal members held 518 acres, with one original allottee still owning his property. Two of the Wyandotte Tribe's original allottees still held their land, part of 1,956 acres in Indian hands. The BIA estimated that state and local governments would gain $526.82 a year in taxes when the Indian property lost is federal status.[6]

The only evidence presented to Congress indicated tribal support for ending federal ties, including resolutions from the Peoria and Ottawa tribes approving termination if certain conditions were met.[7] Even so, the push for terminating the Oklahoma tribes seems odd. The three measures are dated August 1, 2 and 3, 1956, and went into effect three years later. Yet, six months before Congress approved the three measures, Senator Clair Engle of California, one of the staunchest backers of the termination policy, had declared: "There is a change in the attitude of Congress. No bills will be pushed through at this time."[8]

Two decades later, tribal leaders said they were coerced into accepting termination. Representatives of the Peoria and Ottawa tribes told Congress they had no chance to vote on the issue.[9] They appar-

ently saw the situation differently from the government agents of
1956. "We were led to believe termination would be beneficial," said
Chief Lewis Barlow of the Ottawa Tribe in an appearance before a
Senate committee in 1977. "The 1950s constitute one of the black-
est periods in our tribe's history." He said it was hard for his tribal
members to see other tribes getting government benefits while his
people received none. He called it "discouraging and disparaging"
to see the elderly, children, and sick not recognized to get health
care from the Indian Health Service.[10]

By the 1970s, the government attitude had changed. Forrest
Gerard, assistant secretary of the interior, said termination had hindered all four Oklahoma tribes both in development and in planning
for their future. An Interior Department report to Congress stated,
"It is indicative of the lack of genuine concern for their readiness
for termination that no hearings were held."[11]

Chief Rodney Arnett of the Peoria Tribe said the tribe was told in
1956 that its members would be able to get special education and
that tribal claims against the government would be settled more
quickly if the tribe accepted termination. Members did not get the
education, he said, and claims were still pending more than twenty years later. "Helplessly, our leaders have been forced to stand
by and witness this degradation of individual and tribal identity,"
Arnett said.[12]

The Wyandotte chief, Mont Cotter, said the vast majority of tribal
children were living below the poverty level. He stated that at first
some in the tribe thought they were ready to become independent of
the federal government. "Within a year it was quite evident that not
all were capable of making this tremendous change," he said. Like
most tribal members in all parts of the country who have discussed
termination, Cotter said the loss of identity was a severe blow.[13]

As for the Modocs, Chief Bill Follis said, "We didn't know what
it [termination] was."[14]

In 1968 the four terminated tribes joined four still-recognized small northeastern Oklahoma tribes in forming a nonprofit, state-chartered organization. Robert Alexander, the business manager for that Inter-Tribal Council, said the members of the terminated tribes had problems finding jobs, getting education, and getting health care. Members of those tribes were turned away from the Indian hospital. Termination "has definitely hurt the young people," he said. "We have no way to help them."[15]

By 1956 most of the members of Congress and the administration had realized that termination was a flawed policy. By 1961, with the termination of both the Menominees and Klamaths final, the disastrous effects of the policy were looming. But the terminationists had one last gasp; in 1962 Congress issued a final insult to the often-insulted Northern Ponca Tribe, ordering its relationship with the federal government ended.

There seems to be no recorded explanation why the tribe was terminated after the policy had been all but abandoned. A tribal website said only, "In 1962, Congress decided that the Northern Ponca would be one of the tribes terminated."[16] AAIA records show that Senator Frank Church (D-ID) and Representative Ralph F. Beermann (R-NE) introduced the termination bill, which was "initially drafted by the Interior Department."[17] The termination took effect in 1966.

Michael Mason, an Oregon City, Oregon, attorney who represented the Poncas, said, "The Poncas were the last, sort of an afterthought." He said the thinking appears to have been that this is "a little group that resembles some tribes that have been terminated." Their land base had been reduced, and BIA help "already was a pittance."[18] Professor Elizabeth Grobsmith, a University of Nebraska anthropologist who made an extensive study of the Poncas, described the termination measure as "an ill-conceived act with little consideration given to the fate of the Ponca."[19]

The 1962 Senate report accompanying the Ponca termination bill said Ponca tribal members themselves had begun asking for legislation to divide the tribe's assets in 1956 and had been negotiating with the BIA and local officials ever since. The report cited a petition signed by 23 Indians—not all of them Ponca tribal members—living on the reservation as a key factor in the recommendation that the Senate approve termination. At the time the tribe had 525 members. The BIA was managing money accounts for 40 tribal members, and only three loans to tribal members were in effect. Tribal children were attending public schools. The report also noted that "some records have been lost."[20]

The AAIA document notes that "in passing the Ponca bill the 87th Congress reaffirmed the principle established in recent years that termination acts are to include Indian consent clauses." Like most of the consents given by tribes, the Poncas' is in dispute. In a letter submitted to the Senate April 6, 1962, requesting passage of the Ponca termination, John A. Carver, assistant secretary of the interior, listed what he implied was a long history of tribal members' efforts to dissolve the tribe. In reality he was discussing a period of time going back four years, to 1958. Carver cited two unanimous votes, in 1959 and 1961, in favor of the bill he was submitting. However, he also said that the draft bill had been sent to 78 tribal members and only 47 returned the questionnaires, with 29 approving termination.[21] Carver's description of votes does not indicate what percentage of eligible voters participated in any of the balloting. Nor did he mention the tendency of Indians to stay away from a meeting rather than cast a "no" vote, a situation that occurred in at least several earlier terminations. In addition, some tribal members said later that elders had told young members of the tribe they could not vote on the termination resolution. "All the younger generation was against termination in the first place," said one statement submitted to Congress nearly thirty years later. "When the older people told us our vote didn't count we walked out of the last meeting." The statement said that left only half the tribal adults to vote (which could account for the unanimous vote in favor of termination). The statement concluded, "Now they're all dead and gone and we have to live with their mistakes."[22]

Fred LeRoy, who served as chairman of the restored tribe from 1990 to 2002, said not everyone in the tribe was notified about the vote over termination. Many tribal members who left their eastern Nebraska homeland during World War II decided after the war that they had better opportunities in cities than they did in the rural area near the confluence of the Niobrara and Missouri rivers. Those who did vote heard only the good things about termination from the government. Government officials never mentioned the bad things, he said.[23]

The termination ordered on September 2, 1962, was implemented in 1966 with tribal assets divided between the Poncas in Nebraska and the Poncas in Oklahoma. The 442 northern tribal members were removed from tribal rolls and dispossessed from 824 acres.[24]

The Poncas describe themselves as indigenous to Nebraska although some scholars say they were initially a woodland tribe located near Lake Winnipeg north of what is now the Canada-U.S. border and migrated in the 1700s into the South Dakota–Nebraska area, where explorers Lewis and Clark met them in 1804. The tribal members raised crops and lived in villages, but they also hunted, ranging into the Black Hills. The tribe was never involved in armed conflict with the U.S. government or settlers. Between 1817 and 1865 the tribe signed four treaties with the United States, the last one reserving 96,000 acres to the Poncas south of the Missouri River near the Niobrara River. Three years later, in the Treaty of Fort Laramie, the government included the Ponca land in the Great Sioux Reservation, effectively leaving the Poncas homeless. For eight years the tribe appealed repeatedly until the government again changed its Indian policies and decided to move as many tribes as possible to Oklahoma—Indian Territory. Eight Ponca chiefs agreed to look at Oklahoma but found the land barren and unsuitable for agriculture. However, by the time they returned to their Nebraska reservation after a midwinter trek, most of it on foot and without food or money to buy food, they found federal troops already enforcing a removal order. The long trip to Oklahoma and the outbreak of malaria in their new home killed about one-third of the tribal members in 1877–78.

In 1879 Chief Standing Bear's son died. The chief refused to bury the boy in that foreign land and, with sixty-six members of the tribe, started back toward the tribal burying ground in Nebraska. The Indians were captured by the U.S. Army, which prepared to return them to Oklahoma under a law forbidding Indians from leaving their reservations. A story in the *Omaha World-Herald* drew the attention of two prominent attorneys, who filed a writ of habeas corpus to prevent the Indians from being taken back to Oklahoma. The government challenged the writ on grounds that an Indian was not a person under the meaning of the law. The case eventually went to the U.S. Supreme Court, which upheld the District Court ruling that Standing Bear and the others were persons and entitled to go free.

Although they no longer had a home in Nebraska, they continued their journey to the Niobrara River area, and in 1881 the government returned 26,236 acres along the Niobrara and Missouri rivers to the Ponca people. Only 225 tribal members returned to Nebraska, however, while 600 remained in Oklahoma, permanently splitting the tribe between Northern Poncas and Southern Poncas.[25]

The Northern Poncas remained a poor tribe; termination made it poorer still. Through the years after their return to Nebraska, the Northern Poncas continued to face poverty and disease. By 1961, before termination, the AAIA listed the Ponca reservation among those it considered inadequate. The allotment act had whittled the tribally owned property to 690 acres. In addition to the tribal land, 387 individuals shared 2,180 acres divided into 13 allotments. At termination, tribal members who were living on the allotments were allowed to buy them at market value, and many did, continuing to live in their reservation area. The tribal land, trust fund, and federal property on the reservation had a total value of $105,635, about $240 for each of the 442 members listed on the final tribal roll.[26] BIA records do not show how much each person actually received.

Although the tribe's unemployment rate was listed at just 5 percent in 1966, termination began a long deterioration of the tribe's economic status, health, and education. Twenty-five years later, unemployment among tribal members stood at 57 percent, and nearly one-third of tribal members were living below the poverty level. Many of those who did not remain on their own land near Niobrara moved to the Yankton Sioux or Santee Sioux reservations in South Dakota. Even there, they had no access to BIA or Indian Health services because they were officially not Indians. Twenty-five years after termination 40 percent of heads of Ponca households did not have enough money to make necessary visits to a doctor. At least one member of each Ponca household surveyed had been hospitalized within the previous year, and in 37 percent of households at least one person had been kept away from work or school by injury or illness. The household survey showed 27 percent had a member with diabetes, 43 percent with high blood pressure, 33 percent with arthritis, 34 percent with hearing problems, 11 percent with heart disease, 59 percent with dental problems, 39 percent with asthma or allergies, and 16 percent with physical disabilities. Obviously, the figures indicate that most households faced multiple medical problems. One-fourth of the households had no medical insurance.[27]

Three-quarters of the heads of households had graduated from high school or had obtained GEDs. However, many of the younger people hoped to go to college but found they were not eligible for grants or loans available to other Indians. The Ponca culture began to disappear into the Sioux culture.[28]

Fred LeRoy said the loss of identity as a Native American "in some ways meant more than loss of federal services. . . . I was Indian but was not considered to be Indian. . . . That was really important." Two decades later tribal members saw their loss of identity as one of their main losses from termination. "Also, as the government set aside money for programs for minority groups, we could not qualify because we were not Indian," LeRoy said. "That hurt morally and psychologically." He added, "Termination really hurt us. We were told we were not really Indian. That hurts—far more than we thought it did."[29]

Or, as an anonymous tribal member said in the survey, "We are now at a loss as to who we are. How can the government tell me I am no more?"

2. THE WAY BACK

9 Menominees

Pioneers

The board of directors of Menominee Enterprises Inc. (MEI) saw only one way out of the economic and social morass that termination had created for the Menominee people—sell pieces of tribal land to non-Indians for vacation cottages.

That hard-headed business decision roused the tribal people to action that not only restored their own federal status but led eventually to the restoration of most other terminated tribes as well.

Ada Deer, a leader of the restoration movement and later U.S. commissioner of Indian Affairs, said with understandable pride three decades later: "It was the first time in American Indian history that a tribe initiated a policy at the grassroots level and took it all the way to and through the U.S. Congress and got Congress to reverse itself."[1]

Termination had left the tribe demoralized and increasingly divided. Before termination the tribal sawmill was marginally profitable as a tax-free, job-supplying enterprise. After termination a relatively educated elite struggled to turn it into a business generating both profit and enough taxes to finance Wisconsin's new Menominee County. It was an impossible job. The mill was virtually the only source of tax revenue for the fledgling county. Many tribal members were struggling to buy the land under their long-time homes and were unable to pay the newly imposed property taxes. There was little other business to tax in the new county.[2]

So the board of directors of MEI, which had become owner of the tribal land at termination, voted to do the only thing it could find to keep the county afloat: sell some of the land to nontribal members and collect property taxes. The board was made up of five non-Menominee and four tribal members. Not until 1972 was there a majority of Indians on the MEI board. The voting trust for holders of shares in tribal business included four tribal members and three nonmembers. The CEO of MEI, George Kenote, a tribal member, said later he did not remember a dissenting vote on the decision to sell land.[3] But tribal attorneys could not find a record of the vote in minutes of the meetings.[4] Another tribal member, Shirley Daly, a member of the restoration committee, said she and other tribal members believed that Menominee Enterprises was leasing the land, not selling it. She told a Senate committee later that if tribal members had known the land was being sold, there would have been controversy.[5] Certainly when the sales became known they caught the attention of members living away from Menominee County and brought a number of them into the battle to restore the tribe's federal status.

It should have been no surprise that it was the sale of tribal land that touched off the determined move to reverse termination. Tribal members' devotion to their land is deep; Menominees take pride in the fact the tribe is one of the few east of the Mississippi River that has remained on aboriginal land. Their forest is more than a commercial enterprise; it is their home. "As a Menominee I cannot find it in my heart to look upon the land as simply a figure on a balance sheet," Daly told a congressional hearing in 1973. "Our tribal ownership of land is a very personal thing." S. Verna Fowler, president of the College of the Menominee Nation, said, "We have very strong ties to the land. . . . Here I have a sense of belonging I don't have anywhere else." Another tribal member told of a young tribal woman sitting on rocks in the Wolf River watching the sturgeon. A state Department of Natural Resources agent told her she couldn't be there and asked what she was doing. "Watching my relatives," she replied, adding that they were a part of her religion.[6]

On the former reservation, the first protest came after the new—nontribal—land owner ordered several Menominees off a traditional tribal picnic spot in the spring of 1970.

Fowler had just taken her vows as a Catholic nun and had gone home for Memorial Day expecting to go with her family to the usual parade and picnic. Instead, her mother told her they were going to a protest of the Legend Lake land sales. The newly minted nun demurred that she had no clothes other than her order's habit, which she was afraid would draw the attention of reporters. Her mother said she would find her other clothes. So Fowler replaced her flowing black nun's habit with shorts and top and marched off with her family. "At that time I got involved," Fowler said. There she met Deer, a force to be reckoned with.[7]

During hearings three years later on a bill to reverse the Menominee termination, Congressman Lloyd Meeds, a Washington Democrat who was chairman of the House Subcommittee on Indian Affairs, told Deer, "You have been helpful, a constant aid—sometimes too constant."[8] Deer was among the founders of Menominee DRUMS, or Determination for Rights and Unity of Menominee Shareholders. The Menominee effort to restore the tribe's federal status began almost as soon as termination was final in 1961. However, not until the founding of DRUMS in 1970 did the movement begin to have an impact.[9]

The Menominee Council of Chiefs organized in 1962, the year after termination went into effect. It was created as a nonprofit corporation to keep alive the name Menominee Indian Tribe of Wisconsin. Two years later, 789 members of the former tribe signed a petition to President Johnson asking that termination be repealed.[10] A second petition drew 500 signers. "That was all they could think of to do," Deer said.[11] Johnson ignored the petitions. The government could not, however, ignore the Indians' claim that termination did not affect their treaty-guaranteed hunting and fishing rights. In 1968 the U.S. Supreme Court ruled, 6–2, that those rights remained intact. That decision bolstered the Menominee tribal identity and served as a precedent for other terminated tribes.[12]

Meanwhile, a small group of mostly elderly tribal members on the former reservation was keeping traditions and hopes alive. "They would get together for cake and coffee and plan," Fowler said. She said her sister, Shirley, now deceased, had recalled getting up at 3 a.m. for trips to Madison to talk to the Wisconsin Legislature. "They didn't have much money; so they packed a picnic lunch." They went to Madison because they didn't have enough money to go to Washington.[13] It was Deer's non-Indian Quaker mother who got the future Indian commissioner involved in tribal politics. Constance Deer opposed termination, bombarding the Green Bay newspaper with letters to the editor and Ada with admonishments to get involved. She also hitchhiked to Washington DC in the 1950s and spent six weeks there lobbying against termination. Ada Deer was away in college when termination came, and she said she did not fully understand what it meant. She knew only that it was not good and that she needed to get an education and then return and fight.[14]

In July of 1968 Menominee Enterprises made an agreement with a development firm, N. E. Isaacson & Associates, to develop the "Lakes of the Menominee" project, providing for recreation homes along the shore of lakes to be created by construction of three dams. As the first dam rose in 1969, tribal members saw destruction of their aboriginal land and began to organize.[15]

After completing an undergraduate degree in social work at the University of Wisconsin, Ada Deer had spent four years in New York City earning graduate degrees and working. Then she returned to the Midwest, as a social worker in Minneapolis. A friend asked her

Men's traditional dancers take part in the Klamath Tribes' powwow celebrating restoration. Revival of tribal culture was an important part of restoration for all tribes. Photo by Taylor R. David, Klamath Tribes.

In this twenty-four-by-twenty-four-foot shed a handful of people began working toward restoration of the Grand Ronde tribes. Photo courtesy of the Confederated Tribes of Grand Ronde Cultural Resources Department.

Less than two decades later the tribe had built this governance center for the Confederated Tribes of the Grand Ronde Community of Oregon. Photo courtesy of Confederated Tribes of Grand Ronde Cultural Resources Department.

This Ponca Agency building stood empty for thirty years after termination. Restoring it for use as a cultural center was a priority of the restored Ponca Tribe of Nebraska. Photo courtesy Ponca Tribe of Nebraska.

to take a job at the University of Wisconsin–Stevens Point, which was closer to home. "So I started going to meetings and getting involved," Deer said. "I didn't understand. What is this termination? I finally began to understand and said, 'this is wrong—we have treaties.' I saw and felt the suffering of the people. I wanted to do something about it. I couldn't just stand by. We needed a lawyer." She contacted Joseph F. Preloznik, director of Wisconsin Judicare, a federally funded legal service for the poor. Preloznik called the Native American Rights Fund, which dispatched two attorneys. Deer said people were open to the idea of reversing termination but "thought nothing could be done because the government had passed a law."[16]

In the spring of 1970 DRUMS came into being with centers of activity in Milwaukee and Chicago as well as Menominee County, where it coalesced with the resident group that had continued to oppose termination. Jim White, who had left the reservation for Chicago in 1956, was instrumental in forming DRUMS and became its president. Restoration would not have happened without him, according to one tribal member involved in DRUMS.[17] Combining publicity and legal action, the group's stated aims were to stop the sale of land and to restore the reservation to federal status. The group staged a summertime demonstration at the Legend Lakes Lodge protesting the land sales. Then, in October of 1971, dozens of DRUMS members marched 220 miles from Keshena in Menominee County to the state capitol in Madison to call public attention to the tribe's problems and to seek help from Governor Patrick Lucey in restoring the tribe's federal status.

Among DRUMS' early victories was the election of Ada Deer as chairman of the Menominee Voting Trust and of Sylvia Wilbur as chairman of the MEI board of directors. Four DRUMS candidates won election to the seven-member MEI board and two to the trust. The DRUMS activists failed in a challenge to the existence of the trust and then conducted a series of long meetings asking people what they wanted from restoration. "Most were skeptical that we could do it," Deer recalled. "They underestimated the determination of the tribe—and me." At the same time representatives of Menominee Enterprises, Menominee County, and DRUMS began discussions about restoring the reservation to federal status. While White led activities in Wisconsin, Deer went to Washington in 1971. With the National Congress of American Indians providing her a desk and a telephone and VISTA, one of the Johnson administration–era anti-poverty agencies, publishing a newsletter, Deer went to work on Congress and the administration. A delegation of Menominees met with the Wisconsin congressional delegation in January of 1972. Soon afterward attorney Charles Wilkinson of the Native American Rights Fund began drafting a restoration bill for the tribe, and in April the measure was introduced in the Senate. The measure did not pass that year, but back in Wisconsin the Lake of Menominees agreement was dissolved, and a judge ordered an end to the land sales.[18]

The restoration legislation was introduced again in 1973, and in May, June, and September congressional subcommittees on Indian Affairs held hearings in Keshena and Washington. One of the sponsors of the measure was Senator Gaylord Nelson of Wisconsin, who recalled at the September hearing that as governor in 1960 he had opposed termination as "unworkable and a tragic injustice to the Menominee people." He added, "The experiment of termination was a failure."[19] Meeds, the House subcommittee chairman who was elected to Congress after nearly all the terminations had taken place, agreed, stating, "Termination . . . has, beyond question, proven a failure . . . proven a disaster to the Indian tribes and people." Meeds noted that before termination the government had appropriated less than $200,000 a year for the Menominees while afterward the county created on the former reservation required a "massive infusion of public funds." He said, "This must stand as an effective indictment of termination as a national approach to Indian affairs."[20]

Both the House and Senate hearings were almost unbroken recitations of the problems created for the Menominees and the state of Wisconsin by termination. Even the Department of the Interior recommended restoration. Tribal member Wilbur Weber testified: "Holding our assets and people together was the dominant theme for the Menominee for a hundred years. . . . We are not a competitive people. We wish to look after the welfare of our tribe. . . . Termination necessitated competitiveness and it is destroying our tribal values."[21] Said Theodore Boyd, vice president of MEI, "The Menominee have overwhelmingly rejected assimilation."[22]

In addition to the economic and social hardships for the Menominees, testimony and later written statements described the acrimony within the tribe and between the tribe and its non-Indian neighbors that grew out of termination. House subcommittee members appeared sympathetic to the Menominee desire to restore its previous status, except for Representative Manuel Lujan Jr. of New Mexico, the ranking Republican on the subcommittee and later interior secretary under President George H. W. Bush. Lujan raised concerns that the Indians would try to drive out the non-Indians who had purchased land along the lakes.[23] By that time, according to Representative Harold Froehlich (R-MI), non-Menominee people owned 43 percent of the taxable land in Menominee County. The partnership had sold 8,760 acres, and the tribe had bought back 200 to 300 acres. Froehlich's position was an unusual one. He represented Menominee County in Congress and introduced one version of the bill to restore the Menominee tribal status. He also owned one of the lakeside lots the tribe had sold. Seventy of the lot owners lived there full-time, and 33 non-Menominee children from the former tribal land were in the public schools there. The congressman, who had a vacation cabin on his lot, said he was concerned about non-

Menominee on the former reservation. But he made a strong case that the tribe should regain its federal status.[24]

The major opponent of restoration at the hearings was William R. Giese, legal counsel for the Mashawquit Property Owners Association made up of non-Indian land owners. Giese's association claimed 84 landowners with "99 percent" of them living there full-time. Most were retired, but five non-Menominee families had school-age children. Giese feared that restoring the rest of the former reservation to trust status would result in increased taxes for the lakeside property owners. He also charged that the Indians already were making efforts to drive out non-Indians. He claimed law enforcement response was slow, road maintenance was poor, and the county was threatening to close the waste disposal site that served the lake area. He accused DRUMS of trying to drive property values down to get rid of non-Indians. "I think you have a potential for disaster up here between the white people and the Menominee to be truthful about it," Giese told the Senate hearing. "They outnumber the Menominee there." In a parting shot at the Menominees, Giese said termination was structured the way it was "because Indians can't handle money."

Senator James Abourezk (D-SD), presiding over the Senate hearing, asked Giese, "I wonder if you and your people would feel more comfortable if the Menominee people would agree to provide the same type of treatment to your clients as the majority provide to Indian people in other counties where the Indians are a minority? Would that make you feel more comfortable?" Giese did not respond directly.[25]

M. J. Reenhardt, a medical doctor who also owned property at the Menominee lakes, said he and other property owners objected to Giese's opposition to restoration. Services are better and taxes lower in Menominee County than elsewhere, he said.[26]

Andrew J. Pyatskowit, assistant director of the Menominee County

Educational Community, outlined the dispute in the school district encompassing the former reservation. Many Menominee parents viewed school practices as prejudicial to their children. Pyatskowit, a Menominee, said these practices led to an extraordinarily high dropout rate by Menominee children, and these youngsters, unable to find jobs, were turning to drugs and alcohol or other delinquency. By 1972 he said the situation had become so inflamed that Menominee parents formed Menominee County Community School. After the Wisconsin Department of Public Instruction rebuffed a request to form a separate school district, the tribal community financed its school with grants from foundations. At the same time the Native American Rights Fund filed suit against the school district, the U.S. Department of Health, Education and Welfare launched an investigation of the district, and the department later issued an order to eradicate five areas of prejudicial conduct. Those actions by outside agencies led to a series of meetings between local community factions. Pyatskowit described those sessions as "remarkable for the bitterness they uncovered." He added, "Probably the wounds will not be healed for generations."[27] Yet Arnold Gruber, superintendent of the joint school district, said school administrators "did try to develop programs that were culturally sensitive" and were trying to develop a "Menominee curriculum."[28]

Although all the tribal witnesses, including MEI's top executive, George W. Kenote, supported restoration, Kenote later wrote several letters to members of the House subcommittee, stating that tribal members were not totally agreed on the issue. He noted that few tribal members other than DRUMS members testified at the hearings. He claimed that those who did not agree with DRUMS had been harassed, that Judicare and VISTA workers had helped create divisiveness within the tribe, and that a local American Indian Movement (AIM) group "indicated an even more disruptive attitude."[29] Kenote, a Menominee, had been an employee of the Bureau of

Indian Affairs when the tribe asked that he be assigned to write their plan of operation as termination drew near without tribal agreement in the 1950s. The resulting plan was devised by First Wisconsin Trust at Kenote's request, and he remained to administer MEI. His letters indicated he favored restoration of trust status only for the tribal forest and opposed the enrollment as tribal members of those born after 1954. The Council of Chiefs submitted a letter calling DRUMS a pressure group and asking for a referendum on termination and a two-year delay. The council also submitted a resolution saying termination had been "disastrous economically and socially demoralizing" and asking that termination be repealed. The letter was signed only by Richard Dodge, then the chairman of the council. The resolution was signed by Aloysius Frechette, principal chief, and eleven others.[30]

Menominee restoration also had won the support of a variety of outside organizations, Indian and non-Indian. The 1972 Democratic and Republican Party platforms both alluded to the issue. The GOP promised "a complete and sympathetic examination" of the Menominee effort toward restoration. The Democrats merely stated firm opposition to termination. The National Congress of American Indians and a number of tribes, along with groups such as the League of Women Voters, supported restoration for the Menominees. Wisconsin state officials and the Wisconsin Indian Study Committee, established by the state in 1955 to deal with termination issues, endorsed restoration. AIM, however, opposed the restoration bill on grounds it was a compromise.[31]

If numerous witnesses provided substantial reasons for restoring the tribe to federal recognition, Jerome Grignon, chairman of the Council of Chiefs, and James Dickey, who had served as the last chairman of the advisory council before termination, added a sense of urgency. Under the termination law the voting stock in Menominee Enterprises, which owned and managed the assets of the for-

mer reservation, were to become negotiable in January 1974. That
meant that all trust restrictions on the stock owned by individual
tribal members—their share of the former reservation—could be
sold to anyone. When that happens, "control of MEI and the reservation will pass out of tribal hands, including the land," Grignon
said. "Congress must act immediately to save the Menominee from
certain disaster."[32] There was only a brief mention of the Klamath
Tribes' disastrous loss of their reservation as a result of termination,
but that tribe's story was well known in Indian country and must
have increased the Menominee people's sense of urgency.

Congress did act in time. There had been some sentiment that although termination may have been an unfortunate mistake, it would
be best if it were simply forgotten, not corrected. But Abourezk put
that notion firmly aside, setting the stage in his opening statement
at the Senate hearing. "We cannot return to 1953," he said, "but we
can attempt to rectify the injustice which, in all honesty, we must
lay at the feet of Congress and the Bureau of Indian Affairs. Termination threatens the important character of the tribe itself."[33] The
House passed the measure 404 to 3. The Senate made a few changes and passed the bill; the House concurred in the changes. President Nixon signed the measure into law December 22, 1973. The
signing took place without White House publicity and without a
single Menominee present. Nixon did make a forceful statement
to accompany his signing, calling the policy of forced termination
wrong and urging that Congress rescind the 1953 resolution that
made termination congressional policy. Senator Watkins, long out
of Congress, had died less than four months earlier.[34]

Vine Deloria Jr., former executive director of the National Congress of American Indians, called the Menominee restoration measure the single most important Indian issue at the time. "The fear
of termination is almost psychopathic among Indians," he said.
"They don't want to build something and have it taken away . . .

in the last 20 years it has been a stumbling block for progress."
Deloria had also advised the committee to pass the Menominee Restoration Act rather than general restoration legislation. That concrete action will show activists that they can work through the system, Deloria said.[35]

Representative David Obey (D-WI), who introduced the Menominee Restoration Act, said the measure "signals repudiation of the termination policy."[36] Others significantly referred to it as a precedent, which indeed it was.

However, the restoration law was only the beginning of the Menominee Nation's road back to pride and prosperity. Not until April 23, 1975, did Interior Secretary Rogers C. B. Morton preside over a ceremony formally restoring the tribe's federal status.[37] In the meantime, tribal members elected Ada Deer chairman of the committee to lead the tribe through the restoration process. She said after restoration people asked, "What will the BIA do now?" Her response: "We are going to do this." The restoration law for the first time required the government to contract with the tribe for services, giving the tribe control and responsibility for administering its own programs.

Restoration brought people back to the reservation, although there then were no jobs and no housing. "People came anyway," Deer said. "That made additional problems. People are struggling. They thought nirvana was going to occur. Things are better. The land is safe."[38]

The first formal action from the newly recognized tribe came from the Menominee County Education Committee, which in January asked that Menominee County schools be detached from the Shawano School District. The request was granted more than two years later.

The restoration committee presided over reopening the tribal rolls, allowing children born to tribal members after 1954 to be admitted to tribal membership. In three months of 1975, there were 2,342 people added. There was a constitution to write, an election of a permanent Tribal Council and chairman to arrange, and the complicated procedure to restore tribal business to tribal ownership. The tribe wrote a law and order code, established a police force and court system, and in March 1976 took over law enforcement on the reservation from the state. The tribe also regained unquestioned control of hunting and fishing on the reservation. The Menominee Indian School opened in September 1976 with 734 students. The tribe won a $1.4 million federal grant to construct a medical clinic, which opened in 1977. Later expanded, the clinic provided everything from primary care to radiology. It also conducted a dozen health education and community health programs including nutrition, diabetes prevention, and immunization.

When the first legislative election under the new constitution was held in 1979, Gordon Dickie Sr., a longtime tribal leader, opponent of termination, and supporter of restoration, was elected chairman.[39]

The tribe later built a new grade school, a junior/senior high school, and a tribal/county library and created the College of the Menominee Nation, which granted two-year associate degrees and certificates. In 2001 fifteen of twenty-one graduates were attending the University of Wisconsin–Green Bay. College president Fowler said in a 2001 interview that only one student sent from Menominee College to a four-year college had dropped out, and that was because of child care problems. One-fourth of the students were non-Indian, and Indian students came from a dozen tribes in addition to the Menominees. Fowler described the college as a force for good in many ways. It was economic development with nearly ninety people on the payroll. These faculty and staff members with degrees and professional status served as role models. "Obviously, students can look at them and see they did it and say 'I want to be that,'" Fowler said. She added, "Educated tribal members attend meetings, address people. It puts the tribal leadership on edge, to be more responsive." Her memory was full of stories such as the young mother who awoke from a drunken stupor in a ditch wondering where her child was. She walked to the drug and alcohol center across the road, asked for help, and learned about the college; a few years later she was ready to graduate, drug and alcohol free and living in low-cost housing with her son. "I have never given birth to a child," Fowler said, "but I have given birth to a college that gave life to a whole lot of people who would never have had that opportunity."[40]

The tribe built housing for its elderly, and its prize-winning wood-fired plant heated the Neopit School. The sawmill and forest operations, operated by the tribally owned Menominee Tribal Enterprises (MTE), returned to a profitable basis, employing about three hundred people. The pre-termination annual "stumpage" payments resumed with each tribal member getting $200 a year. Also, beginning in 1991, MTE bought back at less than face value the bonds that had been issued to tribal members at termination, averting a financial crisis. Without the buyback the entire multimillion-dollar bond issue would have fallen due in 2000.

Tribal government also resumed its role in providing reservation utilities and services. Menominee Public Transit established regular bus service between reservation communities. Water and sewer lines and some electrical service returned to tribal hands.[41]

The tribe did not attempt to establish other tribally owned businesses, said Llewellyn Boyd, project manager for the Menominee Office of Economic Development. Instead, it encouraged the development of private business. For instance, managers of tribal construction work sought proposals from private contractors on the reservation. The Menominee Business Center offered nine office suites for rent. Occupants in 2006 included a vending machine company, insurance agency, technical services provider, and small business development agency.[42]

Like other tribes, the Menominees turned to gaming for revenue to support tribal programs and to provide jobs. A tribal bingo operation opened in 1981 and a tribal casino in 1987. The casino had a 2006 payroll of more than 450.

The tribe also created a historic preservation department and a language and culture commission. It worked with the state to save the Wolf River sturgeon that are integral to the Indian religion but that were severely reduced in numbers by dams and other development. An annual festival and feast honor the sturgeon.

Not everything went smoothly as the tribe worked its way through the restoration process. In January 1975 the Menominee Warrior Society occupied the abandoned Alexian Brothers Novitiate a few miles outside the reservation, demanding that the order turn the building over to the tribe. The thirty-four-day standoff ended without injuries. In 1983 some 85 acres of woodland burned, threatening a cluster of trailer homes. In December of that year, several miles of ice on the Wolf River resulted in high water in Keshena, flooding some basements. In 1984 two tornadoes blew down 9 million board feet of timber in the Menominee forest and demolished several homes on Legend Lake. Discovery in 1978 of a zinc and copper deposit near the Wolf River upstream from the reservation raised concerns over potential pollution of the river, but two other tribes eventually bought the land to prevent mining there.[43]

And problems continued with the Legend Lake nontribal property owners. Tribal members made up the majority of the Menominee County governing board, and taxes on the nontribal land remained an issue. At one point the property owners attempted unsuccessfully to annex their property to neighboring Oconto County or break off as a separate county. The tribe opposed both proposals. "We'd never give up the most beautiful property on our reservation," Boyd said. On the rare occasion a piece of the land came on the market, the tribe had first option to buy it.

One major goal for the tribe, Boyd said, was to capture on the reservation a larger share of the dollars created there. With few retail stores or service providers, most of the income earned on the reservation was spent elsewhere, Boyd said. "We need to start our own retail." He said it was debatable whether the Menominee had reached the level they would have without termination. "Termination set us back fifty to sixty years," Boyd said.[44]

As Ada Deer told the House committee in 1973, "Termination had three major long-term effects, each one a disaster. One, it created a pocket of poverty. Two, it forced the sale of tribal assets. Three, it denied democracy. We were expected to give up our culture and adapt to a way of life none of us wanted."[45] But the Menominees survived and began to manage their own destiny.

10 Siletz

Fish

No sooner had the Menominees won restoration than the Confederated Tribes of Siletz Indians on the Oregon Coast began working to regain federal recognition. By then, Congress, the administration, and the general public realized that termination had been both a mistake and an injustice to the terminated tribes. The precedent had been set. So restoration should have been easy for the Siletz.

There was just one real stumbling block: fish. And the Siletz confederation wasn't even a major fishing tribe.

The Menominee restoration and the beginning of the Siletz efforts to regain federal recognition came just as Northwest fishing controversies were reaching their height in the mid-1970s. Along Puget Sound in Washington State, Indian fishermen—and women—asserting their treaty right to fish at usual and accustomed places were being clubbed and dragged off to jail. Fishers also were being arrested on the Columbia River between Oregon and Washington, although usually with less violence. In 1969 one federal judge ruled that the Indians were entitled to a share of the fish passing their traditional off-reservation fishing places. In 1975—the year the Menominee restoration was proclaimed—another federal judge ruled that the Indian share was half the fish in those spots. The ensuing uproar roiled politics in the Northwest as few issues have. State officials, white commercial fishers, and sports fishers all denounced the rulings—and Indians.[1]

Before termination the Siletz people had engaged in minimal fishing in some coastal streams far from the Columbia River and Puget Sound battles. Now they found themselves facing opposition over an issue that was far down their list of priorities. The Oregon state fisheries and wildlife director went so far as to recommend that instead of granting full federal status and a reservation, the government should provide the Siletz the same services as recognized tribes and build a museum "to honor the history of the Siletz people."[2]

In congressional hearings, tribal representatives pointed out that few tribal people fished, and when they did it was only for an occasional meal, not for the major share of their diet or for sale like the tribes involved in the long, bitter disputes further north. Non-Indian fishers were not to be placated. One fisher, who repeatedly denounced the Indians as greedy, said the tribal people would take the last fish. The fact that non-Indians had taken the Indians' last land was not mentioned.[3]

The Siletz had begun reviving tribal ties and activities well before Congress passed the Menominee restoration bill. A group of tribal members began in the late 1960s to reestablish some tribal activities. They also began programs to reverse the poverty, alcoholism, and despair that had plagued tribal people after termination. In 1973, as the Menominee restoration bill worked its way through Congress, the Siletz formed an Oregon corporation—the Confederated Tribes of Siletz Indians, Inc., with a constitution, officers, and a goal: full restoration of federal recognition. What the tribal people saw as priorities were education, health care, and revival of tribal culture. The confederation, made up of twenty-seven bands collected from throughout western Oregon to a single reservation in the 1800s, had dispersed after termination as members sought jobs and education elsewhere. However, many remained in the coastal area and eagerly sought to regain their place among tribes.[4]

The Siletz had a model in the Menominee restoration, "but that was a very different situation," said Michael Mason, an attorney who worked on tribal restorations both with the Native American Project of Oregon Legal Services and later as a private consultant.[5] The Menominee land base remained intact, and courts had ruled before restoration that the tribe's hunting and fishing rights were not negated by termination. Restoration of tribal status would not rock the surrounding society's boat. However, the Siletz tribe's little remaining land had been sold at termination, and the hunting and fishing issue was one of the most contentious in the Northwest. If the Siletz acquired land to be placed in trust for a new reservation, it could disrupt ownership, taxes, and, in the minds of non-Indian fishers, the fate of the region's fish.

Tribal leaders approached the issue carefully, moving to secure support on local, state, and federal levels, building a case that restoration was both a matter of justice and a solution to some serious social problems. The Siletz were fortunate in being able to call on two of Oregon's congressional delegation with sympathy for their cause. Senator Mark O. Hatfield, a Republican then in his second term, was vice chairman of the Senate Select Committee on Indian Affairs. Representative Les AuCoin, a Democrat, represented the Siletz home area in the House. The tribe also had the help of attorney Charles Wilkinson, who had served as legal adviser to the Menominees.

For Hatfield and AuCoin, supporting any bill that would confirm Indian hunting and fishing rights would have been political suicide—and the Siletz leaders were politically savvy enough to understand their dilemma. In order to allay fears, a series of public meetings was held along the Oregon Coast. At one of those meetings, according to Doyce Waldrip, who was then assistant area administrator for the BIA, an opponent of Indian hunting and fishing rights stated that if the Indians demanded those rights, they should be confined to their aboriginal hunting methods. Tribal chairman Arthur Bensell started to laugh. He told Waldrip the Siletz hunters traditionally used dogs to run deer to death. Waldrip passed the information to the tribal antagonist; he withdrew his proposal.[6]

When Hatfield and AuCoin introduced the Siletz restoration bill in 1976, it restricted the tribe's hunting and fishing rights to federal land, and it included establishing a reservation. By the time of the Senate hearing at the end of March of that year, the All-Coast Fishermen's Marketing Association, the commercial fishers organization, had withdrawn its opposition. Tribal chairman Bensell said that group's members were "the only people to sit down and discuss with us."[7] The National Congress of American Indians weighed in with strong support for the Siletz restoration and strong opposition to the state's proposed amendment to subject Indian fishing to state regulation. "Termination is not dead," said Susan Shawn Harjo, communications director for NCAI. "Indian leaders look for hidden termination in each piece of legislation." If the Siletz bill were amended as the state wanted, she said, it "becomes an exchange of social programs for rights for every tribe."[8] But sports fishing organizations and the state of Oregon remained adamant that all state fishing and hunting rules apply to the Indians.[9] Congress found that unacceptable. The bill did not pass.

The fishing issue had effectively drowned out all the other testimony explaining why restoration was so important to the people of the Confederated Tribes of Siletz Indians. The witnesses from the tribal government had mostly paid their own way to Washington to plead their case although at the last minute the Presbyterian Church provided some money to help the delegation. Kathryn Harrison, the Tribal Council secretary who later would play a key role in restoration of the Grand Ronde Tribe, provided some of the most compelling reasons for restoration. Describing the importance of Chemawa Indian School in her own life, Harrison noted that after termination Siletz Indians no longer were eligible for the school. "Many of our young people are dropping out, or being kicked out of school without any other option to fall back on," she said. "They do not have the opportunity to attend Chemawa as I had. Many are turning to alcohol and drugs, getting into trouble, even dying at youthful ages as a result." As a licensed practical nurse, Harrison said, "I also am very much aware that our people do not have the means to take care of their medical needs." And as a counselor-trainee she had been witnessing "the anguish and torment among young and old alike due to the disease of alcoholism." Just the prospect of restoration, she said, had "brought a new spring to our step, a feeling of expectation in the air, a hoping that maybe this time we, the Indians, will acquire something, something desperately needed and it would be our very own. . . . restoration is the only way to a decent life for the Siletz Indian."[10]

The following year, 1977, Hatfield and AuCoin, working with the tribe, modified their bill and reintroduced it. This time the measure stated that it neither granted nor restored any fishing and hunting rights. It also directed the secretary of the interior to consult with local interests to determine whether a reservation should be created and, if so, how. In opening the Senate hearing in July of that year, Hatfield said, "It [the measure] would serve as a much needed installment toward paying a moral debt to which this nation has committed its national honor. It is the right thing to do."[11]

Bensell, the tribal chairman, told the committee: "We are not asking for a handout. The things we are asking for will give us the tools which we can work with that will help us, in particular our younger people, to become better citizens of our county, our state and the United States. Education is the most important thing." He said tribal leaders "did not know until two months ago" that the new bill would not include a reservation. "It was hard to go back to the tribe and decide to give it up," he said. He added, "We learned very early we could not have anything controversial."[12] The reservation issue was mildly controversial even within the tribe. Joe Lane, the immediate past president of the confederation, told Congress a reservation would only make the tribe dependent on the government and would not benefit members who had moved away from the tribal area.[13] However, another tribal member, Pauline Bell Ricks, said later, "We need land. We need timber and a steady source of income that will enable the tribe to run our programs."[14]

Hatfield praised the tribe for its flexibility on the land issue. "I know of no group that has been more accommodating or has yielded more on matters that are important to you in order to try to seek a common agreement and to compromise with opposing parties," he said.[15]

The state of Oregon, represented by John Donaldson, the director of the Department of Fish and Wildlife, made another impassioned pitch to specifically deny the tribe fishing and hunting rights. Now a new federal court decision was raising alarms for the state. The terminated Klamath Tribes, like the Menominees before, had won a ruling that termination of the tribe did not end treaty hunting and fishing rights for individual tribal members. Donaldson called the ruling and its potential effects on all tribes "alarming to us."[16] The National Wildlife Federation urged Congress to confirm state control over off-reservation hunting and fishing and to use "other means" to compensate tribes for legitimate claims of lost rights.[17]

In the previous hearing, William A. Luch, president of Trout Unlimited, a sports fishing advocacy group, had raised the specter of tribal members buying river front land, placing it in trust, and then using that land as a base for major fishing operations. Bensell told Hatfield in a later letter that seven tribal members owned a total of 20,708 feet of shoreline on various rivers, including 3,900 feet on Rock Creek, a tributary of the Siletz River, the major fish stream in the Siletz coastal area. Before termination, he said, the Siletz had fishing rights with special permits from the BIA. Fishers caught two to ten fish per set of each net, and "every fish was used." Any surplus to each fisher's immediate needs was smoked, salted, or dried for later use. Fish were shared with elders and others unable to fish. "The tribe does not anticipate a change in habits," he wrote.[18]

Both the House and Senate passed the restoration bill in November, and President Jimmy Carter signed it November 18. The *Newport News-Times*, a weekly newspaper that served the Siletz area had labeled the restoration bill "controversial." But it covered the tribe's celebratory powwow as the social event of the year, complete with pictures and a generous number of quotes from tribal leaders and members.[19]

The celebration was followed by nearly three years of hard work and hard bargaining to reestablish tribal government, acquire a land base, and settle the ever-thorny fishing and hunting issue. In 1980 the tribe approved a constitution and elected a permanent government. Delores (Dee) Pigsley, an employee of the Social Security Administration in Salem, Oregon, and a member of the interim council, was named to succeed Bensell as chairman of the Tribal Council. Lincoln County commissioners had named Bensell, who had served as mayor of the mixed white-Indian town of Siletz for a dozen years, to the Lincoln County economic planning commission. (Pigsley continued to serve in the chairwoman's post in 2006.) Also in 1980 the city of Siletz agreed to return the thirty-seven-acre Government Hill property—the heart of the tribal land. During the termination period the tribe, unable to pay taxes on the land, had given it to the city, although tribal members continued to maintain the tribal cemetery that was on the property. (By 2006 the wooded hill on the edge of the city of Siletz also contained the handsome tribal headquarters and powwow grounds.)[20]

The two most divisive issues also were settled in 1980 with compromises such as those that concerned Harjo in 1976. A federal court consent decree provided that the Indians could take 200 salmon a year from three tributaries of the Siletz River and a total of 400 deer and elk, with a maximum of 25 elk. In addition, the tribe would receive 4,000 pounds of hatchery fish a year.[21] The state approved the decree, but several fish and wildlife groups continued to oppose it. The tribe developed a reservation plan and acquired 3,660 acres of scattered forest land from the Bureau of Land Management, agreeing to pay Lincoln County the same 5 percent of timber receipts that the BLM had paid.[22]

In January 1980, before the tribe had begun to develop its programs, the consulting firm CH2M Hill issued a socioeconomic profile that showed the tribe facing major problems. Just under half the 1,083 enrolled tribal members lived in the tribe's eight-county service area, and more than one-third of them were living below the poverty level. Outside the service area, which then did not include the Portland metropolitan area where many lived, 18 percent of tribal members were below the poverty level. Median household income for all tribal families was less than one-half the state average. There were severe health problems with alcoholism in nearly every family. Half of the adults had not finished high school, and 28 percent of tribal members were living in substandard housing.[23]

Housing was one of the first things tackled by the new tribal government. By 1987 the tribe had purchased land at Siletz, obtained a grant from the U.S. Department of Housing and Urban Development, and built 54 homes. Within three years it had built 15 more homes, and the total later climbed to 126 for elders and low-income tribal members.

Health care had been another major reason behind the tribe's drive for restoration. The return to federal status opened the door to tribal members' care by the Indian Health Service, but the Siletz had grander dreams. In 1991 the tribe opened Siletz Community Health Clinic, available to both tribal members and nontribal members in the area. At times it was one of only two health providers in the immediate area willing to accept Medicare patients. The modern clinic included medical, dental, laboratory, optometry, and pharmacy services. The clinic's inclusive service was part of the Siletz overall policy of sharing with the entire community.[24] Michael Darcy, a former Tribal Council member and retired principal of the public grade school in Siletz, said the general amity between Indian and non-Indian residents of the town was a return to attitudes before termination.[25]

The tribe also developed education programs from Head Start to vocational training for adults. A youth center provided a quiet place to do homework after school—and some tutoring if needed. The tribe used its federal Johnson-O'Malley school funds for grade and high school students to provide tutoring, cultural classes, and college prep courses. The tribe offered college scholarships for members who gained admission to a four-year college or to a community college program leading to transfer to a four-year degree program. For adults, there was assistance for vocational training.

Darcy became principal of the Siletz Grade School in 1981, two years after the tribe's formal restoration. He instituted a program called SMILE—Science and Math Investigative Learning Experience. The program, conducted through the Internet, was made possible by grants from the Siletz tribe and two corporations. Darcy said children in the program even for just one year had a high school graduation rate of 99 percent—this when the graduation rate for Indian children elsewhere was 55 percent. Darcy said during the ten to fifteen years after termination only ten students from Siletz, Indian and non-Indian, went to college.[26] A dozen years after restoration the tribe had an average of thirty-five students in college every year. Where the battle during termination was to persuade youngsters to finish high school, the tribe later could push its young people to obtain advanced degrees.

The Siletz tribe was among the second group of tribes to take up "self governance," a change in federal policy that allowed tribes to contract with the BIA and manage their own programs. Beginning in 1992 the Siletz tribe operated almost totally without BIA supervision.[27] It purchased a state fish hatchery, added three counties in the Portland metropolitan area to its service district to help resident tribal members, established—and later closed as no longer needed—an economic development corporation. It also opened the Chinook Winds Casino and Convention Center in Lincoln City, a major tourist spot on the Oregon Coast. It was among the first tribes to join the Oregon Native American Business and Entrepreneurial Network (ONABEN), a program providing training in business skills and helping individuals start small businesses.

The Siletz first attempted to build a casino just outside the state capital of Salem in 1992, but then-governor Barbara Roberts vetoed the site, her prerogative under the federal Indian Gaming Regulatory Act. The Siletz sued in federal court to overturn her decision but eventually lost when the U.S. Supreme Court refused to hear the case. Meanwhile the tribe, with Roberts's agreement, moved the project to Lincoln City, drawing intense opposition from a local group called No Casino, which said it wanted no gambling in its town—except for the already present Oregon State Lottery video poker machines and twenty local establishments offering varied gambling from keno to off-track betting. Opened in 1996, the casino made it possible for the Siletz to donate money in amounts of $250 to $5,000 to a long list of organizations, tribal and nontribal, including the Salem-Keiser School District for an Indian Education program and the local Veterans of Foreign Wars to repair its headquarters. Donations went to Coastal AIDS Network and Habitat for Humanity, to Siletz tribal elders and a local partnership to build a youth skate park, to Chemawa Indian School and to the Lincoln County Schools auto mechanic program. One of the largest gifts was to the Oregon Coast Aquarium, one of the area's major tourist attractions.[28]

Two decades after restoration the economic consulting company, ECONorthwest, reported that the Siletz tribe, by then with approximately three thousand members, provided more than $9.1 million in wages to Lincoln County from tribal activities and $32.2 million in wages from the casino. In the study, commissioned by the tribe and issued in 2000, ECONorthwest said the tribe added $34.4 million to the county's economy in 1998.[29]

Michael Darcy and Bensell Breon, another former Siletz Tribal Council member, saw some good coming out of termination. Both said it forced tribal members to "make it on our own" in non-Indian society, giving them skills that served well in reorganizing and managing the tribe and its programs. Breon said that difficult experience probably helped speed tribal development after restoration. Darcy said learning to survive was the positive side of termination. The negative side was young people's immersion in non-Indian culture and the loss of their own culture. Restoring the culture presented a unique problem to a confederation of twenty-seven tribes, he said. The question became "which culture?"—and which language. Languages were preserved on video tapes of tribal elders. Ceremonial dances, too, were revived. "Warm Springs [an Oregon tribe that was not terminated] took our dances to keep for us" at termination, Darcy said. "Families brought them back after restoration."[30]

Pride and satisfaction showed as Siltz people recounted their accomplishments since restoration. Their focus, however, remained on their future. "We'll continue to advance our social, economic and political initiatives," said Chairwoman Pigsley on the twenty-fifth anniversary of restoration, "in a manner that respects the sovereign rights of other Indian tribes, the state of Oregon and local governments."[31]

11 Oklahoma and Utah

Flood

After the Siletz there was a flood of restorations. Within a dozen years only one terminated tribe was still seeking restoration. Later, the Mixed-Blood Utes began a campaign to reverse their termination, a battle that remained before the federal courts in 2006. Most of the restorations after Siletz engendered little controversy, and the process became largely routine, although the routine for the Utah Paiute tribes took most of a decade.

Among the tribes that navigated easily through the restoration process were the four based in Oklahoma—the Wyandotte, Peoria, Ottawa, and Modoc tribes. Inspired by the Menominees' success, they began their effort for restoration while the Siletz restoration was in progress. Like other terminated tribes, members of the Oklahoma tribes were convinced they had suffered from the lack of job assistance, education benefits, and health care, especially for children and elders, that recognized tribes received. For their return to federal protection they obtained something missing when their termination legislation was passed—congressional hearings. The hearings in July and September 1977 were almost perfunctory; the Senate hearing lasted less than an hour. Forrest Gerard, the assistant secretary of the interior for Indian Affairs, testified that termination had hindered the tribes' development and ability to plan. He said the Oklahoma measure was "important from a policy standpoint" because it represented a "repudiation of termination."[1] John Ghostbear, attorney for the Inter-Tribal Council of Oklahoma tribes, testified the bill was "extremely acceptable to all the tribes."[2] The chiefs of three of the tribes—Rodney Arnett of Peoria, Lewis Barlow of Ottawa, and Bill Follis of Modoc—testified briefly. Maret Colter of Wyandotte submitted a statement.

The ambiguous nature of the termination of three of the Oklahoma tribes was reflected in the bill, which stated: "Federal recognition is hereby extended or confirmed" to the Wyandotte, Ottawa, and Peoria tribes.[3] Because of conditions in their termination laws, it was not clear that the three had ever been legally terminated, although federal services had been withdrawn. The Wyandotte Tribe had never found an entity to care for its cemetery, a condition of finalizing termination. The Interior Department report on the restoration bill conceded that Wyandotte termination had never gone into effect but said the restoration bill removed the continuing threat of termination. The Peoria termination was to become effective only when all the tribe's claims against the government had been settled. "The last one is still before the Indian Claims Commission," the Interior report stated.[4] Only the Ottawa Tribe appeared to have met the legal standards set in its termination measure, but Chief Barlow testified that, in his view, the tribe was "never lawfully terminated." He said there still were adverse impacts on tribal people two decades later.[5]

For the Oklahoma Modocs, restoration meant the first recognition as a separate tribe. The hundred Oklahoma tribal members were descendants of the Modoc Tribe of Oregon and northern California who had never returned to Oregon after being exiled to Indian Territory—Oklahoma—in 1873. The Modocs who did return became part of the confederation on the Klamath Reservation in Oregon. The Oklahoma Restoration Bill recognized the tribal members in Oklahoma as a separate entity, the Modoc Indian Tribe of

Oklahoma. The Interior Department noted in its report that the governor, congressional delegation, state representatives, other tribes, and local government all had expressed support for the legislation. Despite the lack of opposition, Congress did not pass the measure until the following year, and President Jimmy Carter signed it on May 15, 1978.

The new law ordered the government to help the Modocs create their first independent tribal government and to help the Peorias and Ottawas in reconstituting their government entities. The Wyandotte Tribe had maintained its government as it searched for a caretaker for its burial ground. The four tribes then had a total of about 6,000 members.[6]

The Ottawa, Peoria, and Modoc tribes remained located at Miami, a town of 13,500 in the northeastern corner of Oklahoma. The Wyandotte Nation was ten miles to the southeast in the tiny (population 364) community of Wyandotte. While nominally terminated, all four tribes had become part of the eight-tribe Inter-Tribal Council, Inc., headquartered at Miami. The council managed programs in economic development, employment and training, food distribution, and vocational education. It also operated the Eight Tribes Gift Shop. Each tribe maintained its separate identity and government, but some engaged in joint ventures.[7] The Ottawa and Peoria tribes, along with the never-terminated Miami Tribe, offered language classes, free meals for seniors, and daycare help for tribal members. The Modocs had joined with the Miamis in a bingo and off-track betting facility called the Stables. The Ottawa and Peoria tribes jointly owned a community building used for powwows and other activities.

Like other terminated tribes, those in Oklahoma emphasized education, health care, and housing, especially for elders. The Wyandottes built and operated the Bearskin Healthcare and Wellness Center, an intertribal facility. All four tribes had housing programs to help tribal members obtain or improve housing. The Peorias engaged in a transportation planning program that covered roads in the tribe's reservation area, a maintenance plan, and a survey of transportation needs to, among other things, support tribal economic development. The Modoc Tribe had an environmental protection program. The tribes revived powwows and offered language programs. All four had websites, and the Peoria Tribe's library offered Internet research and other Internet services. A Wyandotte company, Wyandotte NetTel, provided client-server and networking products. In 2005 the company was named among the top ten most successful small businesses in the government market. The Wyandottes also owned a restaurant and convenience store and were developing a casino in Wyandotte County, Kansas. The Peorias had a trading post and a golf course with nontribal memberships going for $1,000 a year.[8]

Leaford Bearskin was not in the tribal area when his Wyandotte Nation was terminated; he had left in 1939 to enlist in the U.S. Army Air Corps. He retired from the U.S. Air Force twenty-one years later as a lieutenant colonel. His final job was as squadron commander and assistant headquarters commandant at Strategic Air Command headquarters in Omaha, Nebraska. He retired again after twenty years in executive positions as a civil service employee of the Air Force and returned to his home area at Wyandotte, Oklahoma. Bearskin brought Air Force management principles and organization charts to the recently renewed tribe when he became the Wyandotte chief in 1983. He led his nation through its two ten-year-plans and into a third, and after twenty-three years in office he gave no indication of being anywhere near a third retirement despite diabetes, heart bypass surgery, and a small stroke.

The 4,410-member tribe was one of the earliest to turn to self-governance, a program under which tribes manage their own programs without BIA supervision. "The first thing to figure out," Bearskin said, "was if we are a sovereign nation, we have to act like a sovereign nation." The Wyandottes rewrote the tribal constitution and reorganized under eight department heads, later to become eleven with the addition of a legal department and others. The tribe settled its land claim against the government for $5.7 million, giving it additional funds for development and programs.

Education programs ranged from preschool to college. Cultural programs included a project to mark historical sites and efforts to revive the tribal language and teach it to the children, and large-scale senior citizen programs. Three items were high on Bearskin's still-to-do list: With only five hundred of the tribal members living in northeastern Oklahoma, he wanted to establish a credit card that could be used anywhere to cover health care expenses. He planned to assure that all the tribe's young people could get an education; sixty-five were in college as of 2006. And there were plans to build a retirement center. At that time the tribe owned three hundred acres and had recently bought a farm that Bearskin hoped would provide a site for small industry. "We have designs on more land," he stated.

Termination "absolutely hurt the people," Bearskin said. He added that with restoration, however, the Wyandottes had as many services for its people as any tribe. "I'm the proudest chief in the country," he said. "We are the best tribe."[9]

The road to restoration was longer and more difficult for the tiny Utah Paiute bands, who had little when they were terminated and even less a decade later. Their fortunes began to rise in 1965. Washington DC attorney Ernest Wilkinson, who represented many Indian tribes, negotiated a land claims settlement of $7.25 million for the 26 million acres taken from them without payment. Even at only 27 cents an acre and after paying the $697,000 legal fees, the bands had more money than they had ever had. However, distribution of the money did not begin until 1971.

The next year the five bands organized the Paiute Tribal Corporation to work with several governmental agencies to improve housing, educational opportunities, and living standards. Like other tribes, the Paiute bands were inspired by the Menominee restoration to try to win back their own federal recognition. Tribal leaders began in 1973 by circulating petitions among members asking for restoration. Later, they enlisted help first from Senator Frank Moss, a Utah Democrat, and later Utah Republicans Senator Orrin Hatch and Representative Dan Marriott, who finally introduced the restoration measure in 1979.[10]

Hatch held a hearing on the proposal in Cedar City, Utah, in August 1979. Reporting to the Senate Indian Affairs Committee in Washington in November, he said twenty-seven witnesses appeared, and "everyone recognizes the Paiutes need help. . . . Restoration is the best means to help."[11] There was no testimony either in Utah or Washington opposing restoration, although initially some county commissioners and a few ranchers who leased grazing land from the Shivwits band questioned the move. One of the major issues raised in the hearings was the status of the Cedar Band. The Shivwits, Kanoosh, Koosharem, and Indian Peaks bands all were listed in the termination law in 1954. The Cedar Band was not, but the BIA ignored it throughout the termination period. The BIA was "not aware they applied for any" services, was the only response from Ralph Reeser, director of the BIA Congressional and Legislative Affairs Office, to sharp questioning by Senator Daniel Inouye (D-HI).[12] To make sure the Cedar Band was covered correctly this time, the bill "restored" the federal trust relationship to the Shivwits, Kanoosh, Koosharem, and Indian Peaks bands and "restored or confirmed" it for the Cedar Band.[13]

House and Senate committees held hearings in November and December of that year with a notable difference from the Paiute termination hearing a quarter of century earlier. This time, with their future at stake, representatives from the Paiute bands testified. The committee's report on the bill indicated that Congress was finally beginning to understand what was at the core of Indians' objection to termination. After enumerating the usual reasons for restoration—termination was unjust, the tribal members need and are entitled to the services provided to other Indians—the report stated, "Above all, the legislation would restore to the bands their dignity and identity as members of an Indian tribe."[14] The bands had lined up an array of supporters who submitted letters to the committees. The Utah Board of Indian Affairs, Utah Legal Services, Judge Reid Blondquist of the Sevier County Justice Court, and the director of Indian Services for the American Indian Services and Research Center at Brigham Young University all urged restoration.[15] Beverly Snow, chairwoman of the Shivwits band, told the committee that if the tribe's federal status was restored, "we may be able to get on our feet, help ourselves to be self-sustaining." She said the tribe had "great potential if the children had an education and know-how."[16]

The only opposition to immediate action came from the BIA, which wanted to do a study before deciding if the bands met eligibility requirements for recognition. But Marriott said, "We don't need to wait."[17] Just over three months later on April 3, 1980—rapid by congressional standards—President Jimmy Carter signed the Paiute Restoration Act. Fulfilling the promise of restoration was not immediate. The measure provided for creation of a reservation of up to 15,000 acres to be designated from "available public, state or private lands" with the acquiescence of state and affected local officials. Getting land took four more years. Then the bands settled for only 4,720 acres in the face of public opposition to letting them have land that was potentially valuable for coal mining or development. A Reagan administration ban prevented giving them Forest Service land. The bands' new land was mostly in small tracts widely scattered over four counties and usable primarily as sites for small businesses. Even before winning restoration, the bands had begun using a federal Housing and Urban Development Department program in 1976 to build homes for tribal members. By 1989 they had constructed 113 units.

The reservation compromise act in 1984 also established a permanent $2.5 million fund for the tribe, with half the annual interest for economic development and half for tribal government. The bands used the money to operate two sewing factories and to improve both their health care and education.[18] By 2002, the bands had awarded $250,000 in scholarships and put millions of dollars into health care. Among problems the bands continued to face was rampant diabetes among tribal members. Lora Tom, the tribal chairwoman, also was a community health representative who worked to teach tribal members the healthy lifestyles and diets that can prevent and help control diabetes and related obesity and cardiovascular disease. The fund financed a tribal headquarters in Cedar City; the five bands were scattered within a 120-mile radius. Other money from the fund went into cultural projects, such as making the traditional cradle boards on which Paiute women carried their babies. The Paiute bands established water rights for 1.38 cubic feet per second from the Santa Clara River and owned 81 acres suitable for irrigation. The Kanosh band obtained a lease for geothermal power development.[19]

The Cedar Band moved into high tech, eventually winning an entrepreneur of the year award from Ernst and Young. Travis N. Parashonts, a Cedar Band member, started an information technology company for the band in 2002. Called Suh'dutsing (the Paiute name for the cedar tree) Technologies, the company engaged in contracting such work as data entry on its reservation and providing high-tech engineering and programming at customer sites. In 2006 it landed a five-year $8-million contract to develop and maintain a fiber-optic telecom system for the Dugway Proving Ground in Utah.

Headquartered in Cedar City, population 20,500, Suh'dutsing had satellite offices just outside Washington DC, and in Salt Lake City, Joplin, Missouri, and Newark, California. In addition to the Dugway contract, the company had contracts in Minnesota with the National Park Service and in Hawaii, Houston, and Tampa.

Parashonts, the Suh'dutsing president and CEO, said that many tribes went into gaming or had natural resources to develop tribal economies. "We don't have those," he said. "This company is going to have to be our casino."[20]

The Paiute bands also were working to retain their culture, which was nearly lost during the termination years. The bands were small and young. The Shivwits band, with 279 members in 2006, was the largest. Cedar Band had 241 members, Kanosh 115, Koosharem 108, and Indian Peaks 38. About one-half were sixteen or younger. Few elders remained to teach children the language and the arts, such as tanning animal hides, said Dorene Martineaux, the cultural resources director. Two dance houses were built after restoration, one at St. George by the Shivwits and the other by the Koosharem. The entire tribe held an annual powwow.

"We're struggling," Martineaux said. "Restoration has been helpful. We've made it this far. We're doing OK."[21]

In contrast, the only other Utah group subjected to termination, the so-called Mixed-Blood Utes, was still trying to regain recognition as Indians as of 2006. As with other terminated groups the Mixed-Blood Utes, using their identity as members of the Uinta band, began seeking to restore their Indian status by winning recognition of their continuing right to hunt and fish on the Uinta and Ouray Reservation in the 1980s. In the 1990s several groups of the Uinta began challenging the 1954 law that divided the Ute Tribe's assets between members who were more than half Indian and those who were less than half Indian. That law left the so-called full-bloods as a recognized tribe and severed the mixed-blood tribal members from the Ute Tribe and from federal ties. More than 250 Uinta band members filed a lawsuit in 2002 claiming that the Ute Partition Act unlawfully removed their status as part of a recognized Indian tribe. By that time an unknown number of the mixed-bloods had vanished from the tribal homeland, presumably fulfilling the goal of termination—absorption into the larger society.[22] It took the federal court until 2006 to decide that the Indians filed their suit too late—the statute of limitations had long since expired. However, a three-judge panel of the U.S. Circuit Court of Appeals for the District of Columbia sent the case back to District Court to determine whether a new law extending filing times for Indian claims could be applied to the Uinta case.[23]

The Uintas contended that more than half the members of their band were children when the Ute Partition Act was passed and therefore had no voice in the decision. Oranna Felter of Roosevelt, Utah, the lead plaintiff in the federal court suit, told the *Deseret News* of Salt Lake City that when the statute of limitations ran out in 1967, "I would have been 17 years old." She asked, "What 17 year old is going to file something in court saying they have been wrongfully terminated?"[24]

12 Cow Creeks and Grand Rondes

Communities

The move to restore federal recognition to terminated tribes gave Sue M. Shaffer the opportunity she had been seeking all her life, a quest handed down from her mother and grandmother. Shaffer, longtime chairwoman of the Cow Creek band of Umpqua Indians, saw the opportunity and acted. The band was one of the few in western Oregon with a ratified treaty with the United States. However, after the tribe refused to move to the Oregon Coast reservation in the 1800s, the government first tried to exterminate the little band and then ignored it for more than a century. In 1954 the government tossed the Cow Creek band in with the five dozen tribes covered in the Western Oregon Termination Act and once more forgot about it. The band found out it had been terminated "long after the fact," said Shaffer. "How do you get terminated from nothing?"[1]

That inclusion, tacitly admitting that the federal government recognized the Cow Creek band's existence, gave Shaffer the opening she needed when the government began restoring recognition to terminated tribes in the 1970s. First, the Cow Creek band showed that the government never notified the tribe it was being terminated. That opened the door to a claim for the promised payment, never made, for the eight hundred square miles the Cow Creeks ceded in 1853. The claim, filed in 1980, was settled through negotiations in

1984 for $1.5 million. A dispute with the BIA over how the settlement was to be paid resulted in a four-year delay before the Cow Creeks received payment. While pursuing the land claim, the tribe also sought government recognition. As an officially terminated tribe—cited in the legislation—the Cow Creek band was not eligible for recognition through the administrative process established for unrecognized tribes. But the BIA also didn't want to admit it was eligible for restoration as a terminated tribe and opposed its recognition.[2]

Before trying to thwart the Cow Creeks, the BIA should have checked with members of the band and non-Indian residents of the little town of Canyonville, Oregon, the Cow Creek home territory. They would have told the bureaucrats that Sue Shaffer was not to be denied. She and her husband, George, were in the bar and restaurant business in Canyonville, population 1,200, for many years, and Shaffer was a longtime civic leader. She knew how to get things done, and she did not give up. In the face of the BIA opposition, the tribe turned to Washington DC attorney Dennis Whittlesey and Oregon historian Stephen Dow Beckham. Those two provided the expertise and the historical information to win the land claim settlement. When the BIA balked at recognition, Representative Jim Weaver, the Democrat who then represented southwestern Oregon in Congress, introduced a bill in Congress to bypass the agency. The measure won unanimous approval in both the House and Senate, and President Reagan signed the measure December 30, 1982.[3]

No land base came with the recognition. Many of the thousand or so tribal members owned property in the area, including Shaffer, who held title to the land near Canyonville that was the Cow Creek band's aboriginal winter camp. Her parents bought the land in 1924; it was the site of tribal meetings through the decades when the government ignored the tribe's existence. Three generations of women in Shaffer's family kept records of those meetings, records that were key to the band's eventual recognition.[4] When the government finally paid the claim settlement in 1988, the Cow Creek band began making up for the lost years. The tribe put its money in the bank and used only the interest as it bought scattered pieces of land for economic development, built a successful casino-resort and more than a dozen other businesses, and provided health insurance for tribal members and employees, scholarships for tribal members, and support to an array of community projects.

Its first purchase in 1985, twenty-eight acres just north of Canyonville, became the site of the Seven Feathers Casino and Hotel. The Cow Creek band was the first Oregon tribe to get into the gaming business after passage of the Indian Gaming Regulatory Act, building a modest establishment in 1992 and later expanding it into an attraction to draw travelers off Interstate 5, the busy freeway that connects California and the Northwest. Canyonville lies seventy miles north of Medford and ninety miles south of Eugene, the two largest southern Oregon cities along the route, making Seven Feathers an attractive stop for truckers and tourists. Local opinion initially was divided on the casino as an industry and because the tribal land was placed in trust, removing it from local tax rolls. Within two years, however, the casino had become a major employer for an area where the basic industry—timber—was rapidly shrinking. The county manager for a regional economic development corporation said the casino had generated enough economic activity to make up for the tax loss "a hundred times over."[5]

In the eight years between 1992, when the casino opened, and 2000 the Cow Creek band built a new headquarters building in Roseburg, the county seat twenty miles north of Canyonville, and a 150-room hotel adjacent to the casino. It opened a clinic with a doctor, a staff nurse, and disease prevention programs. It became a major partner in Rio Communications, a regional telecommunications and data company. It acquired a Canyonville truck stop and travel center, two motels, and a trailer park. It founded Umpqua Indian Foods, which features beef jerky and meat snacks. In 2001 it established its own utility company to distribute electric power from the federal Bonneville Power Administration to its businesses.[6]

As the casino began generating profits, the Cow Creek band began sharing its income with the community. Between 1997, when the tribe established the Cow Creek/Seven Feathers Foundation, and 2002, the twentieth anniversary of recognition, the foundation distributed $2.3 million to nonprofit organizations in southern Oregon. Its grants, totaling $1 million a year and ranging from $100 to $20,000, were aimed at offering "assistance to learning programs, services that strengthen home and family, youth programs" and improving the quality of life in the community. Recipients included a children's theater project and a preschool reading project.[7]

Tribal organizations employed more than a thousand full-time workers, most of them not tribal members. It ranked as Douglas County's second largest employer, and all of its companies paid for their workers' health insurance. The tribe offered members not employed by tribal businesses low-cost health insurance, and tribal members became eligible for tribe-paid college scholarships.[8]

As satisfying as the tribe's economic success was, the salvaging of its culture was a major reason for seeking recognition, said Michael Rondeau, the tribe's chief financial officer. Recognition "was a means to retain our culture and our language and to teach our youth," he said. "We lost a lot of culture. . . . We will never be sure of some things we lost."[9]

While vigorously defending the tribal sovereignty exempting it from property taxes, the tribe was meticulous about working with other local governments. It applied local building codes to all its construction and contracted with the county building department to make inspections. It paid local fire departments the equivalent of other property owners' taxes and paid the Oregon State Police for some regulatory activities on tribal land. Even before its afflu-ence, the tribe donated $25,000 when the city of Canyonville needed $103,000 in matching funds to obtain a $1.3 million federal grant to improve its water system.[10]

Shaffer summed up her philosophy and that of her tribe in 1998 testimony before Congress in a hearing involving tribal sovereign-ty: "Tribal development efforts continue to focus on benefitting our surrounding communities as well as our tribal membership, and we have not asked for any handouts or bailouts. . . . It has always been our Tribal philosophy and practice to build our communities (Tribal and non-Tribal) in a cooperative manner for the common good in furtherance of our desire to help build and support strong and independent families."[11]

While Sue Shaffer was working toward the Cow Creeks' recogni-tion, another determined woman farther north was joining the bat-tle for her tribe's restoration. Kathryn Harrison always knew she'd go back to Grand Ronde someday "and help my people." That day came in 1980. Harrison, whose father was a Grand Ronde tribal member, had spent her early childhood on the Siletz Reservation. When she was ten, both her parents died in a flu epidemic, and she was shuttled to several foster homes, all but one non-Indian fami-lies, until she was sent to the Chemawa Indian School as a teenager. Married young, she had ten children—and a husband who returned from World War II an alcoholic. Her teeth rotted as the result of many pregnancies and poor diet, and with her tribe terminated, she had no way to get dental care. She was in her mid-forties with five of the children still at home when she left her husband and, with the aid of welfare, obtained a degree as a practical nurse. She also got her teeth replaced. When she graduated in 1972, the Siletz tribe, still terminated but trying to create programs to aid tribal members, asked her to help develop its alcohol treatment program. She did; then she ran for the Siletz Council and won, although she never enrolled as a Siletz tribal member. As the secretary of the council, she went to Washington DC on behalf of Siletz restoration in 1976. She used the experience gained at Siletz as she helped guide the Grand Ronde Tribe through the restoration process.

When the Grand Ronde Tribe began its restoration efforts, Harrison was working in the Coos County alcoholism program on the Oregon Coast. The day in 1980 when an especially agitated drunk threatened to hit her, she decided she had enough. "I was so tired of working with drunks," she said. "I quit. It was time to come home." She took a job as enrollment clerk, the lowest paid person on the Grand Ronde staff, and began helping to rebuild a tribe.[12]

By 1980 the process for restoration was pretty well established: the tribe must prove that it continued to function as a tribe after termination, and it must create a roll of members with at least 25 percent Indian blood. (A common comment in Indian Country is that only race horses, dogs. and Indians are subjected to tests of blood quantum.) Then Congress must pass and the president sign a bill recognizing the tribe and establishing the area in which members may receive services such as medical care and education assistance.[13]

Under the pressure from loss of their federal ties the sixty terminated Oregon tribes had gathered themselves into fewer than a dozen tribal communities.[14] Beginning in 1980 the Native American Project of Oregon Legal Services (NAPOLS) provided legal advice and a coordinator, Elizabeth Furse, who later became a member of the U.S. House of Representatives from Oregon's First District. Furse had spent much of the 1970s as an activist on behalf of Indian fishing rights in Oregon and Washington and dropped out of law school to work for NAPOLS aiding tribes seeking restoration. NAPOLS attorney Donald Wharton, who also worked on the restorations, said of the tribes: "They had modest goals. They just wanted medicine for the grandmothers."[15] In seeking funds to help the remaining tribes win restoration, the NAPOLS grant application stated: "Members of the 61 [sic] terminated Oregon tribes were so scattered by financial hardship that maintenance of tribal communities has been extremely difficult. Despite these difficulties a number of tribes have succeeded in holding meetings and maintaining cultural and governmental structure . . . tribal institutions are held together through the sheer tenacity of dedicated individuals and are slipping into obscurity."[16] They raised money to keep going through powwows, bake sales, car washes, and making and selling handicrafts. The NAPOLS application for money to help the other tribes made note—several times—that the Siletz restoration a few years earlier had been successful.

The Grand Ronde Tribe had held onto the little tribal cemetery at the rural community of Grand Ronde along with a twenty-four-by-twenty-four-foot shed and an outhouse. The tribal leaders held meetings in the shed, where it was sometimes so cold that soft drinks froze. As enrollment clerk, Harrison started searching for tribal members among people she knew, asked others on the restoration committee to make lists of those they knew, and she asked everyone she contacted to contact family members. She went door-to-door all through the area around Grand Ronde, sixty miles southwest of Portland, searching for the people listed on the final roll before termination and for their descendants. "I went down every road in the area," she said. When the roll was completed, it contained nearly a thousand names. The number grew to more than five thousand as tribal members returned home and the blood quantum requirement was reduced to one-sixteenth—that is, one great-grandparent had to be a tribal member.[17]

Jackie Whisler, who served as tribal secretary through those early efforts, recalls initial reaction from the members contacted: "You're doing what? You'll never get anywhere. Don't bother." Whisler, who was a child at the time of termination, was at home raising her children, then age nine and seven, when her father called her in 1977 "to come work for my people." Her father, Dean Mercier, was one of the cadre of tribal leaders who organized and pushed through the restoration effort. Whisler learned to write grant applications. The federal Administration for Native Americans (ANA) came through with $50,000 a year for three years to pay staff salaries and meet expenses. Several church organizations also provided help. That ANA grant also allowed Marvin Kimsey, another of the small volunteer group working on restoration, to become the full-time director for the project. With the funding, the restoration group moved its meetings and office out of the shed to an old railroad depot in the community of Grand Ronde and later to a hotel across the street from the depot. The tribe incorporated under state law.

The continuity provided by tending the cemetery and staging the tribe's traditional Memorial Day powwow each year provided the proof of continued existence. The tribe faced an unexpected delay. Both Affiliated Tribes of Northwest Indians (ATNI) and the National Congress of American Indians (NCAI) were slow to support restoration of the Confederated Grand Ronde Tribes. W. Ron Allen, longtime chairman of the Jamestown Sklallam Tribe in Washington State and a former officer in both ATNI and NCAI, said there was a debate within the organizations at that time about restoration procedures. Some approved the tribe-by-tribe restoration through separate congressional action while others believed the terminated tribes should follow an administrative acknowledgment process similar to that required for never-recognized tribes. In addition, the Grand Ronde people were seeking restoration at a time of shrinking appropriations for Indian programs. Whisler said it appeared "there is only one pie and if they have to share it with restored tribes that reduces the amount for the existing tribes." She said there was no guarantee "there would be more money for the pie."[18] Both organizations eventually supported the Grand Ronde restoration.

The Grand Rondes approached Senator Mark Hatfield, an Oregon Republican and a member of the Senate Select Committee on Indian Affairs, and Representative Les AuCoin, a Democrat who represented the district containing the Grand Ronde territory. Hatfield deferred to AuCoin to introduce the bill, and AuCoin told the tribal members they would need to show they had support of the surrounding non-Indian community for restoration.

Harrison, who had become community coordinator for the tribe, went back to knocking on doors. In addition to her work as a tribal staff member, Harrison served twenty-seven years on the Tribal Council, including three terms as chairwoman before she retired in 2001 at age seventy-seven. The tribe got letters of support from city and county governments, civic groups, business people, and tribal neighbors. When the committee had collected 103 letters, AuCoin said it was enough and that he would meet with the tribal committee at Grand Ronde. "We cleaned the office, got cookies and a lace tablecloth," Harrison recalled. "He came with his two kids. . . . He shook hands with everybody."[19]

AuCoin introduced the Grand Ronde Restoration Bill in September of 1983. Five tribal members, paying their own way, went to Washington to testify before a House subcommittee in October. Harrison, then vice-chairwoman of the Tribal Council, took her sixteen-year-old daughter, Karen, a junior at Willamina High School, so she could see the historic occasion. The evening before the hearing, as the tribal delegation planned testimony on the need for BIA programs and problems that termination had brought, the group realized it had no testimony from the viewpoint of a young tribal member. Karen volunteered. "I told her what to say," Harrison recalled, "but being sixteen, she didn't listen to me." Instead Karen wrote her own testimony, which today hangs on the wall of the Grand Ronde tribal headquarters. It reads in part:

All my life I have known only termination. People ask me what
tribe I am and when I tell them, they've never heard of it. That,
in itself, would mean a lot to me: for people to know I am part
of the Molalla Tribe of the Grand Rondes, and how proud I am
to be a member of my tribe. Younger children of the tribe feel
the same as I do. Becoming restored is important to all of the
young people of the Grand Ronde Tribe. The passage of our
bill, HR 3885, will make us one again, a whole, a people, to be
known again by our government as Indians.[20]

Kathryn Harrison led off the tribal testimony, saying, "We are speaking up today for our right to exist." Harrison also made a point,
echoed in other hearings, that the land her tribe lost could have
been supporting tribal members, and the services the government
provides to tribes is payment for the land Indians relinquished. She
stated: "We feel we paid, more than adequately, when we gave up
valuable land in exchange for smaller, less valuable parcels. All of
these services are due for our people; we've already paid dearly for
all of them."[21]

Only one opponent testified, a representative of Trout Unlimited,
which was still concerned about hunting and fishing issues. Like
the Siletz and Cow Creek restorations, the Grand Ronde bill stated
that no hunting or fishing rights were granted or restored by the
bill. That left open whether those rights still existed from before
termination, and the tribe later negotiated a consent decree with
the state spelling out the extent to which the Indians would take
fish, deer, and elk.

The bill passed both the House and Senate by voice votes without audible dissent. President Reagan signed it on November 22,
1983, just two months after AuCoin introduced it. At the urging of
the administration, the House committee had removed provisions
for a reservation, leaving the specifics of the land to be acquired to

be worked out over the two-year period in which the tribe would develop a plan for economic self-sufficiency. The committee report noted, however, that it was the intent of the committee that the tribe receive enough lands "so that the tribe will have a reasonable chance of a viable economy" and land for homes.[22]

The tribe had started to build that economy even before the restoration measure passed. After two and a half years of fund-raising the tribe had bought two and a half acres to add to the six-and-a-half-acre cemetery property. The tribe paid $7,500 for the land it had once sold for $30 an acre. A greenhouse project to raise vegetables for sale was under way, a bead and craft shop had been opened, and tribal members were picking huckleberries on Forest Service land to produce jams and jellies for sale.[23] From those beginnings the Grand Ronde Tribe became probably the most financially successful of the restored tribes.

"Grand Ronde always had a clear vision of where they were going and where they wanted to end up," said LeaAnn Easton, executive director of NAPOLS.[24] It did change its means of getting there, however. Restored years before passage of the Indian Gaming Regulatory Act (IGRA), the Grand Ronde people first pinned their future on timber. But not until 1988 did Congress approve the tribe's acquisition of 9,811 acres of mostly forest land—little more than half the land the tribe had sought. The approval came only after the tribe agreed to sell its timber locally, not build its own mill, and to invest 30 percent of the timber proceeds in tribal economic development. Oregon's timber industry was shrinking rapidly at that time, and the tribe's income from the land would not have matched its ambitions, which included housing, especially for elders, education and jobs for tribal members, and a medical clinic.[25] The alternative turned out to be gambling. First, Congress passed IGRA, which allowed tribes to offer any type of gambling that was legal in the state in which the tribe was located. Then Oregon added video poker to its own state lottery, opening the way to just about every game found in Las Vegas.[26]

Once more, the Grand Rondes made the rounds of their neighbors, seeking support from the heavily timber-dependent community for a casino. There was little opposition. The tribe had a location adjacent to Highway 18, the major route between Oregon's major metropolis, Portland, sixty miles to the northeast, and the Oregon Coast, Portlanders' favorite playground twenty-five miles to the west. The promise of jobs and of travelers finding a reason to stop and drop off money in the rural community muted any anti-gambling sentiment. From its opening in 1995 Spirit Mountain Casino was a success. Within a few years it surpassed Multnomah Falls and Bonneville Dam as Oregon's top tourist attraction, and income from the casino fueled tribal and community development. The tribe acquired additional property, built two housing developments—one specifically for elders—a full-service medical clinic used by non-Indians as well as tribal members, a spacious tribal headquarters, and a resort hotel as part of its casino complex. It funded five sheriff's deputies and a sergeant in the two counties straddled by the new reservation. It offered college scholarships to all qualified tribal members. It sent tribal buses as far as thirty-five miles to pick up members for the weekly luncheon free to all tribal elders. Both the casino and tribal timber operations paid annual dividends to members.[27]

The Grand Ronde special pride, however, was its community development fund, which by 2006 had donated $35 million to nonprofit organizations in its eleven-county service area. More than one-third of the money had gone to education-related groups. Among the recipients were the Institute of Tribal Government at Portland State University, the Oregon Symphony, the Portland Art Museum for construction of a Native American Art wing, local police departments for equipment, the Oregon Food Bank, and emergency shelter programs.

"It's one of the best things the tribe has done," said Tribal Council Member Ed Pearsall. "People recognize that we're not just this sovereign nation out here. We're giving back to the community."[28]

However, with affluence came controversy, both within the tribe and with outside interests. As with any group, there were internal disagreements over the use of money and the future. In addition, the Grand Ronde Tribe made a very public fight to prevent the Confederated Tribes of Warm Springs from building a casino in the Columbia Gorge. The Warm Springs had a small casino in the tribe's Kah-Nee-Ta Resort far from population centers and major highway routes. It proposed a casino just forty-five freeway miles east of Portland at Cascade Locks, where it could draw customers who had gambled at Spirit Mountain. The Grand Ronde Tribe launched a million-dollar ad campaign, sent tribal officials to lobby Congress and the Interior Department, and waded into the 2006 primary election in its efforts to keep the Warm Springs tribes from building on nontribal land in the gorge. Using a carrot as well as a stick, the Grand Rondes also offered to finance a new casino for the Warm Springs on that tribe's Central Oregon reservation near Bend, the fastest growing city in the state. The opposition to the Warm Springs casino in the Columbia Gorge brought criticism both from some Grand Ronde tribal members and other Indian tribes, who feared open controversy would threaten gaming for all tribes.[29] The issue was still being fought as 2006 ended.

13 Klamaths

Troubles

Hunting and fishing issues that nearly derailed other Oregon tribes' efforts toward restoration gave the Klamath Tribes their first boost toward re-recognition. Tribal member Robert Bojorcas filed suit in state court asserting that individual tribal members' treaty rights to hunt and fish at "usual and accustomed places" had not been extinguished by the law terminating federal supervision of the Klamath Tribes. He lost.[1]

Meanwhile, in 1965 another tribal member, Charles E. Kimbol, had received "boxes of documents" from his wife's grandfather, Boyd Jackson, the longtime tribal leader who had tried to forestall termination. Kimbol began reading the documents, and from that grew a federal lawsuit, *Kimball* [court records and references consistently misspell Kimbol's name] *v. Callahan*, in which five Klamath Indians asserted that the hunting and fishing rights of tribal members survived termination. That legal action led to reorganization of the tribe and, eventually, restoration.

After reading the Jackson documents, Kimbol began telling fellow Klamaths, "We didn't sell our rights." Years later he recalled, "Others started getting interested. It was a slow process." In the early 1970s the Native American Rights Fund (NARF) entered the battle, supplying the reorganizing tribe with attorneys. "This is tribal. It has nothing to do with withdrawal or remaining," Kimbol told tribal members. "This is for all of us."[2]

Like Bojorcas, Kimbol lost the first round. Donald R. Wharton, one of the NARF attorneys, recalled that U.S. District Court Judge Gus Solomon of Portland said to Kimbol, "You mean to tell me that if U.S. Steel builds a plant on former Klamath lands you want the right to hunt in their parking lot? No way." Solomon dismissed the suit. Kimbol appealed to the 9th U.S. Circuit Court of Appeals, which found—in an opinion written by Solomon's friend, John Kilkenny—the termination law did not affect the hunting, fishing, and water rights enumerated in the Klamath treaties.[3] The spring after that ruling the tribe held a General Council meeting and conducted its first elections since termination. With rights established, the tribal members created the Klamath Game Commission to regulate tribal hunting and fishing and to deal with state regulatory agencies. A poll of tribal members showed that their number one goal was getting the tribe's federal recognition restored.[4]

While Kimbol was pursuing his lawsuit, other Klamaths had created the Organization of Forgotten Americans (OFA). The group served as a limited Community Action Program, part of the federal Great Society, to provide services to poor people. Another group, Southern Oregon Indian Research (SOIR), was created to develop information in support of grants needed to pursue restoration. OFA was designed mostly to serve Indians in the Klamath County area but had to accept others for service too. By then there were plenty of poor people around the former reservation, most of them Indians. Many families had moved in search of work. Other families had come apart under the stresses of termination, with children sent to foster families elsewhere and individuals wandering off. Even so, when restoration efforts began, 60 percent of those on the termination roll were still living on the former reservation or nearby.[5]

Kimbol, who had been a logger, lumber mill sawyer, and ranch owner, was one who stayed put. Before retiring in 2000 he spent thirty-one years winning affirmation of tribal rights, pushing for restoration, and helping guide the tribe through the first dozen years after winning re-recognition. He also served for several years as chairman of the Oregon governor's Indian Commission. In the late 1970s as Kimbol and the others began their work toward regaining federal recognition, the Menominee restoration served as an inspiration to the Klamath people—as it did for other tribes. The Klamaths started seeking recognition about the same time as the Siletz, but while the Siletz gained restoration within three years of beginning their effort, the Klamaths struggled for a decade. "I can't believe how many trips to Washington it took," Kimbol said. The Klamaths conducted a survey of every tribal household, documenting the impacts of termination on the people. There was opposition to restoration from within the tribe, from other tribes, and from non-Indians. Politicians and other non-Indians said the Klamath people had been paid for their land. That should end it.[6]

Tribal leaders were forced to compromise. Unlike other tribes, the Klamath got no extended service area. Tribal members received such services as medical care and housing aid only if they were in Klamath County. And the tribe got neither land nor the promise of land. Instead, it got authority to create an economic development plan.

A third impetus toward restoration, along with the Menominee success and Kimbol's lawsuit, was Edison Chiloquin's stubborn refusal to let the government take his land when the remaining members gave up their trust with U.S. Bank and sold the rest of the reservation. Congress finally gave up and passed a law recognizing Chiloquin's title. "The legislation letting him retain his land in some ways really affected folks around here," said Jeff Mitchell, a former tribal chairman and later upper basin coordinator for the Klamath River Inter-Tribal Fish and Water Commission. So did another federal court ruling upholding the tribe's senior water right in the Klamath Basin. "It was a combination of events that started to bring the tribe closer together," Mitchell said.[7]

Getting community support was a matter of economics. "Once people understood the economics of restoration, that it would bring federal money into the community, the community approved," said Wharton, the NARF attorney who also worked on the Klamath restoration. After the tribe had patched over some of its own divisions and persuaded the surrounding community that restoration of the tribe would benefit both the Indians and their neighbors, winning congressional approval went smoothly. A House committee hearing was held only to receive a report from the Department of the Interior. The committee approved. The *Klamath Falls Herald and News* noted in an editorial on June 19, 1986, that "there is no overt opposition" to restoration. The House had just passed the restoration bill unanimously, and the newspaper urged the Senate to do the same. Representative Bob Smith (R-OR), who introduced the Klamath measure, told the House the bill did not provide for a reservation, "nor would it suggest that the federal government should ever provide a reservation." He said if the Klamaths wanted a reservation, it "would have to be done the same way any American acquires land"—buy it.[8] The Senate approved the bill in mid-August by unanimous consent, and President Reagan signed it August 28, 1986. Smith said the bill "guarantees a solid foundation for the future of the tribe." Kimbol, then the tribal chairman, said the restoration opened the door to federal services for Klamath tribal members.[9]

The service most urgently needed was health care. "We underestimated the health needs in our planning," said Elwood Miller, the tribe's director of natural resources who served on the Tribal Council during the efforts toward restoration. "There was a forty-year span of unmet dental needs. . . . We had looked at ten years. We did not realize the catastrophic health situation."[10] In 1991 the tribe took over management of the health care program from the Indian Health Service and expanded it to include a clinic and dental office in Chiloquin with a full-time physician, nurse practitioner, dentist, pharmacist, and other professional staff. In addition to primary care, the tribe created public health programs for disease prevention and promotion of good health.

There were other aims too—help for destitute tribal members, education from preschool to college, jobs, and housing. There was progress, but two decades after restoration the Klamath Tribes still struggled. "It seems like we take two steps forward and one step back," said tribal chairman Allen Foreman. A consistent tribal goal, he said in 2006, is "to have a land base, a home to call our own." He added, "We continue to look at all the available processes that will not harm anybody's way of life. This will always be our home."[11] The federal government still had not approved the tribe's economic self-sufficiency plan, which was based on reacquiring 690,000 acres of the Klamath Forest, which had become part of two national forests. There was no move in Congress to approve land for the tribe. There was much opposition to returning any land to the tribe on grounds that they were paid a fair price. The tribe argued, however, that the price they received was the value of the salable timber, not the land itself. And, they said, in little more than two decades the government had collected more than twice as much from timber sales as it paid the Indians for the forest. The two counties containing the forest also profited, receiving an average of more than $2.4 million in annual revenue from federal timber sales on the land.[12]

In 2006 the tribe owned just seven hundred acres, much of it purchased after restoration. The total included ten cemeteries scattered over the area of the former reservation. There were other patches of land in Chiloquin and elsewhere around the old reservation. A handsome two-story tribal headquarters building occupied one piece of land outside Chiloquin. Another piece of land along Highway 97, the major highway route between California and the Canadian border east of the Cascade Mountain Range, was the site of the tribal casino.[13] The casino was not part of the original development plan, nor, according to former chairman Mitchell, was it the answer to the tribe's economic future. The gaming law and Oregon lottery changes that opened the way to Indian casinos had not been passed when the Klamath Tribes were restored.

The plan called for developing a diversity of small businesses and, after the casino was built in 1997, a destination resort in conjunction with the casino. For the Klamath Tribes, the casino was a source of both jobs and tribal income, and Rod Clarke, president of the Klamath Economic Development Corporation, said plans were under way in late 2006 to expand it. Slightly more than half the casino employees were tribal members.[14] With the decline of the timber industry in Klamath County beginning in the 1980s, any additional businesses and jobs were welcomed by both Indians and non-Indians. Together the casino, tribal government, and tribal programs were a major source of jobs, with three hundred employees on the payroll, mostly in the casino, natural resources, and health care.[15] That placed the tribe among the largest employers in Klamath County. In all, with payroll and purchases of goods and services, the Klamath Tribes put $25 million into Klamath County's economy in 2005.[16]

The tribe and its casino were part of the southern Oregon economy's increasing emphasis on tourism. The Great Basin Visitors Bureau welcomed the tribe into membership and began to coordinate tourist promotions with it. The tribe also belonged to the Oregon Tribal Tourism Working Group formed by Oregon's nine federally recognized tribes to promote tourism. The casino was the only tribally owned business, but Clarke said the corporation was looking at investment possibilities in other parts of Oregon. Meanwhile, the casino was bringing in $3 million a year with most of the money distributed to services such as health and education. The 3,500 tribal members also received "a very small" annual per capita payment—perhaps $150.[17]

Some tribal members who left during termination returned, and more were expected to move back when the tribe's economic development program picked up. The economic plan estimated it would take twenty or perhaps more than thirty years for tribal members to achieve parity with their neighbors.[18]

Housing for tribal members was an early priority, with several small projects scattered through the former reservation area. Because it took seven years for the federal government to take the purchased land into trust, the first such action was not finished until the late 1990s. The tribe also had three programs to help low-income tribal members buy, repair, or rent homes. A tribal goal was to broaden the housing programs "so that every Tribal member has a safe, decent and affordable place to live."[19] The Klamath Tribes also instituted a welfare-to-work plan to prepare tribal members for the jobs the leaders hoped to create. By 1999 there were fifty tribal members in college.[20]

The tribe's plans still centered on the forest as an economic base, only partly for sustained yield logging. "This land was our supermarket," Foreman said. Referring to disputes over allocation of water between irrigation farming and maintaining stream flows for fish, Foreman said the forest and streams "are our economic base too . . . it's as valuable to us as irrigation is to farmers." The land, streams, and Klamath Lake continued to be the source of much Indian food—game, fish, and traditional plants.[21] However, one local organization, Klamath Basin Alliance, remained dedicated to preventing the Klamath Tribes from regaining any land. Foreman said the fight to regain the land required an education process that grew increasingly difficult as more people without knowledge of the area's history moved in and acquired former tribal land.[22] "If it takes one hundred years we will wind up with the Winema Forest back," said Clarke.[23] The Winema was created from a major part of the Klamath Reservation after termination.

Restoring the land, whether it is owned by the tribe or not, and reviving the tribal culture that began to slip away during termination were major objectives for the tribe. The Natural Resources Department with fifteen employees was stretched thin, said Director Miller. "Some people are doing ten different jobs. . . . We have thirty-five entities to deal with, state and federal. Each one has us outmanned four to one." He added with some pride, "We usually come up with the best science." The tribe worked with three biologists and a limnologist and with the University of Oregon, Oregon State University, and Washington State University and sent some fisheries samples to the Wyoming Fisheries Department for genetics work. There was a memorandum of understanding between the tribe and the Winema Forest over management. In addition, the Klamath River Inter-Tribal Fish and Water Commission, which also included the Hoopa, Yurok, and Koruk tribes of northern California, had a major role in programs to restore the Klamath River watershed.[24]

Irrigation agriculture, the basis of much of the non-Indian economy in the Klamath Basin, combined with drought brought the area close to armed conflict in the year 2002. The Bureau of Reclamation ordered irrigation gates kept closed to retain stream water for endangered suckers. Armed farmers vowed to open the gates by force to turn water into their fields. Congress intervened. "It became fish v. farmers and Indian v. non-Indians," said Mitchell of the Fish Commission. Non-Indians boycotted the tribal casino. In some ways a shooting spree by three white men through the mostly Indian town of Chiloquin that summer "illustrates how relations have deteriorated," Mitchell said. "It will take a lot to overcome that. People need to recognize that it's not [water] rates; it's not the Klamaths; it's not the farmers. We have over-allocated and over-used the system. It has limits. . . . The U.S. government put all of us in this position. We need creative policies."

Although the situation later calmed, the conflict continued. The farmers resented what they saw as federal subsidies to Indians; the Indians resented what they saw as federal subsidies to farmers. Tribal leaders took the long view. Said Mitchell, "The responsibility I inherited from my ancestors is to ensure this is here for the future. I don't have the right to diminish it. I have to take care of it, not just [for] Indians or [for just] a few generations. Nonnatives have been here three or four generations. They are not going anywhere. We have to find a way to work together."[25]

Unlike the water issue, the Klamaths' cultural resurgence brought more cooperation than conflict with the tribe's neighbors. Gerald Skelton, the cultural resources director, worked for the Klamath County Museum in Klamath Falls early in his career, and other tribal members later worked there under a work-experience program made possible because the tribe was recognized. Skelton said the museum staff was open to suggestions from the tribe about the way it portrayed the Indians and the baskets, bows, grinders, mortars, and pestles that once belonged to them. Most of the objects went to the museum during the termination period. Skelton said after restoration some non-Indians offered the tribe collections of tribal objects, largely to obtain tax deductions. Skelton's department was active in implementing the Native American Graves Protection and Repatriation Act, inspecting proposed federal projects that involve disturbing one-time Indian land to assure there are no graves or Indian artifacts. Restoration was important in that field also; only recognized tribes have the formal relationship with government agencies that makes the work possible. Also, Skelton brought back from Washington DC the bones of Modoc warriors taken by the U.S. Army after the Modoc War in the 1800s.

One of Skelton's favorite projects was a culture camp for tribal kids held during two weeks every summer. In that time tribal members taught the youngsters "the old ways": the making of duck decoys, use of bows and arrows, finding and preparing foods, and telling the traditional tribal stories. The camp started out in tents but later moved to huts made of bent willows and tule mats like the summer lodges of precontact times. Skelton said the Yahooskin band adapted to teepees easily after learning of them late in the nineteenth century because that tribe was mobile. The Klamaths and Modocs didn't need them, Skelton said. "We didn't have to go anywhere. . . . We didn't have to go far for our food."[26]

For the Klamaths, everything goes back to the land. The common thread through nearly every interview was damage done to the land after termination—clear-cutting, reduction in stream flows from removing too much water and logging the headwaters, diminished numbers of game animals from overhunting, loss of fish from rising stream temperatures, and the loss of open space as hobby farms covered once open range. "One of the costs of termination was the land itself," said Kimbol, whose lawsuit set the tribe on the road to restoration.[27]

The tribe offered a hundred-year plan to sustain the forest. "The goal is to restore the forest to where it was in the 1700s," said tribal chairman Foreman. "It will take a hundred years."[28] The Klamath people will wait. They have already waited a long time.

14 Coos and Coquilles

Cooperating

When the Confederated Tribes of Coos, Lower Umpqua, and Siuslaw Indians joined the rush for restoration after the Menominee and Siletz successes, they had little problem showing their continuing tribal identity. Despite being terminated they had kept on holding tribal meetings in their tribal hall and held title to the building as a nonprofit corporation.

In fact, the Coos had not entirely accepted their termination. They had been largely ignored in the years just preceding the removal of federal recognition, but they felt the loss of education aid and the right to use Indian hospitals. Instead of letting the government sell its only building, the tribe made a deal with the town of Empire: the town took over the hall for use as a community center for Indians and others, mostly others, with the proviso that if the town ceased to exist, the hall would revert to the Indians. Nearly two decades after termination the town of Empire was annexed to the adjacent city of Coos Bay. Tribal leaders quickly formed a nonprofit corporation in 1972 and demanded their hall back.[1] They got it in January 1978, but until restoration they struggled to maintain it. Like most tribal activities the hall was sustained to large extent by members' donations. It served as headquarters for a variety of tribal social services under federal Great Society programs—alcohol and drug counseling, job training, and education. Tribal members also used the hall as a store. Two or three members would travel to western Washington to buy groceries from nonterminated tribes who had a cooperative. Then they would sell the goods to other members at lower than retail prices.[2]

Tribal meetings often centered on pursuit of a land claim and recognition of tribal rights. In 1974 the state finally granted the tribe permission to use Sunset Bay State Park overnight for the traditional annual salmon ceremony. There was less success in the effort to win compensation for 1.6 million acres taken without payment by the United States under an unratified treaty. Turned away by U.S. courts on a technical ruling, the Coos took their case to the United Nations in 1956. The UN also rebuffed the tribe, calling it an internal U.S. matter.[3]

The Siletz restoration in 1977 "gave others the idea they could do it," said Donald Whereat, who served on the Tribal Council before and during restoration. He admitted, however, "I didn't think it would ever happen."[4] For Bill Brainard, who served terms as chief, chairman, and Tribal Council member over many years, tribal children were a powerful incentive to work for restoration. Brainard had been a soldier, a logger, a lumber mill worker, and a longtime department manager for a utility company. He looked at the large number of poverty-stricken tribal families and saw their children going without health care. There is no way children should have to go without glasses or dental care, he said, adding, "Health and education are the most important things." Problems getting specific education for a dyslexic grandson spurred his interest in education.[5]

By 1980 the time seemed right, and tribal leaders began exploring the possibility of restoration. Representative Jim Weaver, the Democrat who represented the area in the U.S. House, was willing to sponsor legislation. With Weaver's backing and a grant from the Administration for Native Americans, the Coos began building their case for restoration. Brainard and Ed Bowen, another long-time leader, traveled to Washington DC to lay the groundwork for their return to federal status. At the suggestion of Cow Creek chairwoman Sue Shaffer, they hired Washington DC attorney Dennis Whittlesey, who also was helping the Cow Creek band. The Coos began seeking support from their neighbors. The city councils of most of the communities along their southern Oregon coastal area quickly gave support. One, Florence, approved only on a second vote. Another, Bandon, never did approve. But Coos Bay, the tribe's home base and largest city in the area, approved as did North Bend, the second largest city. So did Kiwanis clubs, Lions clubs, and other civic groups.[6]

The House committee report on Weaver's bill added economic support to the tribal arguments. In 1982, the report said, 75 percent of tribal families lived below the poverty line, compared to 8 per cent of all Oregon families. Unemployment among tribal members was 47 percent compared to just under 10 percent for the southern Oregon Coast as a whole, an area hard hit by the recession of the early 1980s.[7]

Whittlesey and historian Stephen Dow Beckham, who had been serving as a consultant to the tribe, orchestrated the Coos appearance before the House Subcommittee on Indian Affairs in 1984. Each of the five tribal representatives presented a subject related to tribal history, government, and plans. "We were lined up there like crows," recalled Brainard. Committee members asked few questions. Brainard remembered being asked how the tribe intended to govern itself. "We always used Roberts' Rules," Brainard replied.[8] Congress easily approved the restoration bill, and President Reagan signed it on October 17, 1984. The action got little notice in Oregon. It came in the midst of national and state election campaigns and the disintegration of the notorious Oregon ranch of the Bhagwan Shree Rajneesh along with sensational revelations about the cult. The tribe got four paragraphs in the hometown newspaper, the *Coos*

Bay World. The story quoted Brainard, then the tribal chairman, saying members were "on Cloud Nine."[9]

The restoration recognized the tribe's ownership of the 6.2 acres containing the tribal hall and two other small parcels of land. It said a reservation should be established "at no cost to the government."[10] Over the next dozen years the tribe worked out an economic development plan calling for it to take over management of 62,000 acres of the Siuslaw National Forest within the tribe's ancestral homelands. Senator Gordon Smith (R-OR) introduced a bill to redesignate the land to the tribe in 2003.[11] It had not been acted on three years later. However, the tribe continued to refine its proposal in efforts to win support from its neighbors. Among other things, it had agreed to continue paying to local governments the same share of logging revenue the communities received under Forest Service management.[12]

Although tribal leaders saw the forest as the chief component of their economic base and their hopes for self-sufficiency, they had a number of other projects both to strengthen the tribe and to help its members. Even before restoration the tribe had begun work on a fourteen-unit subdivision of single family homes in North Bend. That development grew into twenty-one rental homes for low-income families. Its housing program after restoration included rental assistance for tribal members attending colleges and for low-income families, down payment help—including financial counseling—for tribal families buying their first homes, and aid to homeless families. In all, said Housing Director Laurie Voshall, the tribe was helping seventy to ninety tribal families a month through its housing programs. Even so, there were waiting lists. Because the money came from the federal Department of Housing and Urban Development's Indian Housing Block Grant Program, the Coos projects were a direct result of restoration. There also was a program to help tribal members finance home repairs and weatherization.[13]

The tribe purchased small pieces of land for businesses, housing, and environmental protection. It also re-acquired the first piece of land whites took from the tribe in the 1800s. In 2004 the General Services Administration transferred to the tribe forty-three acres that had been abandoned by the Air National Guard and declared surplus. The tribe planned to build its administrative headquarters there.[14]

As early as 2002, Carolyn Slyter, then vice chairman of the 750-member tribe, said the Coos were well down their checklist of things to accomplish through restoration. Among the major accomplishments were a dental clinic and a health and safety program with ten full-time employees, largely funded by grants.[15] From 1987 to 1995 Muriel Brainard, Bill Brainard's non-Indian wife and a registered nurse, headed the program. It included alcohol and drug prevention and rehabilitation, swimming lessons for children, child safety seats for cars, and smoke alarms for homes. The neighboring Coquille Tribe had a medical clinic that served Coos members, and the Coos dental clinic served Coquille members.[16]

The tribal government also included divisions for welfare, natural resources, and culture. It worked to protect the cultural resources of the tribe—tribally important sites and cemeteries—and to support continued development of its living culture.

With only about five hundred acres in tribal ownership, the Natural Resources Department devoted most of its work to a water quality program on its scattered holdings and to cooperative ventures to restore and improve streams in the tribe's ancestral lands. Working with watershed associations, the tribe fenced stream banks to keep livestock out, planted vegetation along stream banks, and placed logs in streams to improve conditions for salmon and other fish.[17]

Slyter also ticked off a list of educational accomplishments within the tribe—one PhD, a couple more students working toward doctorates, numerous bachelor's degrees, including two of her four grandchildren, and more students in college. Tribal scholarships paid off, as tribal members earned undergraduate and graduate degrees and then returned home. "Restoration has been a good thing for education," she said. "We would have had more if we had not been terminated. We would have been so much farther down the road."[18]

That is especially true for economic development. Most of the tribe's plans for businesses were "on the shelf" for lack of startup money and a land base, said Ron Brainard, chairman of the Tribal Council. An enterprise to make and market fry bread foundered early after restoration because of lack of space, but the Coos Tribe retained the brand label Blue Earth Foods and was considering another effort.[19]

For more than a decade the tribe put a plan for a casino on hold, largely because the Coquille Tribe, although restored later, built first with a giant casino in North Bend, just a few miles up Highway 101 from the Coos location at Coos Bay. In 2004, however, after overcoming legal and financial challenges, the Coos opened its temporary Three Rivers Casino at Florence, fifty miles north of the Coquille resort. The location is at the western end of the major highway from Eugene, Oregon's second most populous metropolitan center, to the Oregon Coast. Work on a larger permanent casino and hotel were under way in 2006. At that time, Three Rivers Casino profits were "paying 20 years of back bills," Brainard said. It also was an increasing source of jobs, with a nine-month leadership training program to prepare tribal members for management positions.

"None of us knew gaming was coming" at the time of restoration, said Whereat, the former council member. But given the decline of the entire timber economy in the Pacific Northwest, even with a timber base "there is no way tribes can support themselves without gaming," he said. He also noted, accurately, that only a few tribes make a major profit from gaming.[20]

With the increasing numbers of tribal members in college and plans for more development, "the future looks good" for the Coos, said George Barton, a former tribal chairman.[21] But noting the chronic problem for Indians and non-Indians alike on the Oregon Coast, he added, "The problem is not education; the problem is permanent employment."

While the Coos federation won restoration with relative ease, its near neighbor, the Coquille Indian Tribe, was the only one to draw active opposition from the Bureau of Indian Affairs when it sought restoration of its federal recognition. The agency had been initially reluctant to support restoration of the first tribes to seek re-recognition but later generally agreed to tribes returning to the federal fold. When the Coquille Tribe began its restoration efforts, however, the BIA insisted the tribe had not existed as an entity separate from the Siletz Reservation after 1855 and opposed its restoration.[22] The agency said evidence of the tribe's continuity as a distinct entity was unconvincing. Coquille people saw it differently. The termination bill had listed both Upper Coquilles and Lower Coquilles as separate entities. A small group of tribal members had kept the tribal organization alive from termination in 1956 until they won re-recognition in 1989. Doris and Bud Chase were active in the effort for more than two decades. Bud Chase, retired from managing the Coos Bay Montgomery Ward auto center, was chairman much of that time. Doris Chase served as secretary. "I gave a garage sale once or twice a year to raise money for stamps and gas," she recalled in a 2001 interview. Between sales, the tribal members sometimes passed a coffee can to raise postage money. One tribal member donated a copy machine. The group had committees that managed an annual tribal gathering, burials, a family cemetery, and a pow-wow. The tribal office was the spare bedroom in the Coos Bay home the Chases occupied during their more than half-century marriage. Tribal records were in Sharon Parrish's sewing room; she became the director of tribal records management and member services and later a Tribal Council member.[23]

When the Coquille people approached Congress for restoration, the tribe inundated the Senate Select Committee on Indian Affairs with documents. The committee inventory listed 145 documents dated between 1922 and 1987, including 15 meeting announcements, minutes from 25 meetings, 53 pieces of correspondence, and 8 newsletters. In addition there were 10 records of application by Coquille tribal members for public domain allotments, a 1955 judgment act awarding land claims to the Coquille Tribe, and a 1961 tribal roll listing 271 members to receive shares of the claim judgment. The tribe also had collected the requisite support from other tribes, county and city governments, civic organizations, and legislators. The committee viewed the evidence and recommended restoration.[24]

During a 1988 congressional hearing on the Coquille restoration, tribal member Michele Burnette, then research and development officer for Western Bank in Coos Bay, summed up the entire social experiment that was termination: "Termination was supposed to allow Indian people to assimilate into non-Indian society, to compete with non-Indian people and thus to advance ourselves and become self sufficient. While on the surface we may appear to have assimilated and to be self-sufficient, the reality is quite different." It was not that the tribal people hadn't tried, she said. Among other efforts, she described Indian Economic Development Inc., a nonprofit corporation formed in the 1970s by several of western Oregon's terminated tribes. That organization tried to "prepare members for future economic growth opportunities that would benefit the total southwestern Oregon area while employing and educating persons of Indian descent." Its projects—aquaculture and a fish waste-processing plant—failed for lack of funding. The federal status would make more economic tools available, Burnette said.[25] The then tribal chairman, Wilfred C. Wasson, told the committee, "Instead of vanishing into the melting pot of American obscurity at the time of termination we have grown stronger in our determination to remain Indian."[26]

Like other tribes, the Coquille sought restoration also for the health, education, and housing programs it would make available, with emphasis on health and housing for the elderly and education for the young. Parrish, the tribal records director, said her grandmother, who was not a tribal member, inspired her to work for restoration, as did her mother, who never accepted termination. Parrish saw the need for medical care, especially for elders, firsthand. Her mother was diagnosed with multiple sclerosis a few years after termination and became totally disabled.[27] Roy Gilkey, then the Coquille chief and the operator of two adult foster homes, outlined for the congressional committee the severe medical problems tribal members faced: 61 percent of Coquille households had at least one member with vision problems; 49 percent of tribal members had dental problems; 39 percent had high blood pressure. One-fourth of tribal members had a problem requiring medical attention but had not seen a doctor because they lacked insurance or money.[28]

"Education has always been our number one priority," said longtime tribal chairman Edward L. Metcalf. "But now it's becoming health care because of the rising cost."[29]

The Coquille restoration appeared to complete the return of the terminated western Oregon Indians to federal status. The Siletz and Grand Ronde confederations each claimed twenty-seven tribes and bands, but David Lewis, manager of the Grand Ronde cultural resources department, said there may be some overlapping—as there was in the list BIA area director E. Morgan Pryse compiled half a century earlier. There became one Coquille Tribe instead of two; the Coos combined three tribes; there remained no entities seeking restoration.[30]

Coquille was the first tribe restored after the Indian Gaming Regulatory Act (IGRA) of 1988, which opened the door nationally to Indian gaming. Oregon's approval of video poker and other casino-type games then opened the prospect of full-scale casinos for Oregon tribes. Many Oregon people remained opposed to casino gambling in general and Indian gambling in particular, however, and the Coquille Tribe ran into a storm of opposition when it announced plans to build an assisted living center on a piece of its historic land in the city of Bandon on the Oregon Coast. Opponents charged that the center was only a front for the tribe's real objective—a casino. The battle raged through construction, sewer connections, water connections, and into the opening of Heritage Place, an upscale home mostly for elderly tribal members but with some nontribal and younger occupants needing help with daily living. The $6-million building opened in December 1994 and began pouring $1.6 million a year in wages and supplies into the local small-town economy.[31]

At the same time, the tribe acquired a closed plywood mill on Coos Bay in the city of North Bend and began converting it into a multimillion-dollar casino and hotel complex. That location drew some opposition too. Among other things, city officials worried about the need for additional fire protection the new development would generate. The tribe responded by buying the city a new fire truck. The casino/hotel operation grew into the major driver of the Coquille economy and gave a major boost to the regional economy, which had lost much of the roller coaster timber and commercial fishing industries that historically sustained the coastal communities. With the hotel filled to capacity in August 2006, the tribe embarked on a ninety-room expansion.[32]

The restoration measure signed by President George H. W. Bush on June 28, 1989, provided for a reservation of up to a thousand acres in Coos and Curry counties, the tribe's original homeland. That was later expanded, and the tribe took over fourteen parcels of Bureau of Land Management forest land totaling 5,410 acres in 1998. It acquired additional land for its various enterprises to push the total to 6,500 acres.[33] The tribe built a 103-unit subdivision using an $8 million Housing and Urban Development Department

(HUD) grant and provided easy terms for tribal members to become home owners.[34]

The tribe's rapid economic development hit a snag in 1996 when HUD and the Environmental Protection Agency raised questions about the use of some of the HUD grant money and some casino construction practices. The tribe suspended the director of its economic development arm, who later resigned. The tribe resolved its difficulties and resumed development.[35] With its enterprises, especially the Mill Casino, on firm footing, the tribe created a community fund that dispersed hundreds of thousands of dollars each year to programs as varied as vaccinations for uninsured children, the Coos Art Museum, and a Port Orford Police Department community involvement project. The board selecting the grant recipients was made up of a community leader, a person appointed by the Oregon governor, and representatives of the tribe and its economic development arm, CEDCO. In 2005 the tribe distributed more than half a million dollars to 55 organizations.[36]

In March 2006 the tribe announced its plan for a fifty-acre site on the Coos Bay waterfront that it bought in 2003. Included were construction of a Home Depot store, an RV park, and other businesses.[37]

The tribal administration office displayed prominently a plaque with the names of members who earned college degrees. The initial listing contained thirty-three names from the six-hundred-member tribe. In addition to college financial assistance, the tribe operated training programs to help members qualify for technical and management jobs both within the tribal operations and elsewhere. Unlike most tribes with casinos or other successful businesses, the Coquille Tribe made no per capita payments to its members. As Joe Thomas, a former teacher, deputy sheriff, and security chief for the tribe's economic arm, explained, "We will provide services—health, etc., but not money . . . We want to provide jobs and opportunities," not welfare.[38]

The Coquille and Coos tribes, close neighbors, often rivals, and sometimes outright antagonists, occasionally joined forces. The two tribes have had a tangled relationship. Both historically occupied lands along the Coquille River. Some portions of the two tribes spoke the same language. There was much intermarriage. Before termination the two tribes shared the tribal hall at Empire. After restoration both established headquarters in Coos Bay. Coos tribal members, rebuffed on a legal technicality in their efforts to obtain compensation for lost lands, resented the Coquille Tribe's success in a similar suit—and the fact that the Coquilles won land for a reservation with restoration while the Coos sought lands for years after being restored. Some Coos questioned the Coquille legitimacy based on a statement in a government document that the government created the Coquille tribe in order to terminate it and on BIA resistance to Coquille restoration on grounds it should be part of the Siletz confederation.[39]

Nevertheless, after restoration the two joined forces on two projects—an abortive aquaculture operation and a traditional Peace-giving Court. The court was a return to traditional ways of dealing with juveniles involved in crime or otherwise troubled. Developed in cooperation with representatives of the non-Indian community, the court was based on traditional approaches of elders working with a youngster's family toward rehabilitation and solving problems rather than on punishment. The processes called for offenders to take responsibility for their actions and for the authorities to treat the person "with respect and generosity," with emphasis on probation, diversion, and alternative sentencing. "I like Peace-giving because you can't make peace—you can only offer," said Tom Younker, vice chairman of the Coquille Council.[40] The court represented both tribes' efforts to use traditional ways while adapting to the modern, non-Indian world.

15 Alabama-Coushattas and California

Legalities

The Alabama-Coushatta Tribe found itself cast as the shuttlecock in a game of badminton between the federal and Texas governments. When the tribe appealed to the Congress in 1986 for restoration of its federal status, the state had barred it from using its own money, and tribal leaders said they felt threatened with extinction. The irony was the Texas attorney general had used the equal protection clause of the Constitution to demolish what had long been an amicable relationship between state and tribe.

The tribe's troubles with Texas began with a March 1983 ruling by state attorney general Jim Mattox. He said the tribe did not exist as an Indian tribe with a legal relationship to the state as spelled out in the 1954 federal termination act and related state legislation. Instead, he ruled, the tribe was "a private unincorporated association." The ruling, according to testimony at a 1986 congressional hearing, extinguished the legal existence of the Alabama-Coushatta Reservation in East Texas and of the tribe. It also subjected the tribal land and enterprises to taxation.[1] The *Tyler County Booster*, published just east of the Alabama-Coushatta Reservation, denounced the ruling as a "dunderhead legal opinion" that would renege on a 174-year-old commitment to the tribe. The newspaper supported the restoration legislation.[2] So did the president of the Citizens State Bank in nearby Woodville, the Tyler County Chamber of Commerce, Polk and Tyler County Courts, the Deep East Texas Council of Governments, and Liberty County judge Dempsie Henley, who had been the first chairman of the Texas Indian Commission.[3] The commission adopted a resolution stating it did not oppose federal status for the tribe if that would ensure its future good and welfare.

After 1954, when the federal government handed off responsibility for the poor and isolated tribe to the state, the state allowed the tribe to lease mineral rights on the reservation. Money from the oil and gas and from the tribe's timber paid for economic development and various health and benefit programs. The state paid for administrators although the amounts appropriated varied widely from year to year.[4] The attorney general's 1983 opinion subjected the tribal mineral revenues to the Texas severance tax, drastically reducing the amount of money available for tribal programs. In 1986 the Texas Legislature allocated money from the tribe's mineral fund, instead of state funds, to pay the salaries of state managers on the reservation and other administrative costs. Then the state controller froze the assets in the mineral fund, depriving the tribe of access to its own money. Attorney Tom Diamond, in a statement to the Senate Select Committee on Indian Affairs supporting Alabama-Coushetta restoration, called the state action "a cruel and callous joke."[5]

Morris Bullard, the tribal chairman, told the House Subcommittee on Indian Affairs, "Without legislation the survival of the tribe is threatened. The reservation won't survive without federal protection." He acknowledged that the ultimate responsibility for the tribe's quality of life lay with the tribe itself. But he said the great threat to tribal survival was the legal issue.[6] Tribal member and attorney Arnold Battise said that even if the tribe won its challenge to the attorney general's ruling, the tribe's long-term security would be no greater.[7]

The state comptroller of public accounts, Bob Bullock, said the state had serious concerns about the possibility the Alabama-Coushattas would bring in high-stakes gambling, but Bullard said gambling was "against our custom and religion."[8] Congress did not pass the restoration act until the following year; President Reagan signed it on August 18, 1987. The act also restored the tiny Ysleta del Sur Pueblo near El Paso, which had been recognized by the federal government only in 1968 and, in the same legislation, terminated from federal trust and turned over to state supervision.[9]

During the period of state trusteeship over the Alabama-Coushattas the tribe developed a thriving tourist destination business to supplement income from the tribe's timberland and revenue from oil and gas leases. The tribal businesses eventually expanded to include a museum, café, gift shop, cabins, and 131 campsites beside a 26-acre artificial lake, grocery store, laundry, a 1,500-seat amphitheater, and a 250-by-150-foot covered pavilion to house its annual powwow and other events. It operated tours of its Big Thicket forest. An estimated 200,000 people visited the reservation each year. At the time the 550-member tribe sought federal restoration, it employed 56 tribal members and had a payroll of $250,000 year. Income had been declining, however, and the tribe was looking for new business ventures along with the health and education benefits federal status would bring. Under state jurisdiction there were no health facilities on the reservation, and health problems were severe. Forty percent of tribal members had high blood pressure, 70 percent had poor eyesight, and 44 percent had diabetes. Unemployment had ranged from 34 percent to 65 percent. However, after he outlined many of the problems the tribe faced, Bullard added, "Our problems are not insurmountable . . . [the reservation] is a beautiful and stable environment to raise kids."[10]

After being restored in 1987 the tribe contracted with the Indian Health Service for medical care and built a 3,300-square-foot health clinic, which later was expanded. With a staff of fourteen, the clinic's services included diabetes prevention and care, safety, community health, outpatient medical and surgical care, and eye care. Much of the tribal administration was housed in a $1.7-million building constructed after restoration. A number of tribal members lived in brick homes built on the reservation beginning in the 1970s under federal housing programs. In 1997 the tribe added a solid waste facility to its enterprises. Its education programs ranged from Head Start to assisting tribal members in obtaining college scholarships. A big part of the education program was teaching the Alabama-Coushatta language and the weaving of the tribe's traditional pine needle baskets. The tribe emphasized its services to children and to elders. For children and teenagers there was financial aid to families in need, summer employment, and protective services. For elders, there was a free lunch every day and a nutrition program, assistance with home repairs, and transportation into nearby towns. The tribe helped its members attend vocational schools and get job training, and it financed on-the-job training and work experience.[11]

In spite of the progress the tribe's income did not cover its needs. Forty-six percent of Alabama-Coushatta tribal members available for work did not have full-time jobs. Only one percent of the members on the reservation had college degrees. Of the 513 reservation residents, 147 were diabetic.[12] Despite Bullard's 1986 statement rejecting gambling, the tribe later opened a casino in its search for additional revenue. However, Texas attorney general (later U.S. senator) John Cornyn ordered the tribal casino closed in 2002 after just nine months of operation on grounds it violated Texas limitations on gambling.[13] The closure was later linked to a complicated scheme by Jack Abramoff, a "super lobbyist" who pleaded guilty to breaking several laws in connection with his representation of Indian tribes and involving campaign donations. The Alabama-Coushatta Tribe had been persuaded to donate $50,000 to a charity operated by Abramoff. At the same time, however, Abramoff was working for the Coushatta Tribe and its casino in Alabama in an effort to close the competing Alabama-Coushatta casino in Texas. A series of e-mails made public in 2005 linked Abramoff to Cornyn's closure of Texas Indian casinos.[14]

Closure of its casino shut off the Alabama-Coushatta Tribe's source of economic development funds and jobs. In an area where few new jobs had been created in decades, the casino added 495 jobs and paid workers $4.3 million in its short life. It employed 87 tribal members, half of whom had been on public assistance. Tribal unemployment dropped from 46 percent to 14 percent, then rose again after the closure. Without investment money, business development was stifled, and funding for tribal programs shrank. "The Alabama-Coushatta Tribe does not want a handout," it proudly proclaimed. "It just wants the opportunity to pursue economic development projects. . . . We want a better life for ourselves and our children. We want to be self sufficient."[15]

Where the Alabama-Coushatta Tribe was spurred by state legal action to seek federal restoration of its federal status, California tribes took a different route: they sued the government and won. They were inspired to act by their increasing poverty, loss of land to taxes, and resentment that the government had not kept the promises it made to win approval of termination. Repairs and improvements to roads, homes, and water systems were not made, leaving the little Indian communities to deteriorate. The tribes also felt the loss of education and health benefits.

Tillie Hardwick, a Pinoleville Pomo Indian woman, gave up on the promises. She reasoned that since termination was conditional on the improvements, and the improvements had not been made, the termination was not valid. Attorneys of the Native American Rights Fund agreed to take that argument to court. They collected five other plaintiffs and in 1979 filed suit. More rancherias and individuals joined the suit. The government finally realized it could not justify the legality of the terminations when it had not carried out its side of the bargain. In 1983 the tribes and government reached agreement on a stipulated order that restored federal recognition to seventeen of the terminated rancherias, mostly in northern California.[16]

At least ten other tribes later won restoration through legislation, administrative recognition, and lawsuits stretching into the 1990s, three decades after termination. The tribes' status varied. Some restored tribes had managed to hang onto property through the termination period. Some had property returned. Some later purchased property. Some remained landless. Some struggled to acquire land and an economic base. Others prospered.

One of the seventeen Tillie Hardwick winners was Big Valley Rancheria at Lakeport in Lake County, a Pomo band as is Tillie Hardwick's Pinoleville Rancheria. Keith Pike, Big Valley's business manager and a member of the neighboring Guideville Tribe, pointed with considerable pride to Big Valley's accomplishments since 1983. By using federal grants "as a way of starting other things," Big Valley prospered. Its casino at nearby Clear Lake provided the money to buy property and build both homes and businesses. With 230 acres purchased by 2002, the band had built a twenty-eight-unit tribal subdivision with fifty additional homes under construction. It also had built a marina, amphitheater, hotel, RV park, and convenience store. Pike described the area as "a premier resort area outside San Francisco and in the wine country." Clear Lake served as a site for marine sports. Gaming "is the big cash cow," Pike said. He wanted to develop other business—possibly in telecommunications, in energy development, or a call center or bill-processing center. Only 130 of the tribe's nearly 1,000 members lived at Lakeport, but Pike said many wanted to come back if there were jobs. He also hoped to see the band build its own school and community college and expand its health care consortium into a clinic with full medical services for all tribal members. Eighty percent of the tribe's workforce, including the casino and construction, were non-Indians. In 2002 the band paid $500,000 to Lake County and contributed additional sums to local charities.[17]

Another Tillie Hardwick tribe, Blue Lake Rancheria, also donated to its local community. When a reduction in state funding left the Blue Lake Union School District without enough resources for a full program, the rancheria donated $50,000. It awarded scholarships both to high school graduates for college and to teachers to further their education.[18]

Other tribes had longer roads back after termination. Cheryl Seidner, chairwoman of the Table Bluff Rancheria of the Wiyott Tribe located near Loleta, California, described her community's journey. "It took twenty years," she recalled. When the tribe was terminated, she was eight years old. Her father, William "Bill" Seidner, was chairman. He gathered his people on the twenty acres of Indian-owned land near Loleta for a meeting with the government agents. The government offered to give tribal members deeds to the land they occupied. First, the agents said, they would bring the houses up to code. They would build a safe water supply. They would construct a sewer system. The people signed the documents and received the deeds to their land. The government went away. "They never did any of it," Cheryl Seidner said. "That's how we beat them in court." Tribal members began gathering information to support their bid for restoration in 1972, took their case to California Legal Services, and finally won restoration of federal recognition and reservation land in court rulings in 1981 and 1991.

Seidner's father died in a logging accident in 1966 before the effort toward restoration began. Cheryl Seidner left Loleta to attend Heald College in San Francisco and graduated from its business school. She was working for the college when her mother became ill and told her it was time to come home. To emphasize her point she kept sending Seidner and her sisters notices of job openings in the tribal area. Seidner and her sister Leona Wilkinson, an artist and later a Tribal Council member, went back. Seidner worked in the Education Opportunities Project at Humboldt State College, a twenty-minute drive from Loleta, as well as serving as tribal chairwoman. Her name is on the lawsuit that restored the tribe. "They wanted an elder, a working person, a middle-aged person, a young person—that was me," Seidner said.

Restoration brought the tribe some property, steps toward revitalizing tribal culture, and establishment of new traditions. The tribe purchased 88 acres sixteen miles south of Eureka, where a hundred tribal members lived in thirty-five homes. The tribe hoped to add half a dozen more homes, and "it may be time for multifamily housing." There also was a community center on the land. The property was not in trust; the tribe paid taxes on it. Tribal membership grew from 250 to more than 550.

The eighteen-person tribal payroll included six tribal members, ten Indians from other tribes, and two non-Indians. The tribe's major effort involved 275-acre Indian Island just off the coast near Loleta, the site of an 1860 massacre that killed most of the tribal members. The city of Eureka owned 90 percent of the island in trust for the state of California. The tribe, with the help of people all over the United States, raised $106,000 to buy one and a half acres of the 10 percent in private hands and was attempting to raise $90,000 to buy eight-tenths of an acre. The tribal piece of land was a boat repair facility; the tribe obtained a grant of $100,000 to clean it up, working with Humboldt Water Resources.[19] "Someday we hope to return it to the place where we can have a dance house," said Wilkinson, who headed the tribal restoration effort. The island, covered with shrubs, berms, dikes, and pasture, also was the base for a yacht club. Non-Indians planted trees on the naturally treeless island. "We'd like to restore the island to precontact stage," Wilkinson said, "but not cut down all the trees. Things change and evolve. People have to change too. We try to make things better."[20]

The tribe also tried to work with the community and found that the community reciprocated. In 1991, when the tribe held its first February candlelight vigil to memorialize victims of the 1860 massacre, about seventy-five to eighty people attended. The second year there were a hundred, the third year two hundred to three hundred, and the number continued to grow. The ceremony included tribal, Christian, and Jewish prayers followed by a community potluck. "We are looking to sing and dance on the island again," Seidner said. The tribe began looking at economic development, and at least some of its leaders resisted the idea of a casino as an economic base.

Scotts Valley, another Pomo band at Lakeport, also won its own way to restoration with legal action. It turned its restored status into jobs, health care, education, and culture. With other bands the Scotts Valley people were working on a Pomo Health Care Center to serve all the rancherias in that northern California area. Members also revived the "big head" dances, and tribal member Elsie Allen was teaching basket weaving. Allen was one of a handful of Pomo women, inspired by Tillie Hardwick and other court actions, who saved the last good source of wooly sedge, the material used in weaving Pomo baskets. The only remaining place where the sedge was readily accessible in 1979 was about to be flooded by the backwater of the Corps of Engineers' Warm Springs Dam. The women did not try to halt the dam construction; they asked only that they be allowed to transplant enough of the sedge to a safe location so they could continue their ancient art and pass it on to future generations. The Corps was slow to respond. Not until 1983, when the Hardwick case was close to conclusion, did the corps offer some money for the transplanting and some assistance in finding a suitable location where the women could plant enough sedges to provide a permanent supply. A non-Indian woman donated land along a stream, and the Ya-Ka-Ma Pomo Learning Center, housed in an abandoned CIA base, added a native plants nursery to its site.[21] Scotts Valley Chairman Don Arnold, a retired train driver for Bay Area Rapid Transit (BART), said he wanted his grandchildren to learn the art of basket weaving. "It's one reason I'm back in [tribal] politics," he said.[22]

Other restored rancherias struggled with trying to obtain land, develop enterprises to sustain a tribal economy, and provide their members, especially the young and elders, with health care, education, and housing.

16 Catawbas and Poncas

Last

Like the California rancherias, the Catawba Indian Nation of South Carolina used the courts as an avenue back to federal recognition. After trying for nearly two centuries to settle the tribe's land claim through negotiations, the Catawbas filed lawsuits. The Indians' challenge to land titles held by more than sixty thousand people finally got the government's attention.

The tribe had reorganized itself in 1973, forming a nonprofit corporation. Although the federal government no longer recognized the tribe's existence, the Catawbas went to the Bureau of Indian Affairs in 1977 for help in pursuing their claim for compensation for the land they were promised but never received. The Interior Department's solicitor general felt the tribe had a strong case, but Attorney General Griffin Bell barred the government from assisting the Indians on grounds the current occupants of the contested land were innocent of wrongdoing. It was the government's responsibility to settle the land claim, not file a suit, Bell said. The government did nothing. Meanwhile, the tribe and the state of South Carolina began negotiating a possible settlement. When the negotiations failed to bring agreement, the state established a commission to investigate the claim and make recommendations to the legislature. The commission included landowners but no Indians. Congressman Ken Holland (D-SC) introduced legislation in 1979 that he hoped would restart settlement efforts, but his plan did not have support of the tribe, the state, or the federal administration.

So in 1980 the Catawba Nation filed suit in the U.S. District Court for South Carolina disputing ownership of the 140,000 acres the Catawbas had been promised but had neither received nor been paid for. Six years later, the Supreme Court ruled that the act terminating the Catawba's relationship to the federal government made the tribe subject to the South Carolina statute of limitations. Justice Harry Blackmun dissented, rejecting arguments that the claim was not valid because the Catawba people had assimilated and dispersed. "The demands of justice do not cease simply because wronged people grow less distinctive," he wrote. Two later rulings held that part of the Catawbas' legal action was subject to the limitation and part was not. The legal action threw a cloud over land titles in the area—mostly in the rapidly developing suburbs just across the state line from Charlotte, North Carolina.

In 1990 the Native American Rights Fund took up the Catawba case, filing two lawsuits. One challenged ownership of the 140,000 acres promised the Catawbas. It named as defendants seventy-six corporations and individuals, including the district's congressman, Democrat John M. Spratt Jr., as representatives of the thousands of landowners. The other case, in the U.S. Court of Claims, sought monetary damages from the government for failure to protect the tribal interest in the land. After the federal court refused to certify the case as a class action, the tribe prepared to serve all 61,767 individual landowners as defendants and stored the summonses in a Falls Church, Virginia, warehouse. These legal actions finally prodded the state and federal governments into serious negotiations with the tribe. Three years later they had reached agreement that the tribal members approved February 20, 1993. The state legislature approved the agreement in June, and Congress took up the measure in July.[1]

There some opposition to provisions of the settlement surfaced. Representative Craig Thomas (R-WY) objected to the federal payment portion of the settlement, arguing that the state should pay more.[2] Representative Bill Richardson (D-NM), chairman of the House Subcommittee on Indian Affairs (and later governor of New Mexico), questioned the "waiver of many sovereign rights of the Catawba" in the portion of the settlement restoring the tribe's federal status. He said the committee needed to understand the reasons behind granting so much civil regulation and civil and criminal jurisdiction to the state.[3] E. Fred Sanders, assistant chief of the Catawbas, also raised the sovereignty issue in a letter to Representative George Miller (D-CA), chairman of the House Natural Resources Committee, complaining that the settlement "deprives the Catawba of sovereign rights." In his written testimony Sanders said the settlement had few advantages for the Catawbas. "As written it will destroy the Catawba's future as an Indian nation," he said.[4]

Chief Gilbert Blue testified, however, that the settlement would "provide economic and government tools with which we can fashion a proud and self-reliant future in partnership with our non-Indian neighbors." He described the issues of jurisdiction as "a product of a consensual, necessary settlement." He said the agreement to allow the state civil and criminal jurisdiction, except for minor offenses involving tribal members, was "the best we can get from the state." He added, "We never had our own courts. Courts would be too much of a burden for our small government."[5]

State senator Robert W. Hayes Jr. told the subcommittee the settlement was necessary for the state's economic development, especially in the northern section. The House committee report on the settlement bill stated, "The pendency of these suits poses a substantial economic and social hardship for large numbers of landowners, citizens and communities in South Carolina, including the tribe . . . continuing this expensive controversy would impair long term economic planning and development for all."[6] Congress added its approval to the agreement, and the Catawba Nation was restored to federal status on October 27, 1993.

The Catawba Indians got $50 million for the 144,000 acres they had been promised in the 1800s. Most of the money went into four trust funds, for land acquisition, economic development, education, and social services and aid for the elderly. The agreement ended the Indians' claims to other land and also extinguished their hunting and fishing rights, water rights, and claims to other natural resources on that land. It did provide tribal members with free hunting and fishing licenses but subjected them to state regulations. It also subjected the tribe to the state gambling law, rather than the more lenient federal Indian Gaming Regulatory Act, but allowed the Catawbas to operate two high-stakes bingo parlors. The land acquisition trust allowed the tribe to buy up to 3,000 acres to add to the 600 it had held through treaty revisions, attempts to move them out of South Carolina, termination, and hard economic times.[7]

During his congressional testimony Blue held up sample pages from the sixteen-inch-thick lawsuit, which he said contained 1.4 million pages. "It is our hope we can soon recycle them," he said.[8] The Catawba Indian Nation never sent out the 61,767 summons stored in Falls Church.

Two issues remained unresolved in the legislation: Catawba potters' access to the beds of special clay required for their unique ceramics and South Carolina's commitment to protecting Indian rights, given the state's unique jurisdiction over the tribe. In a paper prepared for the House subcommittee, Thomas J. Blumer, a Library of Congress historian, noted some troubling incidents and argued that the tribe needed more jurisdiction over its activities. He said the state had held up federal funds for Indian education, and the owner of the clay fields had sought to limit access to those tribal potters who supported a cash-only settlement of the land claim.

In 1990, Blumer said, a local group marching in the annual Spring Hill community parade near the Catawba Reservation portrayed Indians in trash cans, indicating the Indians should be discarded. "To the Catawba that was devastating," he said. Despite protests, there was no apology.[9]

The tribal potters, however, retained access to the clay and did well. About 50 tribal members created and sold the traditional pottery, and an additional 150 tribal members dug the clay and fired the art work. The tribe was attempting to ensure that the art remained alive by teaching the techniques to children in reservation classes. Artists sold much of their work through the craft store operated by the Catawba Cultural Preservation Project, a volunteer nonprofit corporation established before the tribe won federal re-recognition. In addition to working with the potters, the preservation project developed programs to preserve and teach the Catawba language, maintain tribal archives, and work with archeologists studying the tribal homelands.[10]

After restoration the 2,200-member Catawba Nation moved to improve its living conditions and its environment. An ambitious residential/commercial development at Rock Hill, half an hour's drive south of Charlotte, was about one-third completed in late 2006. The development occupied 35 acres of the 300-acre property and included single-family homes, assisted living, and a foster home. It also included retail stores, craft teaching and sales units, a business incubator, a farm, and "learning centers." Designed by Village Habitat Design of Atlanta, the development included a ceremonial area, easy pedestrian routes from homes to commercial areas, and a veterans' park. The entire project was designed to protect water quality and be ecologically sustainable.[11]

The tribe also had agreements with two federal agencies for environmental and wildlife protection. The 2004 pact with the Environmental Protection Agency included monitoring drinking water quality, both indoor and outdoor air quality, and solid waste management. Tribal representatives served on local, state, and national environmental and public health councils.[12] Several agreements with the U.S. Fish and Wildlife Service provided grants to the tribe to develop a natural resources management plan, acquire wildlife habitat, and restore and enhance plant and wildlife environment.[13]

A high-stakes bingo hall in Rock Hill—one of just three "casinos" in South Carolina—furnished much of the money for tribal administration and programs. When South Carolina established a state lottery in 2001, the tribe's bingo income dropped sharply, and tribal leaders asked the state for permission to build a second bingo hall in Santee, as authorized in the law that restored the Catawbas' federal recognition. The state balked, and the issue became a long-running controversy still unsettled in late 2006.[14]

The Ponca Tribe of Nebraska also faced opposition in its efforts to reclaim land. The Poncas made three failed attempts to win restoration of its federal status before a fourth effort succeeded in 1990. Even then, the tribe had to give up the right to a reservation in exchange for recognition, federal programs, and land for uses other than tribal homes. Fred LeRoy, who was chairman of the tribe's restoration committee and the first elected chairman after restoration, said the issue of tribal identity was the most important factor in seeking re-recognition for the tribe. "The only reason I got into it . . . my daughter—she's 28 now; she was 8 or 9—asked me how come there was nothing in the history books about the Poncas. 'Weren't we the first people here?' In 1987 I wasn't working and decided why not try to get us restored. We asked the people if they wanted it. . . . There were two against and 250 to 300 for it." In the postcard survey tribal members listed their identity as Indians as the most important reason for restoration.[15]

The tribe had already reorganized into a nonprofit corporation in 1971 to seek restoration and to maintain its traditions.[16] It obtained a grant from the federal Administration for Native Americans and gathered widespread support from community organizations and institutions. The Nebraska Legislature recognized the tribe in 1988 and supported the federal recognition—but without a residential reservation. The three federally recognized tribes in Nebraska and the Southern Ponca Tribe in Oklahoma also supported the Northern Ponca restoration.[17] Nebraska's two senators, James Exon and Robert Kerrey, both Democrats, introduced the Ponca restoration measure in the Senate, but the tribe had difficulty finding a House sponsor. LeRoy said one House member, whom he did not name, told the tribe in 1987 he would never allow it to be restored.[18] In 1989 the House member from the district containing the Poncas' home territory opposed restoration, fearing the tribe would develop a reservation.[19] Kerrey, in a statement to the Senate Select Committee on Indian Affairs in 1990, said the Poncas' request for restoration was "a just claim." He added, however, "Conditions have changed in their former home. A residential reservation is not feasible."[20] Michael Mason, the Oregon attorney who represented the Ponca Tribe, said tribal restoration without a reservation is incomplete. It is "nice for the individual but doesn't help rebuild the tribe," he said. He called reservation land necessary in the same way self-sufficiency is necessary.[21] Nevertheless, language was added to the restoration bill specifically prohibiting the Poncas from acquiring a residential reservation. The measure, restoring the tribe as the Ponca Tribe of Nebraska, won congressional approval, and President George H. W. Bush signed it October 31, 1990.[22]

After termination, tribal members had scattered, many into cities of Nebraska and elsewhere. However, LeRoy told the Senate committee that "an identifiable community still lives on tribal lands" along the Niobrara River in northeastern Nebraska. He said the tribal members continued widespread use of the native language, customs, and culture.[23] Gloria Chytka, a Ponca living on the Yankton Sioux Reservation in South Dakota, testified, "It will be a slow rewarding experience to bring back to all the Northern Poncas a chance to know their language, crafts, ceremonies, spiritual ways and other cultural ways."[24]

The restoration act allowed the secretary of the interior to place up to 1,500 acres of land in Nebraska's Knox and Boyd counties in trust for the tribes. It allowed tribal members to receive the same services as other Indian tribes and established a service area covering five counties in Nebraska and one in South Dakota, later expanded to nine more counties, including two in Iowa. As did other restoration acts, the Ponca law called for the tribe to create an economic development plan.[25]

The tribe struggled after restoration, but by August 2002 LeRoy was able to say, "We're doing pretty well." By then, the tribe had acquired a little more than eight hundred acres of land in the area around Niobrara. It was operating medical, social service, and housing programs.[26]

The tribe chartered Ponca Economic Development Corporation as a separate entity to oversee all the tribal economic activities. The U.S. Department of Housing and Urban Development granted the tribe $4.5 million for economic projects, and the casino-rich Shakopee Mdewakanton Sioux Community provided $1 million grants for development in 2004, 2005, and 2006. The Poncas became one of fifty-one tribes in the InterTribal Bison Cooperative. The tribal business, Ponca Tribe of Nebraska's Buffalo Programs, operated a tanning facility doing custom tanning of buffalo hides. The business tanned hides brought to it by customers and sold already-tanned hides. In a thwarted business venture, the tribe offered to provide a site for low-level radioactive waste for a regional compact of states. That offer was rejected, but tribal chairman Mark Peniska said the tribe retained an interest in developing a low-level repository. The tribe was developing an industrial park. Nebraska tourism guides listed several Ponca-related sites, but the tribe had not created tourist facilities to serve visitors.[27]

Natural resources and social services drew much of the tribe's development efforts after restoration. As a part of the National Fire Plan, the tribe revived one of its original tools for resource management: fire. In the fall of 2005 the tribe burned 160 acres of its buffalo pasture. Monitors said the burn was successful, and more burns were planned to control exotic plant species that had been supplanting native species. Tribal managers said the change in vegetation was damaging the buffalo herd. The tribe also became a partner in the Nebraska Natural Legacy Project aimed at conserving wildlife. Under that project, the Nebraska Game and Parks Department awarded grants to dozens of organization for work to halt the decline of the more than five hundred endangered, threatened, or declining species of plants and animals in Nebraska.[28]

The tribal housing authority, created in January 1993, owned 120 units worth $12 million by October 2001. The units in Omaha, Lincoln, Niobrara, and Norfolk provided low-rent housing, open to the community as well as to tribal members. The housing authority also helped families make down payments to buy homes. With a fourteen-member staff, the authority managed rentals and other programs, maintained its buildings, and counseled renters and home buyers on housing issues.[29]

The tribe had a medical clinic, open to members of all tribes, in Omaha, home to the largest number of Ponca tribal members. The Ponca Tribe also conducted mental health and substance abuse programs throughout its service area and twice won U.S. Department of Justice grants for a project to combat violence against women. The project included services to victims of violence, documentation of the extent of domestic violence against Ponca women, prevention, law enforcement, and a crisis line.[30]

A priority project for the 1,300-member tribe after it won re-recognition was restoration of the Ponca Agency Building southwest of Niobrara. The building had been used for cultural and social events before termination but stood vacant from 1962 until the tribe acquired the building and site in 1993. It was in a state of such disrepair that it was unusable. In 1999 the tribe obtained an Indian Community Block Grant to restore the exterior of the building. When that was completed the tribe used a loan and grant from the Department of Agriculture's Rural Development Agency to renovate the interior. With the work finished in January 2003, the building was once more in use as a cultural center.[31] Eight months after the work was finished the building served as a backdrop when Mormon Church officials presented the tribe with a wooden plaque thanking the Ponca people for rescuing four hundred Mormons in the winter of 1846–47 by inviting the stranded church members to share the tribe's winter quarters. The ceremony was part of the annual powwow, symbolizing the Northern Poncas' ties to their past and continuing connection to their culture.[32]

Epilogue: The Results

The accounts of termination and its lingering impact on Indian Country leave one nagging question: What were Congress and the federal administration thinking?

There appear to be three answers: 1. Saving money; 2. Getting rid of the Indians as Indians once and for all; 3. They weren't. While that last answer may seem flippant, a study of the records indicates that the policy was largely decided, and then reasons were developed to support it. Some members of Congress talked about freedom and equality for the Indians, but the arguments nearly always went back to the cost of Indian programs to the federal government and the exemption of Indian trust land from state and county taxes. The push came from a small number of members; most in Congress took little interest in Indians and their problems.

It is tempting to place the bulk of the blame on Senator Arthur V. Watkins. While it is true he was the driving force behind most of the termination bills passed in the 1950s, he was building on policies and attitudes that were widely accepted in the United States in the late 1940s and 1950s. In a 1969 report to President Richard M. Nixon, historian Alvin M. Josephy Jr. succinctly outlined the two American impulses that were the basis of the long-term federal policy of assimilation of Indians into the American mainstream. Put simply, the first impulse was a desire to acquire Indian land, and the second was a feeling of moral obligation to give Indians the benefit of a "superior" culture.[1]

There was plenty of evidence—had anyone bothered to study the situations—that even the most successful tribes were not in positions to survive with an abrupt lifting of protected status. Most of the contemporary studies, however, were done after termination bills had become law and were focused on making termination work, not discovering whether termination was feasible. Concerns by the state of Wisconsin in the case of the Menominees and of the Bureau of Indian Affairs in the case of the Klamaths resulted only in delay or minor adjustments in the process of termination; they did not stop either the termination of those tribes or the targeting of more tribes for termination. In the Klamath case there was more concern for the future of the Klamath forest than of the Klamath people. The Indian "consent" promised to terminated tribes was illusory. As Josephy said, the promises to consult with the Indians were never kept. "Instead," he wrote, "threats to freeze tribal money, promises of extra concessions and lies that termination was inevitable with or without consent were among the forms of coercion used to secure a show of consent for the record. Just as often, no consent was even sought. Distance, time pressure, ignorance, and lack of technical assistance precluded any meaningful expression of Indian opposition."[2]

Some tribes targeted for termination managed to escape the process, some by political support, some through their own efforts, and some because members of Congress realized their termination would be a mistake. The Osage Tribe, as mentioned earlier, lined up the entire Oklahoma congressional delegation in support of leaving the tribe alone. The Colville and Yakama tribes in Washington State voted against termination and made their own case. A committee considering the Seminole Tribe in Florida looked at the poor, mostly illiterate tribe and realized termination would be wrong.[3]

Studies prior to the termination era, chiefly the Meriam Report of 1928 and the Hoover Commission Report of 1949, focused on efficiency of government operations, not on what would work best for tribal people. Hoover's report, however, did specify that programs for Indians should be withdrawn over an extended period of time. Neither the Hoover Commission nor various congressional studies considered what the tribes saw as the best policies for their future. In fact, the premise—never seriously questioned—was that Indians should be absorbed into the great melting pot as tribal organizations melted away and individual Indians gave up their tribal ties. As just another in the series of policies dating to colonial times aimed at getting rid of the Indians, termination would prove to be short-lived. Even before the termination process had been completed for the Klamath and Menominee tribes, doubts were being raised in both the administration and Congress. By the mid-1960s the policy was quietly abandoned although not formally repealed. In 1965 the BIA, without legislative direction, shifted its emphasis from termination to community and economic development for tribes that had retained federal recognition. Still, nobody was consulting the Indians although during the 1960s Indians were forming multitribal organizations and task forces and trying to make their voices heard.

Josephy pointed out in his report to President Nixon, "There is no doubt that many of the failures and frustrations that mark the course of federal-Indian relations, past and present, can be ascribed to deficiencies of knowledge about Indians among non-Indians who are involved in managing Indian affairs." Many programs bore no relation to tribal realities, he said, and he noted that the Peace Corps trained its people in the background and culture of the people with whom they were going to work, but the Bureau of Indian Affairs did not. He warned that any new policy would be seen by Indians in the context of history that may be unknown to non-Indian officials but

that is "still intimate and potent in Indian thinking and response."
To Indians, he said, the present is a continuation of an unbroken
narrative of policies, programs, and promises. Josephy added that
the Indian "will color his reaction to a proposal with the evergreen
memories of battles won or lost, of injuries and injustices, of land
taken from his people by fraud, deceit and corruption, of lost hunting, fishing and water rights, and of zigzag policies of administra-
tions that came to office, just like the new one, and then left."[4]

The first steps toward an Indian policy that finally allowed
Indians to plan their own future came from the Office of Economic Opportunity (OEO), one of President Lyndon Johnson's Great
Society programs to combat poverty. OEO allocated money to tribes
and allowed them to design their own programs, just as it did other
communities throughout the country. The terminated tribes generally missed out on this breakthrough, which occurred in the late
1960s after most of the terminations had taken place and before
any restorations. However, some that had maintained an organization did get grants for such programs as alcohol treatment. In
1975 Congress formalized the BIA's change in emphasis to development with the Indian Self-Determination and Education Assistance Act. That law gave tribes the power to contract with the BIA
to provide and manage services themselves. It was passed just as
terminated tribes were beginning to fight their way back to federal
recognition. Later, the self-governance program would give tribes
even more autonomy and flexibility in managing their programs.
Some of the restored tribes were among the first to embrace self-
governance. The Siletz tribe of Oregon was one of the initial twenty-nine tribes in the program, which gave each tribe authority to
manage its share of federal money allocated for various Indian programs. Other restored tribes, such as the Grand Rondes, continued
to contract with the BIA but increasingly took over management of
programs and services.

Josephy said in a 2003 interview that as these governmental shifts were taking place, three events triggered the movement for restoration of the terminated tribes: the takeover of Alcatraz Island in San Francisco Bay by an intertribal group of Indians in 1969, the Indian takeover of the Interior Building in Washington DC at the end of the Trail of Broken Treaties march in 1972, and the deadly standoff between federal agents and members of the American Indian Movement at Wounded Knee on the Sioux Reservation in 1973. "Wounded Knee changed the attitude of the Indian people," Josephy said. "It encouraged a feeling that 'you, too, can win. Stand up and fight.'"[5]

Other historians cite additional key events: the American Indian Chicago Conference of 1961, the Menominee victory in the U.S. Supreme Court in 1968 upholding the tribe's continued fishing and hunting rights, and the return of Blue Lake to the Taos Pueblo in New Mexico in 1970.[6]

Led by the Menominees, who had retained their tribal land and identity, tribes began winning restoration of federal status. They faced numerous and varied obstacles, including a scattering of their members, considerable social disintegration, and in some cases initial opposition from non-Indian neighbors. Despite their two to three decades without traditional organization and the economic and social problems they had faced, the tribes still had some effective leaders. Or perhaps the leaders developed better without the federal umbrella. Senator James Abourezk of South Dakota commented caustically during an American Indian Policy Review Commission hearing: "One thing BIA has done over the years has been to make an effort to destroy whatever Indian leadership has emerged."[7] For the restoration battle, numerous strong leaders emerged, many of them women: Ada Deer for the Menominees, Sue Shaffer for the Cow Creeks, Kathryn Harrison for the Grand Rondes, Dee Pigsley for the Siletz.

By 1976, Task Force 10 (Terminated Indians) of the American Indian Policy Review Commission reported that all of the terminated tribes except the Mixed-Blood Utes wanted to be restored. (That judgment about the Utes was challenged by later events.) At the same time, Hank Adams, chairman of Task Force 1 (Trust Responsibility) said, "We think it is possible to eliminate the whole crippling stigma or effect of termination in any one of its forms by a firm national commitment to permanency for the Indian societal life in the United States."[8]

As the march toward restoration became more routine, attorneys at the Native American Project of Oregon Legal Services, which helped Oregon tribes win re-recognition, identified four stages of the process. One attorney, Michael Mason, later in private law practice, identified the stages as the following: 1) the tribe becomes convinced it is a tribe and convinces its neighbors it is a tribe; 2) the tribe organizes support to get congressional approval of an act recognizing its legal status as an organization; 3) the tribe begins rebuilding its government; 4) the tribe gets services, a land base, and economic self-sufficiency. Mason mentioned one other element important to tribal restoration—a champion in Congress. For the Oregon tribes the champions were Republican senator Mark Hatfield and, for those in his district, Democratic representative Les AuCoin.[9] The first three steps were taken with increasing ease by each restored tribe, although issues of fishing and hunting rights and occasionally land ownership brought heated opposition in some areas. LeaAnn Easton, director of the Native American Project of Oregon Legal Services (NAPOLS), said most of the opposition to restoring land to tribes stemmed from fear that the public would be closed out of recreation and hunting and fishing in forests transferred out of public ownership.[10] Mason said environmentalists also opposed the transfer of forest land to tribes because they feared the Indians would manage the land badly, despite a generally good tribal record of forest management.[11] The land issue was especially difficult for the Klamath Tribes, who were still fighting for return of at least some of the tribal forest twenty years after restoration, and for the Poncas, who were forced to give up efforts to acquire a residential reservation in order to win restoration. Both tribes, however, acquired land for economic uses.

Economic development was a serious problem, and some tribes continued to struggle toward self sufficiency. Most of the restored tribes opened casinos. Their success ranged from the eye-popping income of the Grand Rondes' Spirit Mountain Casino and Resort, which became the number one visitor destination in Oregon, to the late-starting small casino of the Coos Tribe on the southern Oregon Coast and the modest Klamath casino on Highway 97 in sparsely populated south central Oregon. Elsewhere casinos also contributed to tribal income but were not a panacea. In many cases the main benefit of the tribal casino was the jobs it provided for both tribal members and non-Indians. Gaming had a huge impact in making tribes equal partners in their communities, according to Edwin Goodman, another former NAPOLS attorney. This was true especially in some Oregon areas where a declining number of jobs in the timber industry coincided with the rise of casino employment.[12] In addition to the added payroll for communities with Indian casinos, the casinos provided a source of funds for community projects, as most gaming tribes distributed some of their profits to community programs such as law enforcement and education.

In California, tribal casinos boomed into two statewide battles and conflicts between tribes as they competed for casino profits. The tribes saw their sovereignty at risk when the National Labor Relations Board ruled in 2004 that it had jurisdiction over labor practices at the casino operated by the San Manuel band of Mission Indians. The band appealed to the U.S. Court of Appeals in Washington DC and, with the backing of other tribes, sought federal legislation that would overturn the ruling. Back in California, the dispute expanded into a fight over expansion of tribal gaming, with some tribes with successful casinos lobbying to prevent other tribes from getting into the gaming business. The legislature refused to approve additional agreements with the tribes.[13]

Many tribal leaders, however, believed that the gambling would not go on forever and looked to the early bonanza to provide capital for more lasting projects as well as funding for housing and other construction, medical insurance and care, and education benefits.

Some effort went toward developing tribal enterprises; other efforts went toward helping individuals open businesses. Oregon's restored tribes gave strong support to the Oregon Native American Business Entrepreneurial Network, which conducted classes on business management and assisted Indian entrepreneurs to develop business plans and obtain financing. Elsewhere the Menominees and tribes in Utah established small business centers to aid tribal entrepreneurs. Tribal governments grew into multimillion-dollar businesses as tribes managed economic development, casinos, housing projects, medical clinics, health insurance, fish and wildlife protection and enhancement, education programs, welfare and old age assistance, courts, and cultural preservation, including museums. Easton called the progress of tribes since restoration, especially the Grand Rondes, "a phenomenon." She said, in the 2002 interview, "It's hard to imagine in the late 1970s and early 1980s when that small group of people got together, meeting in that little shack at the cemetery . . . then to here in less than twenty years."

Easton spoke of meeting a dying Coquille tribal leader as that tribe was struggling for restoration. He knew "it would be important to his children and children's children that they be recognized as Indians," she said. "For others the reason was as simple as 'I want to be able to get my teeth fixed.' Or sometimes hearing. A woman who grew up in poverty had rotting teeth. After her tribe was restored one of the biggest things was getting her teeth fixed. She came in to show me her new dentures. Reasons for wanting restoration ran the gamut. . . . Family and taking care of family were themes. From everyone it really was about trying to maintain and rediscover tribal practices. . . . Whatever the government says about termination, I don't know anyone who didn't suffer economically from termination. I didn't meet anyone who wasn't worse off."

Easton added, "These people were always on the bubble . . . once the government was gone, families collapsed. Another thing that was harmful, the boarding school kids who were taken away at age eight or so and didn't come home until they were adults. . . . A lot came back just at termination time . . . some things they lost. . . . It was more than one or two generations; it was more like a two- or three-generation gap."[14]

Goodman said he would never say anything good about termination, but it did have the effect of pushing tribal people into the greater society. "They made friendships with non-Indians," he said. "They got education."[15] Mason said small tribes that were not terminated did not advance during the termination period. But, he said, western Oregon's tribes "are much better off than they ever thought of being when they were terminated."[16] Others disagreed, such as Charlie Moses, a member of the nonterminated Colville Indian Nation who worked for the BIA in economic development for many years. Moses said the worst thing the terminated tribes lost was education.[17]

Whether the motivation was education or medicine or simply regaining a lost identity, restoration was often the work of a small dedicated core of people, sometimes as few as eight. Once tribes won restoration, more members became involved, Goodman said. Restoration required lobbyists, advocates, fighters. After restoration, tribes needed managers. In several cases tribes had to buy land for such activities as tribal government and housing. Purchases were complicated by quickly raised prices when land owners learned tribes were seeking property, Goodman said. The situation changed as the tribes became prosperous. Many tribes became major political players as well as major employers in their communities.

"Termination was a very dark cloud," Goodman said. It brought a loss of cultural cohesiveness and identity, but it did not change tribal members' relations with outside society. "Racism didn't go away," Goodman said. "Other tribes that were not terminated looked down on them. So they got it from both ends." That gap was in some ways being bridged as never-terminated and once-terminated tribes tied their futures together in cooperative ventures. A prime example was Oklahoma's Inter-Tribal Council in which eight tribes—four never terminated, four restored—joined to manage a variety of businesses and programs. The Ponca Tribe of Nebraska received grants for development from the never-terminated and casino-rich Shakopee Mdewakanton Sioux Community. Goodman believed some tribes had to agree to too many conditions, such as limiting hunting and fishing rights, to win state and local support for restoration. "Those will be harmful in the long run," he said.[18]

As the restored tribes left the trauma of termination behind, younger members took over tribal government, and as economic success replaced the hard times, the tribes faced new challenges. Kathryn Harrison, the retired chairwoman of the Grand Ronde Tribe, said a veteran leader of a tribe restored several years before the Grand Rondes often asked her, "Are you fighting yet?" When Harrison said no, he would say, "Wait till you get the money. You'll start arguing."[19] Although tribes traditionally keep their internal battles within their own societies, there were indications Harrison's friend was right about more than one tribe. Mounting incomes led to squabbles between tribal members who wanted profits to go largely into per capita payments and those who wanted all or most of the money invested in tribal enterprises and programs. Some tribes saw internal power struggles over tribal government as jealousy arose and factions formed. The most open conflict occurred in California where a baker's dozen tribes, not all of them once-terminated tribes, were embroiled in conflict over "disenrollment" of some members. Circumstances differed, but an organization formed to contest the "disenrollments"—American Indian Rights and Resources Organization—contended the actions occurred after tribes began to see income from tribal casinos.[20]

For tribes the challenge seemed to be whether they could grow rich and still retain the values that held them together during the wilderness of the termination years—the concern for elders and the young, the yearning for community, the need for health care, and above all preserving and continuing their rich culture.

In the meantime the effects of restoration could be seen in a visit to the library of the College of the Menominee Nation, a light-filled room with quiet Indian students working at tables stacked high with books, taking the first step of a higher education. Or at the Grand Ronde Tribe's weekday elders luncheon where the room was filled with friendly chatter and the odor of a hearty casserole. This lunch was free for the tribal elders (there was a nominal charge for outsiders). The diners waved to new arrivals, greeted each other with hugs and smiles, exchanged gossip and memories, showed pictures of grandchildren and bragged about their success in school, in sports, in tribal crafts. This is Indian Country. These are restored tribes.

Appendix: Terminated Tribes and Restorations

Tribe	Term passed	Effective	Restored
Menominee (WI)	1954	1961	1973
Klamath (OR)	1954	1961	1986
Remaining members		1974	
Western Oregon[1]	1954	1956	
Siletz			1977
Cow Creek			1982
Grand Ronde			1983
Coos, Lower Umpqua, and Siuslaw			1984
Coquille			1989
Alabama-Coushatta (TX)	1954	1955	1987
Mixed-Blood Ute (UT)	1954	1961	
Utah Paiute bands	1954	1957	1980
Oklahoma tribes[2]	1956	1959	1978
California			
Lower Lake Rancheria	1956[3]	1956	2000
Coyote Valley Rancheria	1957	1957	1976
30 plus Rancherias	1958	1961[4]	
17 Tillie Hardwick			1983[5]
Catawba (SC)	1959	1962	1993
Ponca of Nebraska	1962	1966	1990

NOTES

1. The Western Oregon Termination Act lists sixty tribes; two of those were confederations, which included some tribes also named separately. The restored Grand Ronde and Siletz confederations each claim twenty-seven tribes or bands with some overlapping. The Coos confederation combined three tribes. The Coquille confederation includes the Upper and Lower Coquilles, which were named separately at termination. No tribes listed in 1953 were known to be seeking restoration in 2006.

2. The Modoc tribal members in Oklahoma were terminated with the larger number of Modocs, who were part of the Klamath, Modoc, and Yahooskin band of Snake Indians in Oregon. When the other three Oklahoma tribes were restored, the Oklahoma Modocs were recognized for the first time as a separate tribe.

3. This rancheria contends it was never legally terminated but lost federal services when its land was sold.

4. Termination for these groups became final over a period of several years.

5. The rancheria termination act is commonly cited as covering thirty-seven or thirty-eight tribes; however, the act itself lists thirty-three, some of which included more than one tribe sharing a rancheria. Seventeen rancherias regained recognition through the "Tillie Hardwick" lawsuit in 1983. Others regained recognition through lawsuits, legislation, or administrative action. Half a dozen of the tribes named in the termination law were not listed as federally recognized in 2006 but may be among tribes that adopted other names or merged with other groups.

Notes

PROLOGUE
1. Gerald Skelton, interview with the author, September 17, 2002.

1. POLICY
1. Joe Thomas, interview with the author, March 26, 2001.

2. Alvin M. Josephy Jr. "Cornplanter, Can You Swim?" in *Now That the Buffalo's Gone*, 303–4; Charles F. Wilkinson, *American Indians*, 19–20.

3. Thomas L. Sloan, "The Indian Reservation System," in Josephy, *Red Power*, 21. The story of European and European-American mistreatment of American Indians has been told by many writers over many years. Helen Hunt Jackson's *A Century of Dishonor*, first published in 1881, set the tone for subsequent studies. She discusses at length President Andrew Jackson's removal policy that sent southeastern tribes on the "Trail of Tears" to Oklahoma, as does Marks in *In a Barren Land*. Marks also provides a good description of Indian boarding schools (202, 213, 248, 292). Boarding school information also is based on the author's discussions with people who attended the schools; also see O'Brien, *American Indian Tribal Governments*, 76. The Sand Creek massacre as an example of the deliberate killing of noncombatants is the subject of Cutler's *Massacre at Sand Creek*. The Nez Perce tribe's battling flight from the U.S. Army is vividly described by Josephy in *Nez Perce Indians*. For a discussion of allotment policy see Wilson, *Earth Shall Weep*, 303–8; and O'Brien, *American Indian Tribal Governments*, 77–79.

4. United States, Bureau of the Census, *Historical Statistics*, pt. 1, PA91–118; the estimate of the total number of tribes is based on the number of tribes (258)

that held IRA (Indian Reorganization Act of 1934) elections by 1944 as reported by Philp in *Termination Revisited*, 11.

5. Charles Wilkinson discusses treaties and other agreements between tribes and the government in *American Indians*, 7–21.

6. "Galen's Indian Page," Native American History and Health, Policies in the 20th Century, http://members.tripod.com/nezperce/indian.htm, accessed January 8, 2002.

7. Meriam, *Problem of Indian Administration*, quoted in "Galen's Indian Page."

8. James E. Sayers, Portland (OR) Area budget officer, Bureau of Indian Affairs (BIA), letter to L. P. Towle, assistant area director, June 9, 1953, folder PAO (Portland Area Office) 1953, annual report, Box 3, Records of the PAO 1, BIA, RG75, National Archives and Records Administration, Pacific Northwest, Alaska Region, Seattle WA (hereafter NARA–Seattle).

9. Philp discusses the postwar issues of tribes and government policy in some detail in *Termination Revisited*, 68–88; also see *Congressional Record* 93, pt. 8, July 21, 1947, S 9466.

10. John Collier, statement, June 30, 1943, folder Indian Office 1943, Office Files of Oscar Chapman, 1933–53, Records of the Secretary of the Interior, RG48, National Archives and Records Administration, College Park MD (hereafter NARA–College Park); folder 1 1948, Tribal delegate notes, AX55-4 Boyd Jackson papers, Special Collections and University Archives, University of Oregon Libraries, Eugene; *Congressional Record* 93, pt. 4, May 2, 1947, Senate, 4457–58; House Committee on Public Lands, Indian Affairs Subcommittee hearing on HR 2502, Klamath Indians, 80th Cong., 1st sess., June 17, 1947, 23.

11. Charles F. Wilkinson discusses Watkins in *Blood Struggle*, 67–71; Watkins's role also is evident in the various hearing records and committee reports from 1954.

12. Commission on Reorganization of the Executive Branch of Government (Hoover Commission), Recommendations on Federal Indian Policy, folder Governors Interstate Indian Council News Letters, July 1, 1952, to June 30, 1953, Area Director's general files 1951–57, Box 3, PAO, RG75, NARA–Seattle.

13. O'Brien, *American Indian Tribal Governments*, 84.

14. *Congressional Record* 93, pt. 14, 1947, Index; pt. 4, 4452–58, 4481–84, 5119; pt. 8, 9465–66.

15. Zimmerman's lists are in Philp, *Termination Revisited*, 75; the congressional directive is described on 70–71.

16. *Governors Interstate Indian Council Newsletter*, September 10, 1952, 4, Container 14, August–December 1952, Administrative Correspondence, Accession 57–98, files of Gov. Douglas McKay, Oregon State Archives, Salem.

17. Philp, *Termination Revisited*, xii; Charles Wilkinson, *Blood Struggle*, 66; Watkins voiced his opinions frequently during the 1954 series of hearings, with one of the best examples his exchange with Billie P. Selgado of the Cohuella Tribe during the hearing on a California tribe's termination plan March 4 and 5, 1954, 473–77; McKay's ideas can be found throughout his correspondence.

18. American Indian Policy Review Commission, chapter 10, "Terminated Indians," 447–48 (from the document collection of the Confederated Tribes of Coos, Lower Umpqua, and Siuslaw Indians, Donald Whereat Collection).

19. Prucha, "America's Indians and the Federal Government," 27.

20. Administrative Committee, Association on American Indian Affairs, report, November 1, 1942, folder 1942 6, Box 14 E768, Indian Office, 1941–42 through 1948–49, 150-12-22 Records of Secretary Oscar Chapman, Office of the Secretary of the Interior, RG48, NARA–College Park.

21. James M. Stewart, "How Can We Improve the Government Policy to Make American Indians Economically Independent Faster, at the Lowest Cost?" 2, folder 1945 U.S. Department of the Interior Post War Resources Institute, Washington DC, November 5–9, 1945, Box 14, Records of the Indian Office, 1942–43 through 1948–49, 150-12-22 Records of Secretary Oscar Chapman 1933–53, RG48, Records of the Office of the Secretary of the Interior, NARA–College Park.

22. Mrs. John J. Kirk, "Withdrawal of Federal Supervision over Indian Affairs," *Congressional Record* 93, pt. 12, May 27, 1947, 3122–24.

23. Record, Conference of Indian Commissioner Glenn L. Emmons with Washington tribes, folder Portland Area Commissioner's Conference, Seattle WA, September 13–14, 1956, Box 4 NN3-075-095-002, Records of the Office of the Commissioner—tribal conference files of Commissioner Glenn L. Emmons,1956–58, RG75, Records of the BIA, NARA–Washington DC.

24. J. R. Heckman, testimony, Senate Committee on Public Lands, Subcommittee on Indian Affairs, August 21, 1947, Klamath Falls OR, on Senate Bill 1222 regarding the Klamath Indians, 366.

25. Will Vernon, testimony, Senate Committee on Public Lands, 369.

26. Record, Governor's Conference on Indian Affairs, July 14, 1950, Salem OR, 1, Administrative Correspondence, Accession 57–98, files of Gov. Douglas McKay, Oregon State Archives, Salem.

27. Statement by Spokane Indian delegation to Commissioner Glenn L. Emmons, January 1, 1955, Spokane WA, folder Colville Long Term and Withdrawal, Box 6, PAO, Director's General Subject Files, RG75, NARA–Seattle.

28. John Collier, handwritten report, "Why Federal Services to Indians Should Be Continued" August 4, 1947, folder 1946–47, Box 14, Records of Secretary Oscar Chapman, 1933–53, RG48, Records of the Office of the Secretary of the Interior, NARA–College Park.

29. Folder Conference of Area Directors 1950, 7, Box 3, PAO, RG75, NARA–Seattle.

30. Circular 3704, John R. Nichols to General Office Staff, July 21, 1949, folder Miscellaneous Activities, Desk Files Box 1, Nichols 1949–50, Office of the Commissioner, RG75, NARA–Washington DC.

31. Documents and letter, Oscar L. Chapman to Hardin Peterson, July 25, 1950, folder Legislation—Miscellaneous, desk files Box 2, Dillon Myer, 1950–55, Records of the Commissioner, RG75, NARA–Washington DC.

32. House Interior and Insular Affairs Committee, Subcommittee on Indian Affairs, hearing on H 1427-2, July 22, 1953, 1–54.

33. Metcalf, *Termination's Legacy*, 23, 30, 116.

34. See Charles Wilkinson, *Blood Struggle*, 67–71, Wilson, *Earth Shall Weep*, 364–65; *New York Times*, obituary for Arthur V. Watkins, September 2, 1973.

35. Harvey Wright to Philip Hitchcock, February 18, 1952; 130 folder 4/5 Klamath Long Range and Withdrawal, Box 6, Area Director general subject files, 1951–57, RG75, NARA–Seattle.

36. Interview with Douglas McKay, *(Portland) Oregon Journal*, September 23, 1953, 2.

37. "Klamath Hearing Report," *Oregon Journal*, August 23, 1947, 22.

38. Charles Wilkinson notes in *Blood Struggle*, "with few exceptions Indian tribes lacked the equipment to make their case in Congress" (66); Philp's discussion of the events leading up to the passage of HCR 108 is notable for the absence of Indian participation in creating policy; he states, "In reality, Indians did not exert much influence over important issues that affected their lives" (85). The records of congressional hearings on specific termination bills in-

clude numerous complaints from Indian witnesses that their ideas and recommendations had been ignored.

39. See text of HCR 108 and Zimmerman's lists in Philp, *Termination Revisited*, 75.

40. Robert Bojorcas, "Profiles of Selected and Non-Federally Recognized Tribes—Oregon Terminated Tribes," report prepared for Task Force 10 of the American Indian Policy Review Commission, 1977, 48 (from Coos Tribal Files—Donald Whereat Collection).

41. For a summary of tribes terminated and their dates see Wilkinson and Briggs, "Evaluation of the Termination Policy," 139, 144.

42. Brophy and Aberle, *Indian*, for a discussion of Public Law 280 (151–52), the transfer of health programs (184–87), and relocation (102).

2. MENOMINEES

1. House Report 93-572 Repealing the Act Terminating Federal Supervision over the Property and Members of the Menominee Indian Tribe of Wisconsin, October 11, 1972, 3.

2. Meriam, *Problem of Indian Administration*, 42–43.

3. Department of the Interior report included in record of hearings by the Indian Affairs subcommittees of the House and Senate on "Federal Supervision over Certain Tribes of Indians," March 10–12, 1954, 585, 586, 589.

4. Monroe Weso testimony, joint hearing by Indian Affairs subcommittees of House and Senate on HR 7135, March 10–12, 1954, 736, 737.

5. Peroff, *Menominee Drums*, 53–57; Weso testimony, 1954 hearing, 736–37; Rep. Melvin Laird, statement at 1954 hearing, 594.

6. U.S. Code Title 25, Subchapter XL, June 17, 1954.

7. Ada Deer, interview with the author, May 15, 2001.

8. Nancy Oestreich Lurie, curator, Milwaukee Public Museum, paper prepared for May 26, 1973, House hearing on Menominee restoration, 193, hearing record; Joseph F. Preloznik, director of Judicare, to Richard Cohen, November 18, 1971, Series III Sub b&c American Indian Civil Rights and American Indian Education, Alvin M. Josephy Jr. Papers Coll. 14, Special Collections and University Archives, University of Oregon Libraries, Eugene.

9. Deer, interview.

10. Don C. Foster, testimony, joint hearing, March 1954, 612–14.

11. Sady, "Menominee," 2, 234/20/17 folder 17, Josephy Papers.

12. Gary Orfield, "Ideology and the Indians: A Study of Termination Policy," undated typewritten manuscript, folder 20, Box 234/20/17, Development of American Indian Policy/Indian Civil Rights: Menominee TP reports and papers (5), 2nd of 3, Josephy Papers.

13. Wisconsin Commission on Human Rights, 1952 Report, quoted in chapter 5, 2, undated, untitled study, 234/16/16, file Wisconsin—Indian—Menominee, Josephy Papers.

14. Foster, testimony, joint hearing, March 1954, 612.

15. Sady, "Menominee," 6, 7, 9.

16. John A. Carver Jr., testimony, Senate Subcommittee on Indian Affairs on S 1934, April 1961, quoted in "Status of Termination of the Menominee Indian Tribe," report to the Committee on Appropriations of the U.S. House of Representatives by the BIA, February 1965, 1, 2, folder Development of American Indian Policy/Indian Civil Rights: Menominee TP reports and papers 234/20/19, Josephy Papers.

17. Beck, *Struggle for Self-Determination*, 142.

18. Gaylord Nelson, testimony, Senate Committee on Indian Affairs, September 17, 1972, S 1687, Repeal Menominee Termination, 25.

19. Harry Harder, testimony, hearing by House and Senate Indian Affairs subcommittees on "Termination of Supervision over Certain Tribes of Indians," pt. 6, Menominee, March 10–12, 1954, 658; Peroff, *Menominee Drums*, 80.

20. Verna Fowler, interview with the author, May 22, 2001.

21. "Liquidation" appears in most early BIA and Department of Interior correspondence, replaced largely by "withdrawal" and later "termination." "Freedom" was the term used most often in public statements.

22. Fowler interview.

23. Arthur Watkins, statement, joint hearing of Indian Affairs Subcommittees of House and Senate, March 1954, 735.

24. Melvin Laird in meeting with Ernest Wilkinson, attorney for the Menominee Tribe; transcript read into record of hearing by Indian Affairs subcommittees of House and Senate, March 10–12, 1954, pt. 6, Menominee S 2813, HR 228, HR 7135.

25. Antoine Waupochick, testimony, hearing by House Indian Affairs Subcommittee, May 25, 1973, on HR 7421, repealing Menominee termination, 67.

26. Ernest Wilkinson, testimony, March 1954 hearing, 700; Charles Wilkinson, *Blood Struggle*, 72.

27. Watkins, March 1954 hearing, 656.

28. Charles Wilkinson, *Blood Struggle*, 73.

29. Watkins, March 1954 hearing, 668.

30. There are numerous examples of Indians citing treaty provisions exempting their reservation lands from taxation. Congressman Melvin Laird of Wisconsin also referred to the treaty provision in testimony before the joint Indian Affairs subcommittees, March 10, 1954, during their Hearing on Termination of Certain Tribes of Indians, pt. 6, 594. A letter from the BIA included in the Utah section of the same series of hearings, February 15, 1954, refers to the immunity from taxation of Omaha land under that tribe's treaty, 29; O'Brien outlines the legal issue succinctly in *American Indian Tribal Governments*: "The courts have long ruled that states cannot tax either individually or tribally owned allotments. First, such lands are technically federal lands, and states may not tax any federal lands (such as national parks). Second, when tribes agreed to cede large portions of their lands and settle on reservations, the federal government promised to protect the lands for the tribes' use. To allow tribal land to be taxed would penalize tribes for using their own land" (284).

31. Jonathan M. Steere, March 1954 hearing, 671, Watkins, 672.

32. James Caldwell and Watkins, March 1954 hearing, 675–78.

33. Weso, March 1954 hearing, 737.

34. Department of the Interior report on S 2813 and HR 7135 included in report of hearing by House and Senate Indian Affairs subcommittees, March 10–12, 1954.

35. John Byrnes, March 1954 hearing, 605–7.

36. H. Rex Lee, March 1954 hearing, 620.

37. Harder, Laird, and Watkins, March 1954 hearing, 651–55.

38. Andrews and Watkins, March 1954 hearing, 734.

39. Gordon Dickie and Watkins, March 1954 hearing, 755.

40. Charles Wilkinson, *Blood Struggle*, 72; *Public Papers of the Presidents*, Dwight D. Eisenhower, 1954, item 147.

41. Ada Deer and other officials of DRUMS testimony submitted to Senate Interior and Insular Affairs Committee, July 21, 1971, on effects of termination on the Menominee, hearing on Senate concurrent resolution 26, 8, 9, 10; materials and legislation 234/20/12, folder Development of American Indian Policy/Indian Civil Rights: Menominee T.P, 14 Series III Sub b&c American Indian Civil Rights and Education, Josephy Papers.

42. Fixico, *Termination and Relocation*, 110; chapter 5, 5–6, paper author and title not listed, file Wisconsin—Indian—Menominee, folder 234/16/16, Development of American Indian Policy/Indian Civil Rights: Menominee TP; reports and papers on TP (1) 234/20/16, Josephy Papers.

43. Orfield, "Ideology and the Indians," undated manuscript, 159.

44. George Kenote, quoted in untitled study, chapter 5, 6, Josephy Papers.

45. Phileo Nash, testimony, 1973 House hearing, 127.

46. Peroff, *Menominee Drums*, 103, 120–21; untitled study, chapter 5, 9–11, Josephy Papers.

47. Quoted in Peroff, *Menominee Drums*, 85.

48. Shames, *Freedom with Reservation*; Preloznik to Richard Cohen.

49. Peroff, *Menominee Drums*, 114, 115, 119; untitled study, chapter 5, 9–11, Josephy Papers.

50. Untitled study, chapter 5, 10, 11, 13, Josephy Papers; Charles Wilkinson, *Blood Struggle*, 183.

51. Untitled study, chapter 6, 13, 14, Josephy Papers.

52. Untitled study, chapter 6, 9, Josephy Papers; Ada Deer and others, testimony at July 21, 1971, hearing, 19; Preloznik to Richard Cohen.

53. Untitled study, chapter 6, 11, Josephy Papers.

54. Harry Harder, Wisconsin Department of Taxation, and George Keith, Wisconsin Department of Public Welfare, statements to Manpower and Employment Subcommittee of Senate Labor and Public Welfare Committee, November 10, 1965, mimeographed copy of record in folder Development American Indian Policy: Indian Civil Rights, Government Legislation Box Series III Sub B American Indian Civil Rights, Josephy Papers; author unidentified, "Plight of Menominee Tribe," folder 234/16/16 Development of American Indian Policy/Indian Civil Rights: Menominee TP reports and papers on TP (1) 234/20/16, Josephy Papers.

55. Ray Pagel series, *Green Bay Press Gazette*, August 10, 1965, 1, and August 13, 1965, 12, Josephy Papers Series III News Clippings 234/20/14.

56. Donald Janson, "Tribe in WI, Deprived of Special Status, Seeks Help in Going It Alone," *New York Times*, September 7, 1965, 29, 234/20/14, Josephy Papers.

57. Ridgeway, "Lost Indians," 18, 234/20/14, Josephy Papers.

58. Author unidentified, "Summary of Fact—Events Directly Affecting Termination of the Menominee Indian Reservation, June 22, 1970, 234/20/11, folder

Development AI Policy—Menominee Termination Policy—correspondence June 1966 to November 1975, Josephy Papers.

59. Reuben La Fave, Senate hearing, 1965, 4.

60. Orfield, "War on Menominee Poverty."

3. KLAMATHS

1. "Problems of Klamath Indians Given Study," *(Portland) Oregon Journal*, September 27, 1956, 19.

2. Haynal, "Termination and Tribal Survival," 271.

3. The preceding narrative was compiled from the minutes of the Klamath General Council in the files of Dibbon Cook and the tribal delegate records of Boyd Jackson, both in the Special Collections and University Archives, University of Oregon Libraries, Eugene; PAO records, NARA–Seattle; and records of congressional hearings in 1947 and 1954.

4. Seldon E. Kirk and Jesse Lee Kirk to Superintendent, Klamath Agency, February 20, 1947, and "Rough draft of bill" by Forest [sic] Cooper, folder 1946–47, Box 14 E768, Indian Office, 1941–42 through 1948–49, RG48, Records of the Secretary of the Interior 150-12-22, NARA–College Park.

5. Ernest Wilkinson to Jesse L. Kirk, November 18, 1950, folder Wilkinson, Jackson Collection AX 55-5, Special Collections and University Archives, University of Oregon Libraries, Eugene.

6. Report on HR 2502, House Committee on Public Lands, May 1, 1947, 2, 3.

7. Boyd Jackson, testimony, Hearing on HR 2502 by House Committee on Public Lands, May 1, 1947, 17, 18.

8. Wade Crawford, testimony, hearing on HR 2502 by House Committee on Public Lands, May 1, 1947, 20.

9. Jackson, testimony, hearing on HR 2502 by House Committee on Public Lands, May 1, 1947, 484, 495–99.

10. Watkins, hearing on HR 2502 by House Committee on Public Lands, May 1, 1947, 504.

11. L. P. Towle to Erastus J. Diehl, July 18, 1951, folder Chronological Misc. Administration, July 1, 1951, to June 3, 1952, PAO 1, Classified files of the area director correspondence reports, Box 4 Correspondence Misc., 1951–52, and Misc. Washington, RG75, NARA–Seattle.

12. Harvey Wright to Philip S. Hitchcock, February 18, 1952, McKay files,

Administrative Correspondence, Accession 57–98, container 14, 4/4, January–July 1952, Oregon State Archives, Salem.

13. Report, House Committee on Appropriations, Interior Subcommittee, Interior Department Appropriations Bill, 1954, P9, folder Interior Department Appropriations Bill 1954, Box 3, Interior Department Appropriations, Records of Secretary Douglas McKay, general subject files 1952–56, RG48, Records of the Department of Interior, NARA–College Park.

14. Forrest E. Cooper to Orme Lewis, November 25, 1953, folder 130, Klamath Long Range and Withdrawal, Box 6, PAO director's general subject files, 1951–1957, RG75, NARA–Seattle.

15. Unsigned handwritten note attached to document titled Proposed Withdrawal of Federal Responsibility over Property and Affairs of the Klamath Indians by E. J. Diehl and J. Morgan Pryse, December 1, 1953, folder Reports on Proposed Withdrawal 1953, Box 85, RG75, PAO 16, Assistant Area Director Klamath Termination, NARA–Seattle.

16. Memo, Pryse to Commissioner of Indian Affairs, August 2, 1953, folder 4 of 4, 130—Klamath Long Range and Withdrawal.

17. E. J. Diehl, testimony at hearing by subcommittees of House and Senate Committees on Interior and Insular Affairs on S 2745 and HR 7320, Washington DC, February 23, 1954, 222.

18. Folder General Council Minutes 1954, July 29 and 30, 1954, 6, Box 6, files of Dibbon Cook, BX 51 Klamath Tribal Records, 1933–58, Special Collections and University Archives, University of Oregon Libraries, Eugene.

19. Jonathan M. Steere, testimony before joint subcommittees on S 2813, HR 2825, and HR 7135, Washington DC, March 11, 1954, 664, 666.

20. Watkins, statement to joint subcommittees on S 2813, HR 2825, and HR 7135, 259.

21. Jackson, testimony before joint subcommittees on S 2813, HR 2825, and HR 7135, 262–64.

22. Employment list, June 30, 1947, Klamath Indian Agency, 241–43, hearing record Senate Subcommittee on Indian Affairs, August 18–23, 1947, S 1222, Appendix B Klamath Management Specialists Records, vol. 3, BX 125, Special Collections and University Archives, University of Oregon Libraries, Eugene.

23. Robert Bojorcas, Robert Coiner, and Dennis DeGross, "A Study of the Process and Effects of Termination on the Lives of Oregon Indians," prepared for American Indian Policy Review Commission Task Force 10, 1976 18, from

the files of Donald Whereat of the Confederated Tribes of the Coos, Siuslaw, and Lower Umpqua Indians.

24. Phil (Bill) Tupper, interview with the author, September 17–18, 2002; Tupper was referring to a survey of tribal members by the Stanford Research Institute.

25. Theodore A. Crume, interview with the author, August 26, 2000.

26. Meeting of July 29–30, 1954, 6–8, folder General Council, Box 6, Files of Dibbon Cook, BX 51 Klamath Indian Tribal Council Records, 1933–58.

27. Lyle F. Watts to unnamed recipient, September 16, 1954, Management Specialists, vol. 2, section N.

28. Unsigned, undated article, "What Will Happen to Indian Timber?" *Timberman*, attached to notes of tribal executive board meeting, November 29, 1955, Box 2, Cook files, BX 51, Klamath Indian Executive Board.

29. McKay to Wallace Turner, April 13, 1955, Letters sent, boxes 46–51, alphabetical 1955 file T-V, Box 51, AX 63, Doug McKay papers, Secretary of the Interior, Special Collections and University Archives, University of Oregon Libraries, Eugene.

30. Report on meeting of management specialists with Klamath Advisory Committee, August 30, 1955, folder 12, General Council, BX 51-5, 1956, Klamath Tribal Council Records, Cook files.

31. McKay to W. L. Phillips, December 15, 1954, and McKay to Thomas B. Watters, folder Klamath Agency, January 14, 1954, to April 29, 1955, Box 297, Great Lakes to Klamath Agency, RG48, Records of the Secretary of the Interior, Central Classified Files, 1954–58, NARA–College Park.

32. B. G. Courtright, report submitted to Senate Subcommittee on Public Lands hearing, August 18–23, 1947, 556.

33. Stanford Research Institute Report, April 1956, 17, 23, BX 125, Klamath Management Specialists Records.

34. Thomas B. Watters to Watkins, vol. 2, Management Specialists reference material, Section J, BX 15, Klamath Management Specialists Records.

35. Watters, letter to Emmons, January 20, 1956, read at tribal executive committee meeting April 16, 1956, folder 17, executive committee April 23, 16, 17, 1956, BX 51-2 Executive council minutes, Cook files.

36. Oregon State Department of Education report entered into Watters testimony before House Subcommittee on Indian Affairs hearing on amendments to Klamath Termination Act, February 12, 1957.

37. Watters to Secretary of the Interior, August 29, 1956, to Fred A. Seaton, November 8 and December 2, 1956, Management Specialists reference materials, vol. 2, section 1.

38. Watters to Hatfield Chilson, January 18, 1957, vol. 2, Management Specialists reference materials, section 1.

39. Minutes, meeting of tribal executive board, BIA officials and management specialists, October 29, 1956, folder 34, BX 51-2, Executive Committee Minutes, Cook files.

40. Senate debate, *Congressional Record*, May 7, 1958, 7354–63, copy in Management Specialists files Section J, vol. 2, Management Specialists reference materials, BX 125.

41. House Committee on Interior and Insular Affairs, Subcommittee on Indian Affairs, hearing on HR 660, 663, 2471, 2578 amending Klamath Termination Act, August 1957, 46, 52, 53.

42. Memorial to Congress, January 29, 1957, 49th Oregon Legislative Assembly, Management specialists reference materials, vol. 3, section J.

43. "Proposed Management Plan Now Available," *Chiloquin (OR) Klamath Tribune* 2, no. 9, September 1957, 1, 4, 9, Collection in Oregon State Library, Salem.

44. Watters to Seaton, April 9, 1958, Management Specialists reference materials, vol. 3, section L.

45. "Certified Election Report Release May 28," *Klamath Tribune* 3, no. 6 (June 1958): 1.

46. Undated memo from Boyd Jackson and J. L. Kirk Sr., folder 22, Resolutions, Management meetings, tribal executive committee, BX 51-5 council records, Cook files.

47. Charles E. Kimbol Sr., interview with the author, August 27, 2000.

48. List of Actions Completed on Sales of Fringe Units, Klamath Indian Reservation, Klamath summary report, 1956–61, Klamath folder, Box 72, PAO assistant area director, 1954–63, RG75, NARA–Seattle.

49. "Remaining Area Management Staff Set," *Klamath Tribune* 4, no. 5 (May 1959): 1.

50. Final Status and Evaluation Report, Klamath Termination, folder Klamath summary reports, 1956–61, USDI BIA, Box 72, PAO assistant area director, 1954–63.

51. Floyd L. Wynne, "Indian Payment Brings Welcome Boost to Basin Business," *Klamath Falls (OR) Herald and News*, April 21, 1961, 1.

52. Truelove and Bunting, "Economic Impact of Federal Indian Policy," 20 (from the files of Hiroto Zakoji).

53. Federal Trade Commission, "Consumer Problems of the Klamath Indians," 8, 9 (copy in Paul L. Boley Law Library, Lewis and Clark College, Portland OR).

54. Allen Foreman, interview with the author, August 27, 2000.

55. Federal Trade Commission, "Consumer Problems of the Klamath Indians," 2.

56. Gail Chehak, interview with the author, November 1, 2000.

57. Haynal, "Termination and Tribal Survival."

58. Elwood Miller, interview with the author, September 17, 2002.

59. Kathleen Shaye Hill, attachment to "The Klamath Tribe: An Overview of Its Termination," unpublished paper, February 20, 1985 (from the files of Hiroto Zakoji).

60. Gordon Bettles, interview with the author, April 19, 2001.

61. Haynal, "From Termination through Restoration," 115.

62. Tupper interview.

63. Foreman interview.

64. Roberta Ulrich, "Ed Chiloquin Told Them Not to Sell," *Portland Oregonian*, December 13, 1993; also Edison Chiloquin, interview with the author, August 27, 2000.

4. WESTERN OREGON

1. "Program for the Early Termination of Selected Activities and Withdrawing Federal Supervision over the Indians at Grand Ronde-Siletz and Southwestern Oregon," PAO of the BIA, December 1950, copy in files of the PAO, BIA.

2. Sharon Parrish, interview with the author, March 27, 2001; June Olson, interview with the author, May 8, 2000; Bensell Breon, interview with the author, February 13, 2001.

3. "Program for Early Termination," 20.

4. Douglas McKay to E. Morgan Pryse, August 21, 1951, entered into record of hearing by joint subcommittees of House and Senate Interior and Insular Affairs Committees, February 17, 1954, on S 2746 and HR 7317, Termination, pt. 3, Western Oregon.

5. Minutes, Governor's Advisory Committee on Indian Affairs, November 29, 1950, 4, 7, 20, specifically minutes, September 11, 1951, 3; Tom Lawson McCall to F. L. Phipps, October 2, 1951, accession 57–98 , papers of Gov. Douglas McKay, 1948–52, Oregon State Archives; McKay to Pryse, August 21, 1951.

6. American Indian Policy Review Commission Task Force 10, 52; Pryse to R. F. Bessey, August 7, 1951, folder Chronological—Misc. Administration, Box 4, Correspondence Misc. and Misc. Washington, 1951–52, PAO 1—area director's classified files, RG75, NARA–Seattle; Pryse to commissioner, September 11, 1951, folder Chronological Correspondence, July 1, 1951, to June 30, 1952, Box 2, general subject files, 1951–57, BIA PAO area director, RG75, NARA–Seattle; Pryse report, December 1953, Box 34, PAO Records related to termination, western Oregon, 1954–56, RG75, NARA–Seattle; Polk County Court, letter to Pryse, October 25, 1951, Yamhill County judge C. F. Haynes to Pryse, November 21, 1951, Lincoln County judge H. M. Haskins to Pryse, November 30, 1951, included in Interior Department report in record of joint subcommittees hearing, February 17, 1954.

7. The preceding historical outline was compiled from sources including an interview with June Olson, cultural director for the Grand Ronde Tribes, discussing the tribal history she was compiling; *The Confederated Tribes of Grand Ronde: Historical Perspective* (a tribal publication); Hall, *Coquille Indians*; and a Cow Creek tribal publication, "Cow Creek Band of Umpqua Tribe of Indians, 1853–1982."

8. Sherman Waters, testimony at hearing by the American Indian Policy Review Commission, March 26, 1975, Portland OR.

9. Parrish interview; House Report 5540, July 25, 1984, Coos Tribe Restoration, 5.

10. Leon Tom, interview with the author, May 8, 2000; tribal elder who asked that her name be withheld, telephone interview with the author, January 30, 2001.

11. Pryse to commissioner, June 13, 1951, Box 4, Correspondence Misc. and Misc. Washington, 1951–52; Resolution Siletz Tribal Council, October 7, 1951, folder Siletz Tribal Resolutions, 1955, Box 1568, Nez Perce, Siletz, Spokane, Tribal council minutes, 1950–65, tribal operations branch, PAO; RG75, NARA–Seattle.

12. Grand Ronde minutes, November 12, 1953, cited in BIA report to

Sen. James Abourezk, April 6, 1976, appended to record of hearing by Senate Select Committee on Indian Affairs on Siletz restoration March 30, 1976. The tribe eventually voted 79-11 to support termination but only after Congress had passed the western Oregon termination measure, making the vote meaningless.

13. Minutes, Siletz tribal meeting, November 1, 1953, folder Siletz minutes and resolutions, 1952–53, council minutes, 1950–65, Box 1568, Nez Perce Siletz Spokane, tribal operations branch, PAO, RG75, NARA–Seattle.

14. Record of joint subcommittees hearing, February 17, 1954.

15. Kathryn Harrison, interview with the author, November 5, 2001.

16. American Indian Policy Review Commission, final report to Congress, May 17, 1977, chapter 10, "Terminated Indians," 454.

17. Wasson testimony before House Subcommittee on Indian Affairs, August 24, 1988, from Coquille tribal files; Michael Darcy, interview with the author, February 23, 2001.

18. Joint subcommittees hearing, February 17, 1954, 187.

19. U.S. Code Title 25 Indians, Subchapter XXX, Western Oregon Indians, 690–95.

20. Report of the Legislative Interim Committee on Indian Affairs submitted to the fiftieth Legislative Assembly (Oregon), October 1958, 49, copy in McKay files, Oregon State Archives.

21. Billie Lewis, interview with the author, March 27, 2005.

22. Darcy interview; Tom interview.

23. "Program for Early Termination," 9.

24. James I. Metcalf, interview with the author, March 27, 2001; "Program for Early Termination," 9.

25. James Stuart, "Oregon Indians Express Views on Impending Emancipation," *Oregonian*, February 24, 1952, 20–21.

26. Wasson, testimony, House Subcommittee on Indian Affairs, August 24, 1988.

27. Foster to commissioner, October 5, 1954.

28. Bill Brainard, interview with the author, March 28, 2002.

29. Greenwood to Foster, December 20, 1954, folder 1, Holm to Foster, April 8, 1955, folder 3, Box 33, Records related to western Oregon termination, 1954–60, PAO, RG75 BIA, NARA–Seattle.

30. Joe Thomas interview with the author, March 26, 2001.

31. Roy Gilkey, interview with the author, March 26, 2001.

32. H. Dushane report, September 30, 1955, folder Grand Ronde-Siletz Administration, 1956–58, Box 36, Records related to western Oregon termination, PAO RG75, NARA–Seattle.

33. Darcy interview.

34. Perry Skarra, acting regional director, to commissioner, August 10, 1956, final report on termination of western Oregon tribes, folder Termination Western Oregon #2, Box 33, records of termination of western Oregon tribes, 1954–60, Box 33, PAO RG75 NARA–Seattle.

35. Harrison, interviews with the author, November 5, 2001, and January 9, 2002.

36. Violet Zimbrick, interview with the author, January 17, 2002.

37. Joint subcommittees hearing, February 17, 1954, 189.

38. Darcy interview.

39. Billie Lewis interview.

40. Darcy interview.

41. Oregon State University Survey Resource Center socioeconomic study of the Coquille Tribe, 1988, quoted by Roy Gilkey in testimony at the Coquille restoration hearing by the Indian Affairs Subcommittee, August 1988 (from Coquille tribal records); House report 98-464, November 2, 1983, Grand Ronde restoration, 3; Profiles of Selected Terminated and Non-recognized Tribes—Oregon Terminated Tribes—a report prepared for Task Force 10 of the American Indian Policy Review Commission, 39.

5. ALABAMA-COUSHATTAS AND CATAWBAS

1. This historical summary is based on Alabama-Coushatta tribal history on the tribal website, http://www.ac-tribe.com/ac/index.php, accessed November 27, 2009), and *East Texas Historical Journal* 17, no. 1 (1979), as quoted by Howard K. Martin, director of research for the Houston Chamber of Commerce, in testimony to the Senate Select Committee on Indian Affairs hearing on HR 1344 restoration June 25, 1986, 362–78.

2. Arnold Battise, testimony to Senate Subcommittee on Indian Affairs, June 25, 1986, 266.

3. Rep. John Dowdy, testimony to joint Interior and Insular Affairs subcommittees on Indian Affairs, hearing on S 2724 and HR 6282 tribal status, February 16, 1954, 123.

4. Dowdy, testimony, 1954 hearing, 99–104; Senate report 1321, Interior and Insular Affairs Committee, May 11, 1954, to accompany S 2744, 9.

5. Dowdy, testimony, 1954 hearing, 108.

6. Report included in Dowdy testimony, 1954 hearing, 102–5.

7. Dowdy, testimony, 1954 hearing, 93, 103, 104.

8. William Wade Head and Dowdy, testimony, 1954 hearing, 118.

9. Dowdy, testimony, 1954 hearing, 106; H. Rex Lee, associate commissioner of Indian Affairs, testimony, 1954 hearing, 117.

10. Record of 1954 hearing, 106–7, 112, 115–16.

11. Senate report 1321, May 11, 1954, "Termination of Federal Supervision over the Property of the Alabama-Coushatta Tribes of Texas"; U.S. Code Title 25, Subchapter XXXI, Alabama and Coushatta Indians of Texas, 539–40.

12. Orme Lewis, speech to Phoenix Press Club, October 5, 1955; folder Assistant Secretary Lewis, VII-7, Box 4, Land Management, Bureau of, to National Park Service Entry 770, general subject files, 1952–56, Records of Secretary McKay, RG48, Records of the Department of the Interior, NARA–College Park.

13. Alabama-Coushatta tribal history; Battise, testimony, 1986 hearing, 411.

14. Gloria Franklin, director/coordinator of Head Start, report to Tony Byars, superintendent, "Head Start Information for the Plan for Restoration Hearing," September 16, 1985, record of Texas Restoration Hearing.

15. This historical summary is based on a statement from Rep. John C. Spratt of North Carolina to the House Natural Resources Committee, Subcommittee on Indian Affairs hearing, July 2, 1993, on the Catawba Land Claims Settlement bill, 137–52, and on Hudson, *Catawba Nation*.

16. D'Arcy McNickle, report to commissioner of Indian Affairs, 1937, Catawba Historical Documents included in record of House Natural Resources Committee, Subcommittee on Indian Affairs hearing on HR 2399, Catawba Land Claims Settlement, July 2, 1993.

17. Report 103–27, pt. 1, September 27, 1993, House Natural Resources Committee, Catawba Land Claims Settlement Act of 1993, 15.

18. Thomas J. Blumer, Library of Congress, to Rep. John M. Spratt Jr., entered into hearing record of House Indian Affairs Subcommittee on Catawba Lands Claims Settlement July 2, 1993, 151.

19. Gilbert Blue, testimony, hearing, July 2, 1993, 214–20.

20. Blue, testimony, House Subcommittee on Indian Affairs 1993 hearing, 19.

21. House Subcommittee on Indian Affairs 1993 hearing, 167.

22. Report to accompany HR 2399 Catawba Land Claims Settlement Act of 1993, 103–27, 15.

23. Rep. John M. Spratt Jr., statement at 1993 hearing, 153.

24. Thomas J. Blumer, Library of Congress, report to 1993 hearing, 282.

25. Blumer, statement for 1979 congressional hearing incorporated into 1993 hearing, 283, 284.

26. Charlotte NC Observer, March 6, 1977, p1C, reprinted in 1977 hearing record and cited in 1993 hearing, 446.

6. UTAH PAIUTE BANDS

1. Rep. Dan Marriott, statement to Senate Select Committee on Indian Affairs, hearing on Paiute Restoration Act, S 1273, November 8, 1979, 14.

2. Bruce Parry, testimony, Select Committee, 1979 hearing, 60; Reid Blondquist to Utah congressional delegation and Paiute Restoration Committee, undated letter, entered in record of Select Committee hearing, 55.

3. Metcalf, Termination's Legacy, 16, 101.

4. Fixico, Termination and Relocation, 63.

5. This historical summary is based on the Utah History Encyclopedia article by Ronald L. Holt, available at http://www.OnlineUtah.com (accessed March 10, 2006).

6. House Interior and Insular Affairs Committee, 2493, 83rd Cong., 2nd sess., report to accompany S 3532, July 26, 1954, folder Terminal Legislation—California, Box 1519, RG75, BIA PAO Tribal Operations Branch, general subject files, NARA–Seattle; also U.S. Code Title 25, Subchapter XXVIII, 512–19.

7. Metcalf, Termination's Legacy, preface, 4, 112.

8. George C. Morris to Watkins, February 12, 1954, printed in record of joint subcommittees' hearing, February 15, 1954, 51; Parry statement to Senate Select Committee hearing, 1979, 50.

9. Watkins, February 1954 joint hearing, 44.

10. Parry, statement at 1979 hearing, 50.

11. Charles H. Harrington to Watkins, February 13, 1954, in 1954 joint hearing record, 61; Henry Gilmore, testimony, February 1954 hearing, 61–62.

12. Joint subcommittees hearing, February 15, 1954, 84.

13. John A. Carver Jr. to Rep. M. Blaine Peterson, August 28, 1962; Ralph Reeser, testimony, 1979 hearing, 21.

14. The criteria are listed in the American Indian Policy Review Commission report, chapter 10, "Terminated Indians," 450.

15. Watkins, February 1954 hearing, 49.

16. The description of the Paiute tribes' economic and social conditions is contained in the Department of the Interior's report made part of the record of the joint subcommittees' hearing on termination of Utah tribes, February 15, 1954.

17. Dillon S. Myer, 1952 Report of the Commissioner of Indian Affairs, 389–95.

18. Dr. Emery A. Johnson, testimony, 1979 hearing, 24.

19. Metcalf, *Termination's Legacy*, 114.

20. Report 96-481 on Paiute Restoration, November 29, 1979, to the Senate Select Committee on Indian Affairs, 2.

21. Carver to Peterson, 1962.

22. Sen. Orrin Hatch, statement, 1979 hearing, 28.

23. Thomas G. Alexander, "Native Americans in Post War Utah."

24. Inouye and Reeser, 1979 hearing, 21, 22.

25. Dr. Emery A. Johnson, written responses entered into 1979 hearing record, 37.

26. Parry, statement, 1979 hearing, 62.

27. Travis Benioh, testimony, 1979 hearing, 45, 46.

28. Beverly Snow, testimony, 1979 hearing, 46.

29. McKay Pikyavit, testimony, 1979 hearing, 46, 47.

30. S. D. Aberle, report on 1958 meeting with Utah bands incorporated into Parry testimony at 1979 hearing, 49.

31. Lezlee E. Whiting, "Members of Uinta Band Lose Bid to Regain Status," (*Salt Lake City*) *Deseret Morning News*, January 31, 2006.

32. Kanosh Band, written statement entered into 1979 hearing record, 53.

33. Patrick Charles to Senate Indian Affairs Subcommittee, November 5, 1979, hearing record, 64.

7. CALIFORNIA

1. Orme Lewis, report to the Senate, January 4, 1954, 358, entered into the record of hearings by the joint subcommittees on Indian Affairs, pt. 5—California, March 4 and 5, 1954, Washington DC, Termination of Federal Supervi-

sion over Certain Tribes of Indians, s 2749 and HR 7322; at the same hearing Leonard Hill, BIA area director in Sacramento, testified, "The number of Indians is difficult to determine" (373). The most recent census, in 1945, provided an estimate of 11,000.

2. Shipik, "Saints as Oppressors," 38.

3. Norton, "Path of Genocide," 114.

4. Orme Lewis, report to the Senate, 357, 358; Josephy, *500 Nations*, 340–49; Norton, "Path of Genocide," 117; O'Brien, *American Indian Tribal Governments*, 63–64.

5. Program for the Termination of Indian Bureau Activities in the State of California, document prepared by the California Indian Agency, Sacramento, 1949, 32, from the files of the BIA, PAO.

6. Hearing, Subcommittee on Indian Affairs, House Public Lands Committee, May 2, 1947, 370.

7. Joint Resolution 7, California State Assembly, read in the U.S. Senate, February 19, 1947, *Congressional Record* 93, pt. 1, 1156.

8. Program for the Termination of Indian Bureau Activities, 37–39.

9. Senate Joint Resolution no. 29, chapter 123, California Statutes, May 18, 1951, quoted in Orme Lewis, report to the Senate, 1954, 359.

10. Robert Lovato, comments at meeting at Auberry Rancheria, December 5, 1956, quoted in report by Fred Quinn to American Friends Service Committee on Indian Affairs, December 12, 1956, File 16272 pt. 1, Box 6, Entry 121, California 4670-1954-013 to 00-1955 015, Central Classified Files, 1940–56, RG75 BIA, NARA–Washington DC.

11. Orme Lewis, report to the Senate, 357, 358; reservations are generally lands that tribes retained when ceding vast portions of their homelands. California Indians lost all of their lands, and Congress in the early 1900s purchased 117 parcels, known as rancherias, for the Indians' use. Both types of land were held in trust by the federal government. O'Brien, *American Indian Tribal Governments*, 64.

12. Dillon S. Myer, memo to area directors, superintendents, school superintendents, and principals, June 17, 1952, folder Indian Bureau, July 1, 1951, to June 30, 1952, Box 4, Correspondence Misc. and Misc. Washington, 1951–52, PAO Classified files, area director correspondence and reports, NARA–Seattle; joint subcommittee hearing, March 1954, 382.

13. Frank Quin, American Friends Service Committee, quoted in summing up AFSC-sponsored conference on California Indians, October 27, 1956, file

16272 pt. 1, folder 00-1953, Box 6 entry 121 CA 4670 1954-013 to 00-1955-015, Central Classified Files, 1940–56, RG75, NARA–Washington DC.

14. Orme Lewis, report to the Senate, 359.

15. Joint subcommittees hearing, 1954, 365.

16. Joint subcommittees hearing, 1954, 422–27.

17. Joint subcommittees hearing, 1954, 453–57.

18. Joint subcommittees hearing, 1954, 462–74.

19. Joint subcommittees hearing, 1954, 474–80.

20. Joint subcommittees hearing, 1954, 481–84.

21. Joint subcommittees hearing, 1954, 485–94.

22. Joint subcommittees hearing, 1954, 488, 494–501.

23. Joint subcommittees hearing, 1954, 504, 506.

24. Joint subcommittees hearing, 1954, 509–12.

25. Joint subcommittees hearing, 1954, 509–15, 535–36.

26. Joint subcommittees hearing, 1954, 338–52.

27. Joint subcommittees hearing, 1954, 572–74.

28. Joint subcommittees hearing, 1954, 575, 576.

29. Wilkinson and Briggs, "Evaluation of Termination Policy," 139, 144.

30. Cheryl Seidner, interview with the author, November 12 and 13, 2002.

31. Don Arnold, interview with the author, November 12, 2002.

32. Viola Pack, interview with the author, November 12, 2002.

33. Sue Masten, interview with the author, November 13, 2002.

34. Keith Pike, interview with the author, November 13, 2002.

8. OKLAHOMA TRIBES, NEBRASKA PONCAS

1. Rodney Arnett, chief of the Peoria Tribe, Lewis Barlow, chief of the Ottawa Tribe, and Mont Cotter, chief of the Wyandotte Tribe, testimony before the Senate Select Committee on Indian Affairs on the status of Oklahoma Indian tribes, September 27, 1977, 82, 88, 99; Senate report to accompany s 661 95-574, Status of Oklahoma Indian Tribes, 2.

2. Report of Senate Select Committee on Indian Affairs to accompany s 661 95-574, 2, 3.

3. "A Brief History of the Wyandotte Nation," http://www.wyandotte -nation.org/history/general_history/brief_history.html, accessed November 27, 2009).

4. These tribal histories are based on the Senate report to accompany s

661 restoration of Oklahoma tribes, on histories presented on tribal websites (http://www.wyandotte-nation.org, http://www.peoriatribe.com/, http://www.ottawatribe.org/, all accessed November 27, 2009, and on Josephy, 500 Nations, 243–44, 261, 279, 306–7.

5. Vine Deloria Jr., statement on behalf of National Congress of American Indians to House Subcommittee on Indian Affairs hearing on HR 7421, Menominee restoration, June 28, 1973, 321.

6. Senate report 2516 to accompany s 3969, 5, 2517 to accompany s 3970, 6, and 2519 to accompany s 3968, 3, 4.

7. Ottawa tribal resolution, February 18, 1956, contained in Senate Report 2516; Peoria tribal resolution.

8. Rep. Clair Engle statement to meeting at Lone Pine Rancheria, February 18, 1956, quote in memo by John C. Dibbern to acting chief of coordinating staff, March 2, 1956, folder 00-1953 California 015, BIA Central Classified Files 1940-56 California 4670 1954-013 to 00 1955 05, Box 6 entry 121, RG75, NARA–Washington DC.

9. Report s 963, 3, 6.

10. Lewis Barlow, testimony, Senate Select Committee on Indian Affairs hearing on s 661, September 27, 1977, 90.

11. Forrest Gerard, testimony, 1977 hearing, 10; Report s 963, 10.

12. Rodney Arnett, testimony, 1977 hearing, 94.

13. Mont Cotter, testimony, 1977 hearing, 99, 100.

14. Bill Follis, testimony, 1977 hearing, 15, 16.

15. Robert Alexander, testimony, 1977 hearing, 15.

16. Ponca Tribe of Nebraska, "About Us," http://www.poncatribe-ne.org/about.php, scroll to "Termination," accessed November 27, 2009.

17. Legislative and administrative memo no. 62-1 covering 1961–62 from general counsel to Board of Directors, Association on American Indian Affairs, 7, folder Association on American Indian Affairs, 14-61-3 1954–64, American Indian Charter Convention, Alvin Josephy Papers Coll. 14, Special Collections and University Archives, University of Oregon Libraries, Eugene.

18. Michael Mason, interview with the author, February 19, 2002.

19. Elizabeth R. Grobsmith, associate professor of anthropology at the University of Nebraska, statement to Senate Select Committee on Indian Affairs hearing on s 1747, Ponca Restoration, March 28, 1990, 228.

20. Senate report 1623, June 25, 1962, to accompany s 3174.

21. John A. Carver Jr. to Lyndon B. Johnson, April 6, 1962, in Senate Report 1623 to accompany s 3174, June 25, 1968, 3, 4.

22. Grobsmith, statement at 1990 Ponca restoration hearing, 236.

23. Fred LeRoy, telephone interview with the author, August 29, 2002.

24. House report 101–776, October 1, 1990.

25. Grobsmith, statement at 1990 Ponca restoration hearing, 206–20; LeRoy interview; "Ponca Trail of Tears," Nebraska state historical marker viewed at http://www.nebraskahistory.org/publish/markers/texts/ponca_trail_of_tears .htm, accessed January 2, 2010; Ponca Tribe of Nebraska viewed at "About Us," http://www.poncatribe-ne.org/about.php, scroll to "Trial of Chief Standing Bear," accessed January 5, 2010; the story of Chief Standing Bear is related in Wilson, Earth Shall Weep, 293–95, and in Tibbles, Standing Bear and the Ponca Chiefs; Mordock recounts the Ponca history in detail in Reformers and the American Indians.

26. Thomas, Indian Voices, 8, Folder AAIA 14-61-3, Josephy Papers.

27. Gloria Chytka, testimony, 1990 Senate hearing, 189, 190.

28. Grobsmith, statement, 1990 Senate hearing, 231.

29. Leroy interview.

9. MENOMINEES

1. Ada Deer, interview with the author, May 15, 2001.

2. Descriptions of the problems in Menominee County abound in the testimony before both the House Subcommittee on Indian Affairs and the Senate Select Committee on Indian Affairs in 1972 and 1973 in hearings on Menominee restoration, including statements by tribal members Ada Deer and Andrew J. Pyatskowit, Theodore Boyd of MEI, Sen. Gaylord Nelson, and Nancy Lurie, curator of the Milwaukee Public Museum, who also submitted a lengthy paper detailing the tribe's problems; in addition, the problems of the tribe were the subject of numerous newspaper and magazine articles, including an August 1965 series by Ray Pagel in the Green Bay Press Gazette, Ridgeway's "Lost Indians" in the New Republic, and Homer Bigart, "Menominee Problems," New York Times, February 27, 1972, 57; Peroff, Menominee Drums, discusses conditions, 169–73.

3. George Kenote, testimony, hearing by Senate Select Committee on Indian Affairs, September 17, 1972, 175.

4. Joseph Preloznik, testimony, hearing by Senate Select Committee on Indian Affairs, September 17, 1972, 176.

5. Shirley Daley, testimony, hearing by Senate Select Committee on Indian Affairs, September 17, 1972, 176.

6. Daly statement to House Indian Affairs Subcommittee hearing on Menominee restoration, May 25 and 26, 1973, 83; Verna Fowler, interview with the author, May 22, 2001; interview with anonymous tribal member, May 22, 2001.

7. Fowler interview.

8. Rep. Lloyd Meeds, statement at Menominee restoration hearing by House Subcommittee on Indian Affairs, May 25, 1973, 31.

9. Peroff, *Menominee Drums*, 173.

10. The Menominee Indian Tribe of Wisconsin, "MITW History—1960–1979," http://menominee-nsn.gov/history/1960–1979.php, accessed January 4, 2010.

11. Deer interview.

12. Peroff, *Menominee Drums*, 214; Menominee Indian Tribe, "MITW History—1960–1979."

13. Fowler interview.

14. Deer interview.

15. Menominee Indian Tribe, "MITW History—1960–1979," 1968; Peroff, *Menominee Drums*, describes the development and opposition to it, 147–52, 182.

16. Deer interview; Lurie document for House subcommittee hearing on restoration, 190–98; Joseph F. Preloznik, director of Judicare, to Richard Cohen, November 18, 1971, Series III B&C American Indian Civil Rights and American Indian Education, folder Development of American Indian Policy, Menominee termination policy correspondence, June 1966 to November 1975, Josephy Papers, Coll. 14, Special Collections and University Archives, University of Oregon Libraries, Eugene.

17. Beck, *Struggle for Self-Determination*, 161.

18. Menominee Indian Tribe, "MITW History—1960–1979," 1970, 1971, 1972, described in more detail in Peroff, *Menominee Drums*, 185–89; Deer interview.

19. Sen. Gaylord Nelson, statement, at 1973 House hearing, 1, 2.

20. Meeds statement, 1973 House hearing, 6.

21. Wilbur Weber, testimony at 1973 House hearing, 40.

22. Theodore Boyd, testimony at 1973 House hearing, 88.

23. Rep. Manuel Lujan Jr., comment, House hearing, June 28, 1973, 282.

24. Rep. Harold Froehlich, testimony, House hearing, June 28, 1973, 258.

25. William R. Giese, testimony, 1973 Senate hearing, 107–22.

26. Dr. M. J. Reenhardt, letter submitted to House subcommittee, hearing record, 396.

27. Andrew J. Pyatskowit, testimony, 1973 Senate hearing, 81–85; Beck, *Struggle for Self-Determination*, 158.

28. Arnold Gruber, testimony, House hearing, June 28, 1973, 101.

29. George Kenote, letters to Reps. Lloyd Meeds, Harold V. Froehlich, and David R. Obey, all dated June 18, 1973, and contained in record of Senate hearing, 204–5.

30. Council of Chiefs, letter, June 24, 1973, and resolution, June 13, 1973, House hearing record.

31. House hearing record: League of Women Voters letter, 396; John Perote testimony for AIM, 63; Wisconsin Legislature memorial to Congress, 127; Democratic platform referenced in Ada Deer testimony, 35; Vine Deloria Jr. for National Congress of American Indians, 323; Wisconsin state senator Reuben LaFave on behalf of Wisconsin Indian Study Committee, 17.

32. Jerome Grignon, House hearing, May 26, 1973, 209–11.

33. Sen. James Abourezk, statement opening Senate hearing, 1.

34. Menominee Indian Tribe, "MITW History—1960–1979," 1973; President Nixon signing statement, *Public Papers of the Presidents*, Richard Nixon #369, 1023, Senate library.

35. Deloria, testimony, House hearing, May 25, 1973, 223–26.

36. David Obey, statement, House hearing, May 25, 1973, 8; Obey may have jumped the gun—the measure did not pass until later in the year, or perhaps he meant that the serious consideration given the Menominee restoration amounted to repudiation of termination.

37. Menominee Indian Tribe, "MITW History—1960–1979," 1975.

38. Deer interview.

39. Menominee Indian Tribe, "MITW History—1960–1979," 1974–79.

40. Fowler interview.

41. Menominee Indian Tribe, "MITW Housing Department," http://menominee-nsn.gov/housing/housing/housingHome.php; Menominee Indian Tribe, "Department of Transit Services" http://menominee-nsn.gov/community development/transportation/services.php; Boyd interview.

42. Llewellyn Boyd, telephone interview with the author, November 3, 2006.

43. Menominee Indian Tribe, "MITW History—1960–1979"; Menominee Indian Tribe, "MITW History—1980–1990," http://menominee-nsn.gov/history/1980-1990.php, accessed February 4, 2010; Menominee Indian Tribe, "MITW Historic Preservation," http://menominee-nsn.gov/laborEdu/historic/historicHome.php; William E. Farrell, articles in the *New York Times*, January 10, 1975, 35, and February 10, 1975, 15; Matt Pommer, "Fire Damages Forest," *Madison (WI) Capital Times*, October 28, 2003, 1, available online at http://www.highbeam.com, accessed October 22, 2008.

44. Boyd interview.

45. Deer, testimony at 1973 House hearing, 293.

10. SILETZ

1. Charles Wilkinson describes the rulings and the combustible Northwest atmosphere over salmon and Indian fishing rights in the chapter "The Salmon People," of *Blood Struggle*, 150–73.

2. John Donaldson, testimony, Senate Select Committee on Indian Affairs hearing, July 13, 1977, on s 1560 Siletz Restoration, 30–32.

3. Forrest L. Mueret to Teno Roncallo, House Subcommittee on Indian Affairs, July 13, 1977, entered as additional material in record of hearing by Senate Select Committee on Indian Affairs, July 13, 1977.

4. Interior Department statement at the July 13, 1977, hearing, 16, 23.

5. Michael Mason, interview with the author, February 19, 2002.

6. Doyce Waldrip, interview with the author, January 30, 2002.

7. All Coast Fishermen's Marketing Association statement included in Arthur Bensell testimony, hearing by Senate Select Committee on Indian Affairs, Siletz restoration, March 30, 1976, 56. The committee held hearings on Siletz restoration in both 1976 and 1977.

8. Susan Shawn Harjo, testimony to 1976 Senate hearing, 89.

9. Testimony at 1976 hearing by Beverly Hall, Oregon Department of Fish and Wildlife, 64, William Luch, Trout Unlimited, 101, Forrest L. Meuret, Save Oregon's Resources Today, 102, 103.

10. Kathryn Harrison, testimony, 1976 Senate hearing, 54, 55.

11. Sen. Mark O.Hatfield, statement opening 1977 Senate hearing, 2.

12. Bensell, testimony, 1977 Senate hearing, 25.

13. Joe Lane, statement in additional materials in 1977 Senate hearing record.

14. Pauline Bell Ricks, testimony, House Committee on Interior and Insular Affairs, May 29, 1980, on HR 7267 to establish a Siletz Reservation.

15. Hatfield, statement opening 1977 Senate hearing, 26.

16. Donaldson, testimony, 1977 Senate hearing, 30; although it was not mentioned in the Siletz hearing, the Menominee Nation had won the precedent-setting ruling on continuation of hunting and fishing rights in 1968.

17. Laura Clapper, statement for National Wildlife Federation, in additional material in 1977 Senate hearing record, 41.

18. Arthur Bensell to Mark O. Hatfield, April 14, 1976, inserted in 1976 hearing record, 96.

19. "All Indian Celebration Is Planned by Siletz," *Newport (OR) News-Times*, November 16, 1977, 1, Trend section, Oregon Historical Society files.

20. Confederated Tribes of Siletz Indians of Oregon twenty-fifth anniversary restoration celebration, November 16, 2002, program accomplishments, 10; "Tribe Restored," *Newport News-Times*, September 28, 1977, 11; "Deal Reached on Land," *Newport News-Times*, May 7, 1980.

21. Bensell, testimony, House Committee on Interior and Insular Affairs, May 29, 1980, on HR 7567 to establish a Siletz Reservation.

22. William R. Blosser, testimony, hearing by House Interior and Insular Affairs Committee on HR 7267 Siletz reservation bill, May 29, 1980.

23. Blosser, testimony, hearing, May 29, 1980.

24. ECONorthwest, *Economic and Social Impact Study*.

25. Michael Darcy, interview with the author, February 23, 2001.

26. Darcy interview.

27. Roberta Ulrich, "Indians Do Better Job than Feds," *Portland Oregonian*, July 19, 1995, D01.

28. "Siletz Tribe Contributions," *Siletz (OR) News*, 28, no. 5 (May 2000), 22.

29. ECONorthwest, *Economic and Social Impact Study*, 3, 12, 13.

30. Darcy interview; Bensell Breon, interview with the author, February 13, 2001.

31. Delores Pigsley, "The Blessings of Siletz Tribal Sovereignty," *Oregonian*, November 16, 2002.

11. OKLAHOMA AND UTAH

1. Forrest Gerard, testimony, Senate Select Committee on Indian Affairs, September 27, 1977, 10, 12.

2. John Ghostbear, testimony, Senate Select Committee on Indian Affairs, September 27, 1977, 13.

3. s 661 (U.S. Code Title 25, Subchapter XXXVII e), 557.

4. Senate Report to accompany s 661, Select Committee, September 27, 1977.

5. Lewis Barlow, testimony, 1977 Senate hearing, 90.

6. U.S. Code Title 25, Subchapter XXXVII—Wyandotte, Peoria, Ottawa, and Modoc Tribes of Oklahoma: Restoration of Federal Supervision; see specifically article 861a, organization of tribes.

7. Helen Christie, acting executive director, Inter-Tribal Council, Inc. of Oklahoma, telephone interview with the author, December 29, 2009.

8. Wyandotte Nation, http://www.wyandotte-nation.org; Peoria Tribe of Indians of Oklahoma, http://www.peoriatribe.com; Ottawa Tribe of Oklahoma, http://www.ottawatribe.org, accessed March 9, 2006, and November 27, 2009.

9. Leaford Bearskin, telephone interview with the author, November 9, 2006; Wyandotte Nation, http://www.wyandotte-nation.org.

10. Thomas G. Alexander, "Native Americans in Post War Utah."

11. Sen. Orrin Hatch, statement to Senate Select Committee on Indian Affairs, Hearing on Paiute Restoration Act, s 1273, November 8, 1979, 27–29.

12. Ralph Reeser, testimony, Senate Select Committee on Indian Affairs, Hearing on Paiute Restoration Act, s 1273, November 8, 1979, 18, 19.

13. Public Law 96-227, section a, U.S. Code Title 25, Subchapter XXXII-A.

14. House Report 96-712 to accompany HR 4996, Paiute report, December 18, 1979, 4.

15. Letters entered into record of 1979 Senate committee hearing: Robert K. Chicago, undated, 56; Utah Legal Services, October 24, 1979, 54; Reid Blondquist, undated, 55; Dale T. Tingey, October 24, 1979, 55.

16. Beverly Snow, testimony at 1979 Senate hearing, 46.

17. Rep. Dan Marriott, prepared statement in record of 1979 Senate hearing, 14.

18. Thomas G. Alexander, "Native Americans in Post War Utah."

19. Paiute Indians of Utah, PL 96-227, http://www.onlineutah.com/paiutehistory.shtml, accessed October 27, 2004.

20. Suh'dutsing Technologies website, http://www.suhdutsingllc.com; Steven Oberbeck, "Paiutes Land $8M Telecom Contract at Dugway," *Salt Lake Tribune*, August 25, 2006, available at http://www.suhdutsingtelecom.com/PR _PaiutesDugway.htm, accessed November 28, 2009.

21. Dorene Martineaux, telephone interview with the author, January 9, 2007.

22. Metcalf, *Termination's Legacy*.

23. Nancy Hobbs, "Mixed Blood Indians Seek Reinstatement in Ute Tribe," *Salt Lake Tribune*, August 1, 1993, 1, b2; Larry Weist, "Mixed Bloods Seek Indian Status," *Salt Lake City Deseret Morning News*, June 29, 2003; Tatel (David S.), Appeals Court Opinion, United States Court of Appeals for the District of Columbia Circuit, January 19, 2007, http://undeclaredutes.net/AppealCourtsOpinion .html, accessed November 28, 2009.

24. Lezlee E. Whiting, "Members of Uinta Band Lose Bid to Regain Status," *Deseret Morning News*, January 31, 2006.

12. COW CREEKS AND GRAND RONDES

1. Sue M. Shaffer, interview with the author, March 13, 2001.

2. Cow Creek Band, "Cow Creek Band of Umpqua Tribe of Indians, 1853– 1982," based on tribal historical records, Roseburg OR, 2002, 2, 3; Christopher Hamm, "Reagan Signs Bill Recognizing Cow Creek Indians," *Roseburg (OR) News-Review*, December 30, 1982, 1; House Report 97-862 on HR 6588, December 29, 1982.

3. Hamm, "Reagan Signs Bill," 1.

4. Shaffer interview.

5. Roberta Ulrich, "A Future Chance," *Portland Oregonian*, December 5, 1994, B01.

6. "Cow Creek Band of Umpqua Tribe of Indians," 7; Michael Rondeau, chief tribal financial officer, interview with the author, March 13, 2001.

7. Alice Tallmadge, "Cow Creek Tribe Flourishes despite a Rocky Past," *Portland Oregonian*, April 28, 2002; Cow Creek Seven Feathers Foundation, "A History of Giving," Roseburg OR, 2001.

8. Cow Creek Band, "History of Giving," 10; Tallmadge, "Cow Creek Tribe Flourishes."

9. Rondeau interview.

10. Ulrich, "Future Chance."

11. Sue M. Shaffer, testimony, Senate Committee on Indian Affairs, April 7, 1998, http://www.cowcreek.com/govt/index.html, scroll to "Sue Shaffer Senate Testimony," accessed January 2, 2010.

12. Kathryn Harrison, interview with the author, November 5, 2001.

13. The process was not contained in regulations, although there were several criteria imposed. However, each restoration followed the same basic pattern, as indicated in the various hearings records and restoration legislation.

14. Native American Project, Oregon Legal Services, Grant proposal for 1980–81, from files of the Confederated Tribes of the Grand Ronde Community of Oregon.

15. Donald Wharton, telephone interview with the author, March 12, 2001.

16. NAPOLS 1981 application for funding to Campaign for Human Development, from Grand Ronde files.

17. Kathryn Harrison, interview with the author, January 9, 2002.

18. Interviews conducted by the author with Jackie Whisler, May 8, 2000, June Olson, May 8, 2000, Elizabeth Furse, October 31, 2001, and Donald Wharton, October 28, 2001; Jackie Mercier Colton, testimony, House Interior and Insular Affairs Committee, October 18, 1983, from Grand Ronde files.

19. Kathryn Harrison interview, 2002.

20. Karen Harrison, testimony, House Committee on Interior and Insular Affairs, October 18, 1983, from Grand Ronde tribal files.

21. Kathryn Harrison, testimony, House Committee, 1983.

22. Report 98-464, 98th Cong., 1st sess., to accompany HR 3885, 4, from Grand Ronde tribal files.

23. Marvin Kimsey, Frank Harrison, and Jackie Mercier Colton, testimony at 1983 hearing, from Grand Ronde tribal files.

24. LeaAnn Easton, interview with the author, December 11, 2001.

25. Rep. Les AuCoin, testimony, House Interior and Insular Affairs Committee, April 12, 1988, on HR 4143, Establishing a Reservation for the Confederated Tribes of the Grand Ronde Community of Oregon, 3, 4, from Grand Ronde tribal files.

26. *Oregon Blue Book*, 1995–96 ed., 83.

27. Jeanie Senior and Kris Brenneman, "Tribal Giving," *Portland Tribune*, September 16, 2003, 1, 8.

28. Angie Sears, "Spirit Mountain Community Fund Reveals New Logo,"

Smoke Signals (Grand Ronde tribal newspaper), September 15, 2006, 4; Ed Pearsall, qtd. in Sears, "Spirit Mountain Community Fund."

29. Harry Esteve, "Tribe Takes Gamble in Turf War," *Oregonian*, June 25, 2006. A01.

13. KLAMATHS

1. Donald Wharton, interview with the author, October 28, 2001.

2. Charles E. Kimbol Sr., interview with the author, August 27, 2000.

3. Wharton interview; the ruling in the Kimbol case followed by seven years the similar Menominee ruling by the U.S. Supreme Court. The Menominees, however, still largely controlled their traditional hunting and fishing areas through Menominee County or the tribal enterprise corporation; the Klamath Tribes no longer owned or controlled any of their lands.

4. Kimbol interview.

5. House report 99-630, June 11, 1986, 3, House Interior and Insular Affairs with HR 3554, Klamath Restoration.

6. Kimbol interview.

7. Jeff Mitchell, interview with the author, September 16, 2002.

8. Editorial, *Klamath Falls (OR) Herald and News*, June 19, 1986, 4; "Klamath Tribes Standing Restored," *Herald and News*, August 16, 1986, 1.

9. "Senate Passed," *Herald and News*, August 15, 1986, 1; "Klamath Tribes Exist Again," *Herald and News*, August 28, 1986, 1.

10. Elwood Miller, interview with the author, September 17, 2002.

11. Allen Foreman, telephone interview with the author, January 11, 2007.

12. Klamath Tribes, "The Klamath Tribes Economic Self Sufficiency Plan," http://klamathtribes.org/information/background/ESSPWeb03.html, accessed February 10, 2010.

13. Foreman interview, January 11, 2007.

14. Rod Clarke, telephone interview with the author, December 12, 2006.

15. Clarke interview.

16. Klamath Tribes Public Information/News Department, communication to author, December 30, 2009.

17. Clarke interview.

18. Klamath Tribes, "Economic Self Sufficiency Plan."

19. Klamath Tribes, "Housing Department," http://klamathtribes.org/departments/#tribalhousing, accessed December 30, 2009.

20. "Klamath First to Receive Federal TANF Approval," *Indian Country Today*, June 1997.

21. Foreman interview, August 27, 2000.

22. Foreman interview, January 11, 2007.

23. Clarke interview.

24. Elwood Miller interview.

25. Mitchell interview.

26. Gerald Skelton, interview with the author, September 17, 2002.

27. Kimbol interview.

28. Foreman interview, August 27, 2000.

14. COOS AND COQUILLES

1. Bill Brainard, interview with the author, March 28, 2002; deed copy in papers of Donald Whereat.

2. Bill Brainard interview.

3. Stephen Dow Beckham, "historical perspective" prepared for the Coos, Lower Umpqua, and Siuslaw Indian Tribe, undated copy in Whereat papers; "Coos Indians Address Land Petition to UN," *Portland Oregonian*, August 17, 1956, 1.

4. Donald Whereat, interview with the author, March 28, 2002.

5. Bill Brainard interview.

6. Bill Brainard interview; Carolyn Slyter, interview with the author, March 27, 2002; Whereat interview.

7. House report 98-904, July 25, 1984, to accompany HR 5540, Coos Restoration.

8. Bill Brainard interview.

9. "Confederated Tribes Status Restored," *Coos Bay (OR) World*, October 18, 1984, 2.

10. PL98-481, Section 714e, U.S. Code Title 25, Subchapter XXX-D.

11. Fact sheet—Forest Land Restoration Plan, April 2003, Confederated Tribes of Coos, Lower Umpqua, and Siuslaw document.

12. Fact sheet, 2.

13. Laurie Voshall, telephone interview with the author, December 15, 2006.

14. Associated Press, "Feds Give 43 Acres on Coast to Tribes," November 24, 2004, from Coos tribal files.

15. Slyter interview.

16. Bill Brainard interview.

17. Howard Crombie, natural resources director, Coos tribe, telephone interview with the author, December 15, 2006.

18. Slyter interview.

19. Ron Brainard, telephone interview with the author, December 28, 2006.

20. Whereat interview.

21. George Barton, interview with the author, March 29, 2002.

22. Profiles of Selected Terminated and Non-federally Recognized Tribes, Oregon Termination, undated report prepared for Task Force 10 of the American Indian Policy Review Commission, 28, 29; House Report 1061 to accompany HR 881, Coquille restoration, August 5, 1988.

23. Doris and Bud Chase, interview with the author, March 26, 2001.

24. Senate Report 101-50 to accompany s 521, Select Committee on Indian Affairs, June 13, 1989.

25. Michele Burnette, testimony, hearing by House Interior Committee, August 5, 1988, from Coquille tribal files.

26. Wilfred Wassson testimony, hearing by House Interior Committee, August 5, 1988, from Coquille tribal files.

27. Sharon Parrish, interview with the author, March 27, 2001.

28. Roy Gilkey, testimony, 1988 House hearing, from Coquille tribal files.

29. Edward L. Metcalf, telephone interview with the author, December 19, 2006.

30. David Lewis, telephone interview with the author, November 2 and 3, 2008.

31. Roberta Ulrich, "Casino Opens in North Bend," *Portland Oregonian*, May 19, 1995, B01.

32. Edward L. Metcalf interview.

33. Parrish interview.

34. Roberta Ulrich, unpublished notes from May 1995 interview with Bruce Anderson, then CEO of CEDCO, Coquille Tribe's development arm.

35. Courtney Thompson, "Loan Deals New Hand to Coquille Casino," *Oregonian*, October 10, 1996, D03.

36. "Money Distributed," *Tribal Tidbits* (Coquille Tribal newsletter), February 2006, 1, 8.

37. "Development Plans," *Tribal Tidbits*, March 2006, 1.

38. Thomas interview.

39. Robert Bojorcas, Robert Coiner, and Dennis DeGross, study of termination effects on Oregon Indians prepared for Task Force 10 of the American Indian Policy Review Commission, 29, from the files of Donald Whereat; Profiles of Selected Terminated and Non-federally Recognized Tribes, prepared for Task Force 10, 28–29.

40. "Peacegiving Court," *Tribal Tidbits*, March 2006, 6, reprinted from Affiliated Tribes of Northwest Indians newsletter, February–April 2006.

15. ALABAMA-COUSHATTAS AND CALIFORNIA

1. Arnold Battise, testimony, House Subcommittee on Indian Affairs hearing on HR 1344, Alabama-Coushatta Restoration, 99th Cong., 2nd sess., June 25, 1986, 27.

2. *Tyler County Booster*, September 12, 1985, copy in House hearing record, 352.

3. 1986 House hearing record, 98, 348, 349, 350, 353, 354, 355.

4. Alabama-Coushatta Tribe of Texas, "Tribal History," http://alabama-coushatta.com, click on "History," click on "Tribal History," accessed December 29, 2009.

5. Tom Diamond, statement to Senate Select Committee, incorporated in appendix to House hearing.

6. Morris Bullard, testimony, 1986 House hearing, 24; Bullard, statement in hearing appendix, 344.

7. Battise, testimony, 1986 House hearing, 26.

8. Bob Bullock, statement, 1986 House hearing appendix, 436; Bullard testimony, 24.

9. Alabama-Coushatta Tribe, "Tribal History"; 1986 House hearing, 21.

10. Bullard, statement in 1986 hearing appendix, 342.

11. Alabama-Coushatta Tribe, "Tribal History."

12. Alabama-Coushatta Tribe of Texas, "Economic Opportunities," http://alabama-coushatta.com, click on "Economic Dev.," click on "Economic Opportunities," accessed December 29, 2009.

13. Alabama-Coushatta Tribe, "Economic Opportunities."

14. "Return Money to Alabama-Coushatta," http://Indianz.com, January 12, 2006, accessed April 5, 2006; Suzanne Gamboa, Associated Press, November

11, 2005, posted on the *San Antonio Express-News* website, http://mysantonio
.com/global, accessed April 5, 2006.

15. Tribal chairman Carlos Bullock in a telephone interview with the author
January 4, 2010, said that this statement remained tribal philosophy although
it had been temporarily removed from the tribe's website during a redesign.

16. *Tillie Hardwick, et al., plaintiffs v. United States of America, et al., defendants*,
Stipulation of entry of judgment, July 13, 1983, available at http://humboldt
.edu/ffinasp/hardwick, accessed May 24, 2004.

17. Keith Pike, interview with the author, November 13, 2002.

18. Blue Lake Casino Hotel, http://www.bluelakecasino.com/Rancheria.htm,
accessed April 7, 2006.

19. Cheryl Seidner, interview with the author, November 12 and 13, 2002.

20. Leona Wilkinson, interview with the author, November 13, 2002.

21. "Lake Sonoma Dam Drowns Basket Plants," http://kstrom.net/isk/art/
basket/warmdam.html, accessed April 7, 2006.

22. Don Arnold, interview with the author, November 12, 2002.

16. CATAWBAS AND PONCAS

1. The preceding narrative was compiled from House report 103-27, September 27, 1993, Catawba Land Claims Settlement Act of 1993, HR 2399; section (a) Findings of PL 103-116 Title 25, Subchapter XLIII-A, Catawba Indian Tribe of South Carolina: Restoration of Federal Trust Relationship, U.S. Code, and testimony at the House Subcommittee on Indian Affairs hearing on HR 2399, July 2, 1993.

2. Rep. Craig Thomas, additional views entered into Report 103–27, 35.

3. Rep. Bill Richardson, opening statement at 1993 House subcommittee hearing.

4. E. Fred Sanders to Rep. George Miller, June 30, 1993, entered in record of House hearing, 300–301.

5. Gilbert Blue, testimony, 1993 House hearing, 14.

6. State Rep. Robert W. Hayes Jr., testimony, 1993 House hearing, 226.

7. PL 103–116 section 9411i, Tribal trust funds, section 941, Games of chance.

8. Blue, testimony, 1993 House hearing, 223.

9. Thomas J. Blumer to Rep. John M. Spratt Jr., entered in 1993 House hearing record, 256–58.

10. Catawba Cultural Presentation Project, http://www.ccppcrafts.com, accessed January 13, 2007.

11. Village Habitat Design, "Catawba Indian Reservation," http://villagehabitat.com/project_menu/Catawba/Catawba.htm, accessed November 27, 2009.

12. U.S. Environmental Protection Agency, "Catawba Indian Nation, EPA Sign Environmental Agreement," http://www.epa.gov/, search by press release title, accessed November 27, 2009.

13. U.S. Fish and Wildlife Service, "Fish and Wildlife Service Issues Call for Proposals," http://www.fws.gov/southeast/news/2005, November 2, 2005, accessed January 13, 2007.

14. Jim Largo, "Governor Stalling Catawba Plans for Second Bingo," *Indian Country Today*, December 17, 2003, http://indiancountrytoday.com, click on "Archive," search for "Catawba," accessed January 4, 2010.

15. Fred LeRoy, telephone interview with the author, August 29, 2002.

16. Fred LeRoy, testimony, hearing by Senate Select Committee on Indian Affairs, March 28, 1990, 69, CIS90 S411–23, hearing 101–762.

17. Sen. Robert Kerrey, statement and letters in record of 1990 Senate hearing, 78, 147.

18. LeRoy interview.

19. Ponca Tribe of Nebraska, "Restoration," http://www.poncatribe-ne.org, click on "About the Ponca Tribe," scroll to "Restoration," accessed January 25, 2006.

20. Kerrey, statement, 1990 Senate hearing, 78.

21. Michael Mason, interview with the author, February 19, 2002.

22. Ponca Tribe, "Restoration."

23. LeRoy, testimony, 1990 Senate committee, 69.

24. Gloria Chytka, statement to 1990 Senate committee, 187–89.

25. PL 101–84 sections 983b, c, h, Title 25, subchapter XLVI-A, U.S. Code.

26. LeRoy interview.

27. Ponca Economic Development Corporation, http://www.poncatribe.biz, accessed April 13, 2006; "Local NE Tribe Reveals Prior Nuclear Waste Site Proposal," *Nuclear Power Today*, August 19, 2004, available at http://www.allbusiness.com/utilities/electric-power-generation/202105-1.html, accessed February 3, 2010; Mark Peniska, qtd. in "SMSC Donates $1 Million to Ponca Tribe of Nebraska," Shakopee Mdewakanton Sioux Community, October 3, 2006, http://www.shakopeedakota.org/press/2006/20061003.html, accessed November 27, 2009; "Ponca Tribe Offered to Host Radioactive Waste Dump,"

August 11, 2004, http://64.38.12.138/News/2004/003786.asp, accessed November 27, 2009; search for Ponca Earthlodge or Ponca Tribal Museum at the Nebraska Department of Economic Development website, http://visitnebraska .gov, accessed February 9, 2010.

28. National Fire Plan, "Fire Regime and Rangeland Restoration on Ponca Land," http://forestsandrangelands.gov/success/index.cfm, click on "Nebraska," click on "Fire Regime and Rangeland Restoration," accessed February 3, 2010; Nebraska Game and Parks Commission, "The Natural Legacy Project," http:www.ngpc.state.ne.us/wildlife/programs/legacy, accessed February 4, 2010.

29. Northern Ponca Housing Authority, http://www.poncahousing.org, accessed January 5, 2010.

30. Ponca Tribe of Nebraska Department of Social Services, communication to the author, February 5, 2010.

31. "USDA Rural Development Assists in Historic Tribal Building Restoration for Use as Tribal Cultural Center," http://www.rurdev.usda.gov/ne/FY03SuccessStoryPoncaTribeofNECFLN&GRT.pdf, accessed January 6, 2010.

32. Associated Press, "Mormon Church Thanks Ponca Tribe for Saving Lives," August 19, 2003, posted to website, http://64.38.12.138/News/archives/000896.asp, accessed January 6, 2010.

EPILOGUE

1. Alvin M. Josephy Jr., "The American Indian and the Bureau of Indian Affairs," 1969, Box 52, folder 14/72 Citizens Advocacy Center, 8, Josephy Papers, Coll. 14, Special Collections and University Archives, University of Oregon Libraries, Eugene.

2. Josephy, "American Indian and the Bureau of Indian Affairs."

3. Charles Wilkinson discusses the Colville battle over termination in *Blood Struggle*, 179–82; minutes, Committee on Jurisdiction, Tribal Leaders Conference, October 18, 1966, 413; Doyce Waldrip, former superintendent of Seminole Reservation, interview with the author, January 30, 2002.

4. Josephy, "American Indian and the Bureau of Indian Affairs."

5. Josephy, interview with the author, September 3, 2003.

6. Wilson, *Earth Shall Weep*, 378–79; Charles Wilkinson, *American Indians*, 124; Charles Wilkinson, *Blood Struggle*, 216.

7. James Abourezk, comment at meeting of the American Indian Policy Review Commission, June 4, 1976, from record printed for Senate Select Committee on Indian Affairs Meetings of AIPRC, 81.

8. Hank Adams, statement at AIPRC meeting, 104.

9. Michael Mason, interview with the author, September 19, 2002.

10. LeaAnn Easton, interview with the author, December 11, 2001.

11. Mason interview.

12. Edwin Goodman, interview with the author, February 27, 2002.

13. Randal C. Archibold, "Governor's Push to Expand Indian Casinos Fails in California," *New York Times*, September 2, 2006, 11; Erica Werner, "Tribe Battles over Labor Laws," Associated Press, *Spokane Spokesman-Review*, Spokane September 4, 2006, A3; Michael Pfeffer, "Gaming Legislation and Land-Divestiture Negotiations," *News from Native California*, Winter 2005, 21–23.

14. Easton interview.

15. Goodman interview.

16. Mason interview.

17. Charlie Moses, interview with the author, April 25, 2001.

18. Goodman interview.

19. Kathryn Harrison, interview with the author, January 9, 2002.

20. American Indian Rights and Resources Organization, "Genocide in California Indian Country," flyer distributed at the organization's protest rally at the California State Capitol, October 6, 2006.

Bibliography

ARCHIVES

Bureau of Indian Affairs, Office of the Commissioner. John R. Nichols, 1949–50; Dillon S. Myer, 1950–51; Glenn L. Emmons, 1956–58. Record Group 75, National Archives and Records Administration. Washington DC.

Bureau of Indian Affairs, Portland Area Office Records. Portland Area Office, Portland OR. Record Group 75, National Archives and Records Administration, Pacific Northwest Region. Seattle WA.

Chapman, Oscar. Records of the Secretary of the Interior, 1933–53. Record Group 48, National Archives and Record Administration. College Park MD.

Confederated Tribes of the Coos, Lower Umpqua and Siuslaw Indians. Donald Wheat Collection. Coos Bay OR.

Confederated Tribes of the Grand Ronde Community of Oregon. Tribal Records. Grand Ronde Archives. Grand Ronde OR.

Cook, Dibbon. Papers (Klamath General Council minutes). Special Collections and University Archives, University of Oregon Libraries, Eugene OR.

Haynal, Patrick. "From Termination through Restoration and Beyond: Modern Klamath Cultural Identity." PhD diss., University of Oregon, 1995.

Hill, Kathleen Shaye. "The Klamath Tribe: An Overview of Its Termination." Unpublished manuscript, February 20, 1985.

Jackson, Boyd. Papers, Special Collections and University Archives, University of Oregon Libraries, Eugene OR.

Josephy, Alvin M., Jr. Papers. Special Collections and University Archives, University of Oregon Libraries, Eugene OR.

Klamath Indian Education Program, Records. Hiroto Zakoji files, Beaverton OR.

Klamath Management Specialists. Records. Special Collections and University Archives, University of Oregon Libraries, Eugene OR.

McKay, Douglas. Papers. Oregon State Archives, Salem OR.

———. Papers. Special Collections and University Archives, University of Oregon Libraries, Eugene OR.

———. Records of the Secretary of the Interior, 1952–56. Records Group 48, National Archives and Records Administration, College Park MD.

Orfield, Gary. "Ideology and the Indians: A Study of Termination Policy." Undated manuscript.

———. "The War on Menominee Poverty." Unpublished manuscript, May 1966.

PUBLISHED SOURCES

Alexander, Thomas G. "Native Americans in Post War Utah." In *Utah, the Right Place: The Official Centennial History.* Salt Lake City: Gibbs Smith, 1995. http://byustudies.byu.edu/showTitle.aspx?title=6451, accessed February 5, 2010.

American Indian Policy Review Commission. *Final Report to Congress.* May 17, 1977.

Beck, David R. M. *The Struggle for Self-Determination: History of the Menominee Indians since 1854.* Lincoln: University of Nebraska Press, 2005.

Brophy, William A., and Sophie D. Aberle, comps. *The Indian: America's Unfinished Business; Report of the Commission on the Rights, Liberties and Responsibilities of the American Indian.* Norman: University of Oklahoma Press, 1966.

Bureau of the Census. *Historical Statistics of the United States Colonial Times to 1970.* Bicentennial ed. Part 1. Washington DC: U.S. Department of Commerce, 1975.

Bureau of Indian Affairs, California Indian Agency. *Program for the Termination of Indian Bureau Activities in the State of California.* Sacramento CA: Bureau of Indian Affairs, 1949.

Bureau of Indian Affairs, Portland Area Office. *Program for the Early Termination of Certain Activities and Withdrawal of Supervision over the Indians at Grand Ronde-Siletz and Southwestern Oregon.* Portland OR: Bureau of Indian Affairs, 1950.

Caldera, Melody F., Chuck Hulbert, and Melody Caldera. *South Slough Adventures.* Coos Bay OR: Friends of South Slough, 1995.

California State Assembly. Joint Resolution 7. February 1947.

California State Senate. Senate Joint Resolution 29. Chapter 123 California Statutes. May 18, 1951.

Congressional Record 93 (1947 and 1948), 80th Cong., 1st and 2nd sess.

Costo, Rupert, and Jeanette Henry Costo, eds. *The Missions of California: A Legacy of Genocide.* San Francisco: Indian Historian Press, 1987.

Cutler, Bruce. *The Massacre at Sand Creek.* Norman: University of Oklahoma Press, 1995.

ECONorthwest. *An Economic and Social Impact Study: A Report for the Confederated Tribes of Siletz Indians.* Portland OR: ECONorthwest, 1999.

Federal Trade Commission Staff. *Consumer Problems of the Klamath Indians: A Call for Action.* Seattle WA: Federal Trade Commission, 1973.

Fixico, Donald Lee. *Termination and Relocation: Federal Indian Policy, 1945–60.* Albuquerque: University of New Mexico Press, 1986.

Hall, Roberta L. *The Coquille Indians: Yesterday, Today and Tomorrow.* Restoration ed. Corvallis OR: Words and Pictures Unlimited, 1991.

Haynal, Patrick. "Termination and Tribal Survival: Klamath Tribes of Oregon." *Oregon Historical Quarterly* 101, no. 3 (Fall 2000).

Hudson, Charles M. *The Catawba Nation.* University of Georgia monographs, no. 18. Athens: University of Georgia Press, 1970.

Jackson, Helen Hunt. *A Century of Dishonor.* 1881. Norman: University of Oklahoma Press, 1995.

Josephy, Alvin M., Jr. *500 Nations: An Illustrated History of North American Indians.* New York: Alfred A. Knopf, 1994.

———. *The Nez Perce Indians and the Opening of the Northwest.* New York: Houghton Mifflin, 1977.

———. *Now That the Buffalo's Gone: A Study of Today's American Indians.* New York: Alfred A. Knopf, 1982.

———, ed. *Red Power: The American Indians Fight for Freedom.* 2nd ed. Lincoln: University of Nebraska Press, 1999.

Kirk, Mrs. John. "Withdrawal of Federal Supervision over Indian Affairs." Speech prepared for delivery to the National Conference on Indian Welfare. *Congressional Record* 93, pt. 12 (May 27, 1947).

Marks, Paula Mitchell. *In a Barren Land: Indian Dispossession and Survival.* New York: William Moss, 1998.

McNeil, Michelle. "Tribal Gaming Expansion in Calif. to Boost Revenues for Education." *Education Week* 27, no. 13 (February 13, 2008).

Meriam, Lewis. *The Problem of Indian Administration*. Report of a survey made at the request of Hubert Work, Secretary of the Interior, and submitted to him February 21, 1928. Baltimore: Johns Hopkins Press, 1928.

Metcalf, R. Warren. *Termination's Legacy: The Discarded Indians of Utah*. Lincoln: University of Nebraska Press, 2002.

Mordock, Robert Winston. *The Reformers and the American Indians*. Columbia MO: University of Missouri Press, 1971.

Norton, Jack. "The Path of Genocide: From El Camino Real to the Gold Mines of the North." In *The Missions of California: A Legacy of Genocide*, ed. Rupert Costo and Jeanette Henry Costo, 111-29. San Francisco: Indian Historian Press, 1987.

O'Brien, Sharon. *American Indian Tribal Governments*. Norman: University of Oklahoma Press, 1989.

Oregon Blue Book. 1995–96 ed. Salem OR: Secretary of State.

Oregon. Legislature. Interim Committee on Indian Affairs. *A Reintroduction to the Indians of Oregon: A Report Submitted to the 50th Legislative Assembly of Oregon*. Salem OR, October 1958.

———. Legislature. 49th Legislative Assembly Memorial to Congress. January 29, 1957.

Peroff, Nicholas C. *Menominee Drums: Tribal Termination and Restoration, 1954–1974*. Norman: University of Oklahoma Press, 1982.

Ppfeffer, Michael. "Gaming Legislation and Land-Divestiture Negotiations." *News from Native California*, Winter 2005.

Philp, Kenneth R. *Termination Revisited: American Indians on the Trail to Self-Determination, 1933–1953*. Lincoln: University of Nebraska Press, 1999.

Prucha, Francis Paul. "America's Indians and the Federal Government, 1900 to 2000." *Wisconsin Magazine of History*, Winter 2000–2001.

Public Law 103-116.

Public Law 101-84.

Public Papers of the Presidents of the United States. Washington DC: Federal Register Division, National Archives and Records Service, 1953 and 1973.

Ridgeway, James. "The Lost Indians." *New Republic*, December 4, 1965.

Sady, Rachel Reese. "The Menominee Transition from Trusteeship." *Human Organization* 6, no. 2 (Summer 1946).

Shames, Deborah, ed. *Freedom with Reservation: The Menominee Struggle to Save Their*

Land and People. Madison WI: National Committee to Save the Menominee People and Forests, 1972.

Shipik, Florence Connally. "Saints as Oppressors." In *The Missions of California: A Legacy of Genocide*, ed. Rupert Costo and Jeannette Henry Costo. San Francisco: Indian Historian Press, 1987.

Thomas, Robert K., ed. "Ponca Lands." *Indian Voices*, April 1965.

Tibbles, Thomas Henry. *Standing Bear and the Ponca Chiefs*. Lincoln: University of Nebraska Press, 1995.

Truelove, W. T., and David Bunting. "The Economic Impact of Federal Indian Policy: Incentives and Response of the Klamath Indians." Paper presented at the 45th annual conference of the Western Economic Association, Burnaby, BC, August 30, 1971.

U.S. Code. Title 25, Subchapter XXX, Subchapter XXX-D, Subchapter XXXII, Subchapter XL, Subchapter XLIII, Subchapter XLVI, Subchapter XXXVII.

U.S. Commission on Reorganization of the Executive Branch of Government (Hoover Commission). Recommendations on Federal Indian Policy, 1948.

U.S. Congress. House. Committee on Appropriations, Subcommittee on Interior Appropriations. *1954 Interior Department Appropriations Bill*. Rpt. 98-464. 98th Cong., 1st sess. November 2, 1983.

———. House Interior and Insular Affairs Committee, Subcommittee on Indian Affairs. Hearing on H 1427-2, Termination Policy. 83rd Cong., 1st sess. July 22, 1953.

———. House. Committee on Interior and Insular Affairs. Hearing on S 3532. *Division of Assets of the Ute Tribe of Utah*. Rpt. 2493. 83rd Cong., 2nd sess. July 26, 1954.

———. House. Committee on Interior and Insular Affairs, Subcommittee on Indian Affairs. Hearing on HR 660, 663, 2471, 2578 amending the Klamath Termination Act. 85th Cong., 1st sess., August 1957.

———. House. Committee on Interior and Insular Affairs, Subcommittee on Indian Affairs. *Repealing the Act Terminating Federal Supervision over the Property and Members of the Menominee Indian Tribe of Wisconsin*. 92nd Cong., 2nd sess. October 11, 1972, Rpt. 93-572.

———. House. Committee on Interior and Insular Affairs, Subcommittee on Indian Affairs. Hearing on HR 7421 *Repealing the Act Terminating Federal Supervision over the Property and Members of the Menominee Indian Tribes of Wisconsin*. 93rd Cong., 1st sess. May 25–26, June 28, 1973.

———. House. Committee on Interior and Insular Affairs. HR 4996, *Paiute Restoration*. 96th Cong., 1st sess. Rpt. 96-712 December 18, 1979.

———. House. Committee on Interior and Insular Affairs. Hearing on HR 7267, *Establishing a Siletz Reservation*. 96th Cong., 2nd sess. May 29, 1980.

———. House. Committee on Interior and Insular Affairs. Hearing on HR 3885, *Grand Ronde Restoration*. Rpt. 98-464. 98th Cong., 1st sess. October 18, 1983.

———. House. Committee on Interior and Insular Affairs. Hearing on HR 5540, *Restoration of Coos Tribe*. Rpt. 98-904. 98th Cong., 2nd sess. July 25, 1984.

———. House. Committee on Interior and Insular Affairs. Hearing on HR 3554, *Restoration of the Klamath Tribes*. Rpt. 99-630. 99th Cong., 2nd sess. June 11, 1986.

———. House. Committee on Interior and Insular Affairs, Subcommittee on Indian Affairs. Hearing on HR 1344, *Restoration of Federal Supervision over the Alabama and Coushatta Tribes of Texas*. 99th Cong., 2nd sess. June 25, 1986.

———. House. Committee on Interior and Insular Affairs. Hearing on HR 4143, *Establishing a Reservation for the Confederated Tribes of the Grand Ronde Community of Oregon*. 100th Cong., 2nd sess. April 12, 1988.

———. House. Committee on Interior and Insular Affairs. Hearing on HR 881, *Coquille Restoration*. Rpt. 1061. 100th Cong., 2nd sess. August 5, 1988.

———. House. Committee on Interior and Insular Affairs. Hearing on S 1747, *Restoration of the Ponca Indian Tribe of Nebraska*. Rpt. 101-776. 101st Cong., 2nd sess. March 28, 1990.

———. House. Committee on Natural Resources. Hearing on HR 2399, *Catawba Land Claims Settlement Act of 1993*. Rpt. 103-27. 103rd Cong., 1st sess. July 2, 1993; Sept. 27, 1993.

———. House. Committee on Public Lands. HR 2502, *For the Welfare of the Klamath Indian Tribe of Oregon*. 80th Cong., 1st sess. Rpt. May 1, 1947.

———. House. Committee on Public Lands, Subcommittee on Indian Affairs. Hearing on *Authorizing a Census of California Indians*. 80th Cong., 1st sess. May 2, 1947; June 17, 1947.

———. House and Senate. Committees on Interior and Insular Affairs. Subcommittees on Indian Affairs. Hearings on *Termination of Federal Supervision over Certain Tribes of Indians*. February 13, 15, 16, 17, 23, March 4–5, 10–12, 1954.

————. Senate. Committee on Interior and Insular Affairs. Hearing on s 2744, *Termination of Federal Supervision over the Property of the Alabama and Coushatta Tribes of Texas.* Rpt. 1321. 83rd Cong., 2nd sess. May 11, 1954.

————. Senate. Committee on Interior and Insular Affairs. Hearing on Senate Concurrent Resolution 26: *Effects of Menominee Termination.* 92nd Cong., 1st sess. July 21, 1971.

————. Senate. Select Committee on Indian Affairs. Hearing on s 2670 and HR 7674, Paiute termination. 83rd Cong., 2nd sess. February 15, 1954.

————. Senate. Interior and Insular Affairs Committee. Rpt. 1321, to accompany s 2744, Alabama-Coushatta Termination. 83rd Cong., 2nd sess. May 11, 1954.

————. Senate. Select Committee on Indian Affairs. Hearing on s 3968, 3969, 3970, *Termination of Ottawa, Peoria and Wyandotte Tribes of Oklahoma.* Rpts. 2516 (ottawa), 2517, 2519. February 18, 1956.

————. Senate. Select Committee on Indian Affairs. Hearing on s 1687, *Menominee Restoration.* 92nd Cong., 2nd sess. September 17, 1972.

————. Senate. Select Committee on Indian Affairs. Hearing on s 2801, *Restoration of the Siletz Indian Tribe.* 94th Cong., 2nd sess. March 30, 1976.

————. Senate. Select Committee on Indian Affairs. Hearing on s 661, *Status of Oklahoma Indian Tribes.* 95th Cong., 1st sess. Rpt. 95-574. Sept. 27, 1977.

————. Senate. Select Committee on Indian Affairs. Hearing on s 1560, *Siletz Restoration.* 95th Cong., 1st sess. July 13, 1977.

————. Senate. Select Committee on Indian Affairs. Hearing on s 1273, *Restoration of Paiute Indian Tribes of Utah.* 96th Cong., 1st sess. Rpt.96-481. November 8 and 29, 1979.

————. Senate. Select Committee on Indian Affairs. Hearing HR 1344, Texas Tribes Restoration. 99th Cong., 2nd sess. June 25, 1986.

————. Senate. Select Committee on Indian Affairs. Hearing on s 521, *Restoration of the Coquille Tribe.* 101st Cong., 1st sess. Rpt. 101-50. June 13, 1989.

————. Senate. Select Committee on Indian Affairs. Hearing on s 1747, *Restoration of the Ponca Indian Tribe of Nebraska.* 101st Cong., 2nd sess. March 28, 1990.

————. Senate. Committee on Public Lands, Subcommittee on Indian Affairs. Hearing on s 1222, regarding the Klamath Indians. 80th Cong., 1st sess. August 21, 1947.

Walch, Michael C. "Terminating the Indian Termination Policy." *Stanford Law Review* 35, no. 6 (July 1983): 1181-215.

Wilkinson, Charles F. *American Indians, Time and the Law: Native Societies in a Modern Constitutional Democracy.* New Haven: Yale University Press 1987.

————. *Blood Struggle: The Rise of Modern Indian Nations.* New York: W. W. Norton, 2005.

Wilkinson, Charles, and Eric Briggs. "Evaluation of the Termination Policy." *American Indian Law Review* 5 (Summer 1977).

Wilson, James. *The Earth Shall Weep: A History of Native America.* New York: Atlantic Monthly Press, 1999.

Wisconsin Legislature. *Memorial to Congress.* 1972.

Index

Gerard, Forrest, 134, 170–71

Ghostbear, John, 171

Giese, William R., 150

Gilkey, Roy, 84, 211

Goodman, Edwin, 241, 243–44

Governors Interstate Council on Indian Affairs, 13

Grand Ronde, Confederated Tribes of the, 71, 72, 74, 76, 78, 85–86, 87, 162, 184, 211, 242, 245; agency, 71; clinic, 191; community development fund, 191–92; council, 76; economy, 190; and gaming, 190–91, 242; housing, 191; hunting and fishing rights, 189; land, 85, 190; reservation, 189; and restoration bill, 188, 189; and restoration efforts, 185; Spirit Mountain Casino and Resort, 191, 192, 241; and termination effects, 85–87; and timber, 190; and Warm Springs Tribe, 191

Great Basin Visitors Bureau, 198

Green Bay Press-Gazette, 42

Greenwood, W. Barton, 82

Grignon, Jerome, 152–53

Grobsmith, Elizabeth, 135

Gruber, Arnold, 151

Guidiville Rancheria: termination effects, 129

Harder, Harry, 27–28, 34

Hardwick, Tillie, 219, 220, 221, 223

Harjo, Susan Shawn, 162, 165

Harrington, Charles H., 103

Harrison, Karen, 188

Harrison, Kathryn, 77, 85, 162–63, 184–85, 186, 188, 189, 239, 244

Hatch, Orrin, 175

Hatfield, Mark O., 161, 162, 163, 164, 188, 240

Hayes, Robert W., Jr., 227

Haynal, Patrick, 66, 68

Head, William Wade, 91

Heckman, J. R., 12–13

Hemphill, Robert, 97

Henley, Dempsie, 216

Hill, Leonard, 123

Holland, Ken, 225–26

Holm, Martin, 82

Hoopa Tribe, 118–19

Hoover Commission, 7–8, 14, 16, 237

House Concurrent Resolution 108, 14–15, 17; and California Indians, 115; and Klamaths, 50; and Menominees, 22

Humboldt Water Sources, 222

Indian Affairs, Office of. *See* U.S. Bureau of Indian Affairs

Indian Affairs, Senate Select Committee on. *See* U.S. Senate

Indian Affairs subcommittee, House. *See* U.S. House of Representatives

Indian Affairs subcommittee, Senate. *See* U.S. Senate

Indian Claims Commission. *See* U.S. Indian Claims Commission

Indian Committee, Senate. *See* U.S. Senate